MATTERING PRESS

Mattering Press is an academic-led Open Access publisher that operates on a not-for-profit basis as a UK registered charity. It is committed to developing new publishing models that can widen the constituency of academic knowledge and provide authors with significant levels of support and feedback. All books are available to download for free or to purchase as hard copies. More at matteringpress.org.

The Press's work has been supported by: Centre for Invention and Social Process (Goldsmiths, University of London), Centre for Mobilities Research (Lancaster University), European Association for the Study of Science and Technology, Hybrid Publishing Lab, infostreams, Institute for Social Futures (Lancaster University), Open Humanities Press, and Tetragon.

MAKING THIS BOOK

Mattering Press is keen to render more visible the unseen processes that go into the production of books. We would like to thank Endre Dányi, who acted as the Press's coordinating editor for this book, the reviewers Anna Tsing and Margaret Wiener, Jenn Tomomitsu for the copy-editing, Tetragon for the production and typesetting, Sarah Terry for the proofreading, and Ed Akerboom at infostreams for formatting the html versions of this book.

COVER

In 1693, the French Académie des Sciences introduced a new, supposedly more rational system for categorising letterforms and constructing them according to an underlying grid. This was employed in the design of Romain du Roi, a new typeface for Louis XIV's royal printer. The grid-engraved plates, on which the 'B' on the cover is based, were produced to demonstrate the typeface's geometrical construction at a time when letterforms were generally derived from stylised handwriting. The tight grid, however, would have been of little use to the type cutter having to sculpt type on a minuscule scale. So, it is said that the skilled hand of Philippe Grandjean, who spent half a century honing Romain du Roi, has altered and arguably improved its now only partially grid-determined shape. Type cutters already knew what Science and Technology Studies scholars have since established: that carving out scientifically precise inscriptions requires situated work, which is why letter-shapes are not easily captured solely by the material-semiotic net of a grid. Knowing this does not require a critical analyst. The committee announced publicly that 'experience has shown us that it is in the harmony of parts that an agreeable letter consists, and that often enough it depends on an indefinable quality… that can be felt rather than defined'. The letter grid remains vibrant, involving different modes of knowing, some of which defy definition. This is what secures the place of the 'B' on the cover as a proto-baroque object, in the sense of this book.

The cover design, and this cover note, draw inspiration mainly from Robin Kinross's 'Modern typography: an essay in critical history' (1992, Hyphen Press). Mattering Press also thanks Łukasz Dziedzic and tyPoland for Lato, available under the free, libre and open source Open Font License.

Cover art by Julien McHardy

MODES OF KNOWING

*Resources from
the Baroque*

EDITED BY

JOHN LAW

AND

EVELYN RUPPERT

MATTERING PRESS

First edition published by Mattering Press, Manchester.

Copyright © John Law and Evelyn Ruppert; chapters by respective authors, 2016.

Cover art © Julien McHardy, 2016.

Freely available online at www.matteringpress.org/books/modes-of-knowing

   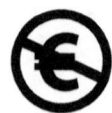

ISBN: 978-0-9931449-8-1 (pbk)
ISBN: 978-0-9931449-9-8 (ebk)

Mattering Press has made every effort to contact copyright holders and will be glad to rectify, in future editions, any errors or omissions brought to our notice.

CONTENTS

LIST OF FIGURES

ILLUSTRATIONS

EQUATIONS

CONTRIBUTORS

MARIO BLASER is the Canada Research Chair in Aboriginal Studies at Memorial University of Newfoundland. He is the author of *Storytelling Globalization from the Paraguayan Chaco and Beyond* (Duke University Press, 2010), and co-editor of *Indigenous Peoples and Autonomy: Insights for the Global Age* (University of British Columbia Press, 2010), and *In the Way of Development: Indigenous Peoples, Life Projects and Globalization* (Zed, 2004). His current research examines how heterogeneous life projects fare under the shadow of the Anthropocene.

ANTOINE HENNION is Professor at MINES ParisTech and the former Director of the Centre for the Sociology of Innovation, where he has developed a problematisation of mediation crossing cultural sociology and Science and Technology Studies (STS). He has written extensively on the sociology of music, media and cultural industries, and is now exploring a pragmatist approach to various forms of attachment – from taste and 'amateurs', to home care and issues about vulnerability, ageing, and disability. Recent books include *The Passion for Music* (2015), *Le vin et l'environnement* (with G. Teil 2011), and *La grandeur de Bach* (with J.-M. Fauquet 2000).

JOHN LAW is Emeritus Professor in Sociology at the Open University and Honorary Professor in Sociology in the Centre for Science Studies at Lancaster University. His publications have worked through empirical case studies in a range of areas including large technological projects, nature and culture, and postcolonial knowledge relations to develop STS theory and methods in material semiotics. His publications include *After Method, Aircraft Stories*, and *Organising Modernity*.

ADRIAN MACKENZIE is Professor in Technological Cultures at Lancaster University and works at the intersections of science and technology studies, media and cultural studies, and social and cultural theory. He is mainly interested in the overlaps and entanglements associated with network and computational media, with sciences as forms of practice and thought, and with social production of value. Much of his current work also focuses on the invention of data-related methods. He is author of *Wirelessness: Radical Empiricism in Network Cultures* (2010), *Cutting Code: Software and Sociality* (2010), *Transductions: Bodies and Machines of Speed* (2002) and *Into the Data: An Archaeology of Machine Learning* (2017).

ANNEMARIE MOL is Professor of Anthropology of the Body at the University of Amsterdam. She has published *The Body Multiple,* and *The Logic of Care,* and has also co-edited *Differences in Medicine, Complexities* and *Care in Practice.* Her articles explore human bodies, fluid machines, social topologies, and intranslatable words. Thanks to an ERC Advanced Grant and a Spinoza Prize, she currently works with a spirited team on questions to do with eating and/or normativities.

HUGH RAFFLES teaches anthropology and directs the Graduate Institute for Design, Ethnography & Social Thought at The New School in New York. He is the author of *In Amazonia: A Natural History* (2002) and *Insectopedia* (2010), which will be appearing this year in French and Chinese. His forthcoming book project is an ethnography of stone.

MATTIJS VAN DE PORT is an anthropologist who works at the University of Amsterdam and the VU University Amsterdam. At the latter he holds a chair on 'popular religiosity'. Intrigued by the observation that the world does not comply with our narrations of it, his anthropology is an ongoing exploration of the tensions that follow from this existential given. Recently, he has moved to filmmaking to explore the potential of images to express his research findings. He did fieldwork in Serbia and the Netherlands, and since 2001 he has been studying the Candomblé religion in Bahia, Brazil.

EVELYN RUPPERT is Professor of Sociology at Goldsmiths, University of London. She works on questions of method, data, and digital life, and is currently leading a project funded by an ERC Consolidator grant, 'Peopling Europe: How Data make a People' (ARITHMUS; 2014–19). Evelyn is the founder and editor-in-chief of a SAGE open access journal, *Big Data & Society*. Her book, *Being Digital Citizens* (with Engin Isin) was published in April 2015.

HELEN VERRAN and BRIT WINTHEREIK have worked together on several projects since 2010. Helen is University Professorial Fellow, Charles Darwin University, Australia. Brit is Associate Professor in the Technologies in Practice Group at IT University of Copenhagen. They are joint book review editors for *Science & Technology Studies*, which brings joy when young scholars approach them with a book they wish to review. Helen is less known for growing bumper crops of organic garlic in a hillside garden. Brit is less known for being a lead singer in a woman's band and for her obsession with composting.

ACKNOWLEDGEMENTS

We are grateful to the participants of 'The Baroque as Empirical Sensibility' workshop held from June 11th–13th 2011 at the Manchester Museum. The workshop was sponsored by the UK's Economic and Social Research Council (ESRC) Centre for Research on Socio-Cultural Change (CRESC) within its cross-cutting Social Life of Method theme. The chapters included in this collection come from participants at that workshop and we are especially thankful for their responsiveness to our provocations, endurance, and collegiality. We are also grateful for reviews of an earlier version of this collection by Margaret Wiener and Anna Tsing. Finally, we wish to acknowledge funding that supported the publication of this collection as open access: the European Research Council (ERC)-funded project led by Evelyn Ruppert (ARITHMUS; ERC-2013 CoG 615588) and the NWO Spinoza Prize awarded to Annemarie Mol.

I

MODES OF KNOWING: RESOURCES FROM THE BAROQUE

John Law

INTRODUCTION

By dint of quartering the subjective, the cognitive, the objective and the collective, how can we say the right word and live a happy life? The analysis that unties these four components comes from the hate that divides. What love will reunite them? That's the project of a thought, the program of a language, the hope of a life (Michel Serres 2012: 75).

I do not want to fix or represent the self as self, but to recognize the existence of the self in relationship with otherness and perceive the world in a place where such a relationship exists (Lee Ufan 2011: 121–22).

The Two Boys began playing at the Kantju waterhole, mixing the water with the surrounding earth. They piled the mud up, getting bigger and bigger, until it was the size that Uluru is now. Then they started playing on it. They sat on the top, and slid down the south side of their mud pile on their bellies, dragging their fingers through the mud in long channels. The channels hardened into stone and now form the many gullies on the southern side of Uluru (Tommy Manta, reprinted in Anne Kerle 1995: 18).

The soul is suspended in such a way that it seems to be completely outside itself. The will loves; the memory, I think, is almost lost; while the understanding, I believe, though it is not lost, does not reason – I mean that it does not work, but is amazed at the extent of all it can understand; for God wills it to realize that it understands nothing of what His Majesty represents to it (Teresa of Àvila 1964: 68).

HOW SHOULD WE KNOW THE WORLD? THAT IS THE QUESTION.

Michel Serres (2012), philosopher and historian of science, is a wordsmith. But he's writing in a way that isn't really philosophy any more. The citation comes from a book that reveals its learning, but is also personal and poetic. It is excessive to analysis, too: he's resisting what he calls 'quartering' and he's telling us that we need to love the world and give up on control if we are to stop destroying it. Instead we need to tell stories that work with emotions and avoid the divisions common in Western ways of knowing. For the book is a declaration of love for a world on the verge of destruction.

Lee Ufan (2011), a Korean artist-philosopher, creates texts and minimalist artworks. Like Serres, he's interested in relations and he's critical of Western boundedness and separation. For him, selves are in patterns of relations that extend ever so far and take different materially heterogeneous forms. His sculptures absorb the viewer into a field, cultivating a sense of otherness, of that which is not present, of incompleteness. Bodies, then, and sensibilities to absence and relationality – these are crucial to his mode of knowing.

Tommy Manta was from the Pitjantjatjara nation of Central Australia.[1] His story is a small excerpt from a longer 'dreamtime' story about ancestral beings and the creation of the world. The 'dreamtime' happened in the past, but it is also done and redone in continuing narratives and rituals by particular guardians at particular sites. This is a world of radical performativity. If the rituals stop, then the world gets hollowed out. It stops being realised. And the stories and the rituals are site-specific, belonging to particular groups. So his story isn't just 'a story' but rather the redoing of events that materialise the world, its geographical features, its animals and plants, its weather, and its people.

Santa Teresa d'Ávila (1964) was a sixteenth-century Spanish Carmelite nun and mystic. Her memoirs offer techniques for dissolving the self and embracing – being embraced by – the grace of God. These demand the disciplines of prayer and penitence in which knowing is corporeal and may lead to ecstatic communion with God. There is little that is analytical here. This is a mode of knowing that is embodied, goes out to seek and to experience that which is invisible – the fire of the Christian Holy Spirit – and to be swallowed up in it.

So here we have four different ways of knowing the world. And in what follows we're going to look at a fifth – the baroque. For this is the starting point: there are many ways of knowing and knowing well, and academic styles for doing so might be revitalised by looking beyond their current boundaries.

KNOWING PRACTICES
Social Science and its Others

Like other human activities, knowing is embedded in practices (Latour 2013). In varied ways knowledge practices seek to make sense of the world.[2] They find significance in the flux of experience by filtering, relating, deleting, and discovering regularities. But neither can we think about knowing without attending to institutions. The world needed for – and enacted by – Lee Ufan's art is quite unlike Tony Manta's mode of knowing. Similarly, Saint Teresa's ecstasy is far distant from the world inhabited by Michel Serres. None, however, with the possible exception of Serres, begins to fit with academic ways of knowing. The implication is that notwithstanding their strengths, academic ways of knowing bracket, forget, and conceal much. And if we focus more particularly on the social sciences we can ask: what do their modes of knowing have most difficulty with? Here are some possible responses.

PASSION. How does *feeling* link with social science *knowing*? No doubt it affects our choice of topics, and some have written about their passions,[3] but more often in social science we hide our loves (or hates). We may know through love, but unlike Serres we do not talk about it. Or we may know through spiritual experience (Saint Teresa), but then, like Karl Jung, we hide this reality too.

Perhaps, then, as Mattijs van de Port argues in his chapter, passions constitute the way we know, but more usually they are othered.

BODIES. The idea that the body might be *part* of method is difficult. Science and Technology Studies (STS) talks of tacit knowledge (Polanyi 1958) and of care as embodied relationality (Mol, Moser, and Pols 2010). Disability studies knows well that knowing is embodied (Barton 1996), as do many feminists (Despret 2004). But despite the exceptions, social science modes of knowing depend on but also tend to other the methodologically salient body.

MATERIAL HETEROGENEITY. STS tells us that knowing is materially heterogeneous, but the 'methods and materials' sections of academic papers are a pale and rationalised reflection of the messy heterogeneity of social science in practice (Latour and Woolgar 1986). And academic use of other forms of material communication – sculpture, performance, pilgrimage – is limited. There are growing exceptions[4] – see the piece by Evelyn Ruppert in this volume – but mostly the material heterogeneities of knowing are denied.

EXCESS. Academics write *about* ecstasy, eroticism, or religious enthusiasm, but as forms of social science method these would be unusual. The idea that love or ecstasy might count as method doesn't sit easily with what the methods guidelines lay out. Perhaps (unlike passion, bodies, and material heterogeneity) excess isn't allowed in at all. Or perhaps it powers academic knowing, and then it is repressed. At any rate, social science realities are *made* to be austere and moderate. They other excess.

SPECIFICITY. Academic modes of knowing are usually universalist and assume that valid findings may safely be moved from place to place. But STS tells us that knowing is situated (Haraway 1991b). Can you move that knowing elsewhere? The answer is unclear. Perhaps knowing is not a matter of accumulation but of apprehension on a journey, or of site and person-specific practices (Verran 2001). So despite the STS warning, the universalism of purportedly generalisable knowledge tends to overwrite situated knowing.

FORMLESSNESS. In the academy researchers mostly look for regular forms: in the Western tradition it is usually assumed that the cosmos has an underlying order (an assumption that does not hold in the dominant traditions of Chinese philosophy (Hall and Ames 1995; Lin and Law 2014)). There are important exceptions,[5] but social science modes of knowing mostly search out structures behind the confusion of the empirical. The idea that we might open ourselves up to the possibility that there is no form, or that we could not catch those forms (Santa Teresa), makes little sense.

PERFORMATIVITY. In recent decades it has become easier to argue in social science that knowing practices are performative.[6] This is also, of course, what the story about Tommy Manta is all about: knowing as enacting. But I add performativity to the list because it suggests that alternatives to social science modes of knowing might generate alternative realities. Opening ourselves to the possibility of what *is* may be a form of ontological politics.[7]

Knowing Continuities

Blind spots and forms of othering: all modes of knowing work to exclude; they have no choice. Necessarily they work by pushing experience through a screen of presuppositions to produce workable forms of knowledge or experience. As a part of this, they distinguish the probable from the improbable, and the possible from the impossible (Foucault 1979). But as I noted above, knowing is also institutional. Serres works in a particular Parisian intellectual space that is not simply academic in a standard disciplinary sense. His audience – catered for by publishers and media – is broader than that of most English-language philosophers. Lee Ufan is painting and sculpting in an international art-world space with its museums, patrons, and collectors. Tommy Manta is reporting from a place in which knowing resides in particular ceremonial forms of particular privileged elders. And Saint Teresa lived, wrote, and worshipped as a Carmelite nun. It is such conditions of institutional possibility that allows for their modes of knowing and makes them resilient. You cannot know differently without tackling the institutional and material correlates that go with the normative modes of knowing. Failure to do this leads to silence or expulsion.[8]

This begs the question as to what the spaces of academic knowing afford and allow. There are many differences and discontinuities, but there are also continuities. A large story might start by saying that the Greeks organised high-status knowing in the agora, where it was debated between free men who distinguished bodies from minds and privileged reason in a search for pattern lying behind complexity.[9] It might be added that significant elements of this configuration were reproduced in the Judaeo-Christian tradition and especially the Catholic Church. Schismatic and diverse though this was, it took it for granted that the world was endowed by a structure given by its maker; it stipulated appropriate ways of knowing the agency of that maker, his creation, and the regularities behind the confusions of the world; and it reproduced all this thanks to appropriate material and institutional forms. The story would continue with the birth of modern empirical experimental science in the seventeenth century.[10] The natural philosophy established in the Royal Society of London created a basis for a continuing investigation of God's enduring reality, now transformed into an experimental mode. Matters of fact about nature were distinguished from speculation, and institutional as well as literary arrangements to sustain this distinction were put in place. In the nineteenth century these morphed into disciplinarily organised universities with their specialist audiences and their 'modest witness' modes of textual representation.

Perhaps things are changing.[11] Nevertheless, this oversimplified story suggests why there might be continuities in – and family resemblances between – different modes of academic knowing. In content, academic disciplines are different, but at least until recently they have all been lodged within similar institutional structures (academic, or academically structured institutions), have implied particular economic arrangements (state and/or private sector funding), life course patterns (salaried bureaucratic posts with career paths), and modes of circulation (academic publications with appropriate forms of modest witnessing). These are modes of knowing in which there has been little space for unruly passions, messy materials and bodies, excesses, the idea that knowing might be situated, the possibility of formlessness, or performativity. This is a settlement that has, to be sure, been highly productive. At the same time it has systematically produced and reproduced forms of otherness. Perhaps it is time to move on.

So how might we think differently? This book is an attempt to respond to this question. Its contributors are all interested in non-standard modes of knowing. They are all more or less uneasy with the restrictions or the agendas implied by academic modes of knowing, and they have chosen to do this by working with, through, or against one important Western alternative – that of *the baroque*.

Why the baroque? One answer is that the baroque made space for and fostered many of the forms of otherness listed above. It *knew* things differently. It knew *about* different things. It knew extravagantly and excessively, it knew in materially heterogeneous ways, and it apprehended that which is other and could not be caught in a cognitive or symbolic net. It also knew in ways that did not gather to a single point, and knew itself to be performative. A part of a great Western division between rationalist and non-rationalist modes of knowing, the baroque is therefore a possible *resource* for creating ways of knowing differently, a storehouse of possible alternative techniques. To say this is not to say that it is the right mode of knowing. The book's authors do not seek to create a 'baroque social science', whatever that might be, and they also work in very different ways. But before moving on to an overview of what they are after, it will be useful to ask: what is, or was, the baroque?

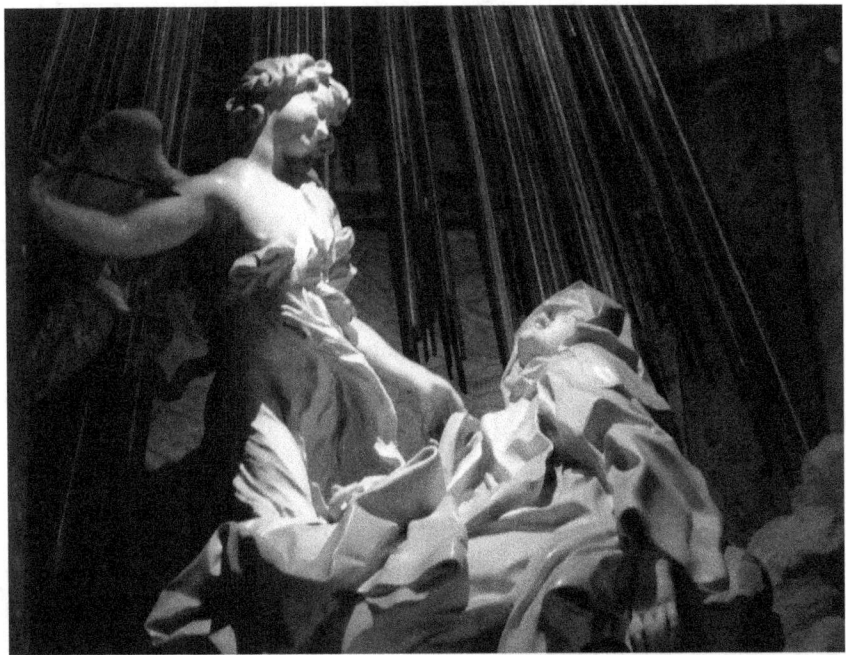

FIG. 1.1 Bernini, Ecstasy of Santa Teresa d'Ávila[12]

THE BAROQUE

Otherness and the Baroque

The first answer is that it was many things. But I want to make it real and sensuous, so I set off in a specific place with a particular work of art. This is a sculpture by Gian Lorenzo Bernini created around 1647. It is the Ecstasy of Santa Teresa d'Ávila in the church of Santa Maria della Vittoria in Rome. As I noted earlier, Santa Teresa was a Spanish Carmelite and a visionary mystic. Canonised in 1622, she was an inspirational figure for the Catholic Counter Reformation. Highly literate, in the memoirs cited above she famously describes how she was visited by an angel:

> 'He was not tall, but short, and very beautiful', and added that his face was 'all afire'.
>
> 'In his hands', she continued, 'I saw a long golden spear and at the end of the iron tip I seemed to see a point of fire'.
>
> 'With this he seemed to pierce my heart several times so that it penetrated to my entrails. When he drew it out, I thought he was drawing them out with it and he left me completely afire with a great love for God'.
>
> 'The pain [from the angel's spear] was so sharp that it made me utter several moans; and so excessive was the sweetness caused me by this intense pain that one can never wish to lose it, nor will one's soul be content with anything less than God'. (Teresa of Ávila 1964: 164)

In Bernini's sculpture the angel has just withdrawn his spear. He is looking down on Santa Teresa with the love and affection that a parent might show for a child or the Christian God might feel for his children. At the same time she is in a place of ecstasy, 'afire', as she puts it, with his love.

Here we have entered the world of the baroque. Bernini's 'Ecstasy of Santa Teresa' was created in Rome in the middle years of the seventeenth century, and the term 'baroque' was a label retrospectively pinned onto artworks such as this. The label is iffy because it implies a chronology and teleology, but it has been conventional in art history to talk of work in Rome at this time as the

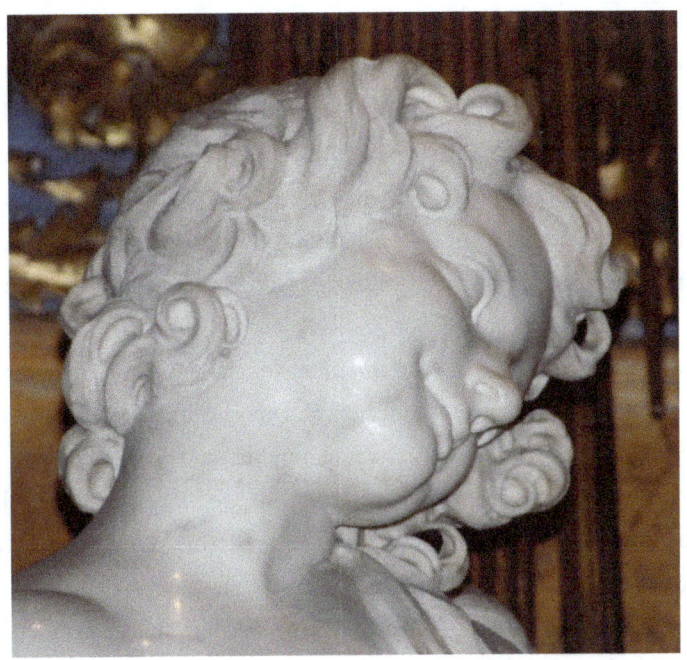

FIG. 1.2 Bernini, Ecstasy of Santa Teresa d'Ávila, Angel (detail)[13]

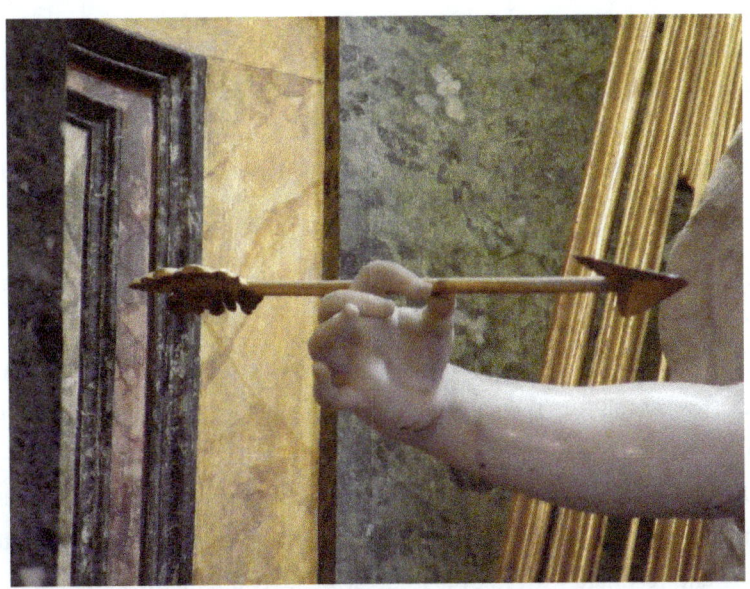

FIG. 1.3 Bernini, Ecstasy of Santa Teresa d'Ávila, Spear (detail)[14]

'High Baroque'. The sculpture itself is canonical. It exemplifies a style of Italian art which flowered with extraordinary energy in a particular 'space of knowing', enjoying and celebrating the patronage of popes, princes, and cardinals in Italy in the middle fifty years of the seventeenth century. But what is the statue *doing*? How does it *differ* from how we might otherwise go about *knowing*? And most important, what do we want to *learn* and *take* from the baroque – or not – as we think about bodies, affects, excesses, and the elusive now? Here are three preliminary reflections.[15]

First there is the issue of *subject matter*. In academic social science we are sometimes inspired by spiritual concerns, and may be interested in the techniques for *representing* religious ecstasy, but we rarely set out to write texts intended to induce ecstasy – or loss of self in any form – in the reader. Academic knowing does not have much to do with unbounding the person, spiritually or otherwise. The knowing subject is much more self-contained. In this respect it is far removed from the baroque – though the latter wasn't necessarily religious, so Bernini worked with classical mythological subjects too and endlessly mixed with patronage and political power. Below, for instance (Fig. 1.4), is his bust of Louis XIV.

But that said, in one way or another, baroque work was very often about transcending the person. So there are several points here.

- Straightforwardly, the baroque recognised *different kinds of realities*.
- Those realities often had to do with the *spiritual* life.
- They belonged to a world that was *extra-ordinary* and only partially fitted with mundanity.

In short, the baroque offers a way of acknowledging *otherness* and unrepresentable *absences and gaps*.

Second, the baroque mobilises particular *subjectivities*: the *argument* of the Santa Teresa sculpture is *emotional*, not reasonable. Below (Fig. 1.5) is another Bernini sculpture, also from Rome.

This is of the nun Ludovica Albertoni, on her deathbed in pain and in ecstasy. Is the latter sexual? Many say so. Do we share whatever it is she is depicted as feeling and resonate with it, or is it idolatrous? Again, many say yes to the last of these questions. But whatever our response, it is in part *emotional*. So here's a

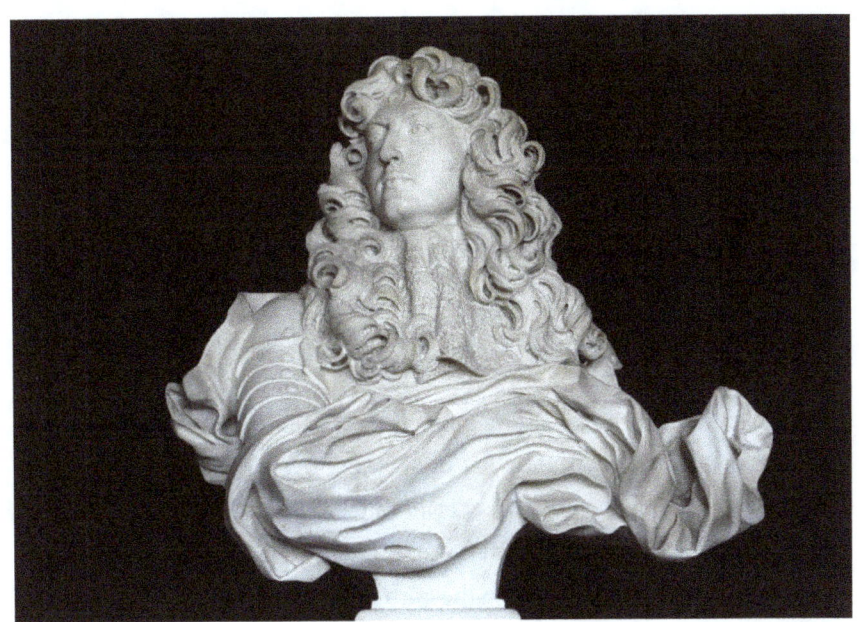

FIG. 1.4 Bernini, Bust of Louis XIV[16]

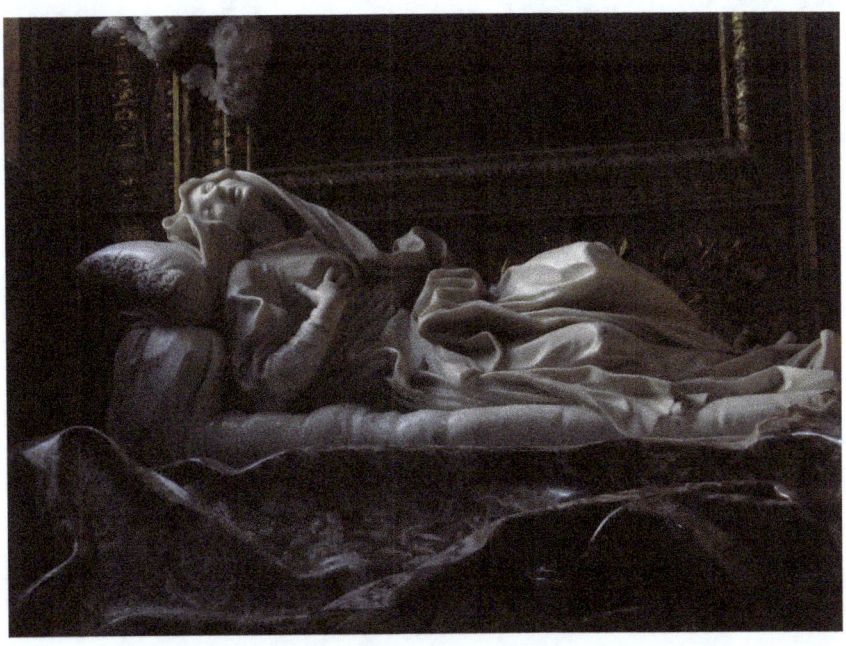

FIG. 1.5 Bernini, Ludovica Albertoni on her Deathbed[17]

second possibility. The baroque might be a resource for reflecting on *emotional* modes of knowing and learning.

One: otherness. Two: emotions. And three? Straight away, we are moved to *embodiment*. Baroque ways of knowing or experiencing have to do with pleasure, and pain, and the flesh, often in ways that are transgressive.

Look, for instance, at Caravaggio's *Doubting Thomas* (Fig. 1.6). Here Thomas doesn't just doubt. He doubts so much that (and seemingly at Christ's invitation) he presses his finger into the gaping wound left by the centurion's lance. The picture has been understood in many ways, for instance as an expression of homoeroticism, but a more straightforward reading is that it is only the flesh that can vanquish Thomas' doubts – and our doubts too.

So what's at issue is *sensuousness*, *bodily* but also and more generally *materially*. For if baroque forms of experience are about bodies, they are about textures in other material forms as well. In the baroque, experience comes in forms of bodily sensibility that are far removed from those of Protestant asceticism. This is a place where mind-body dualisms don't work. *Cogito, ergo sum*? Not at all:

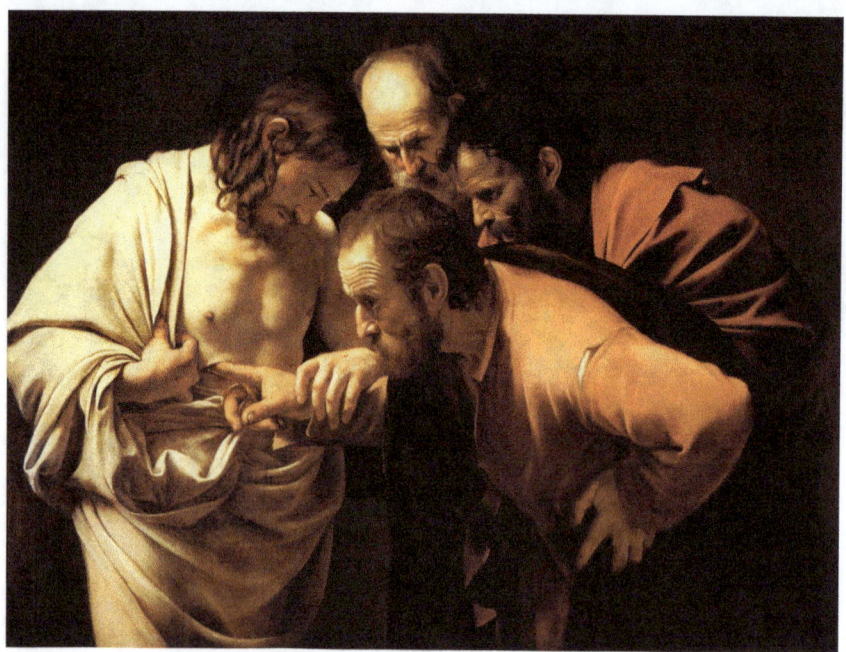

FIG. 1.6 Caravaggio, Doubting Thomas[18]

there are no seats of consciousness removed from the flesh. So that's the third issue: being a body and knowing go together.

I have made a small list here. I am engaged in a version of Serres' quartering. And I will shortly characterise the baroque as a mode of knowing in terms of a longer list of attributes too. This means that I am working very much within a standard social science mode, burdened by its restrictions as much as reacting to these. I am trapped. But I hope that this does not mean that the exercise is entirely self-defeating. For the three points about otherness, emotion, and embodiment all interfere with academic social science modes of knowing in ways that resonate with concerns shared by many among us. And not only are these substantive concerns potentially inspiring, but they also have implications for the methods, or more broadly the techniques of knowing.

To think about this I draw on art history and read Bernini's sculpture as a mode of knowing that indeed works through a set of techniques.

SIX TECHNIQUES OF THE BAROQUE
Theatricality

The baroque works as *theatre*.

This seventeenth-century painting (Fig. 1.7, overleaf) shows us the whole chapel around the sculpture of Santa Teresa, and it reveals that this is a space that has been set out like a stage.[20] In the middle you can see the saint and the angel. They are being brightly lit from above by a hidden source of light. They are inside a pediment with columns on either side set at the back of a shallow chapel. In front there is an altar and a low balustrade. And then on either side of the chapel there are onlookers in *prie dieux* that look uncannily like theatre boxes. All in all it is like a stage in a theatre. So this is the first and perhaps the most fundamental point about Bernini's baroque technique – and the baroque more generally. Its effects, its dialogues, its scenery, and the multiplication of its artifices are *theatrical*. Indeed, the artifice is self-conscious, which works to highlight the limits of human modes of representation and, in a church setting, the not-knowing we confront when we face the divine.

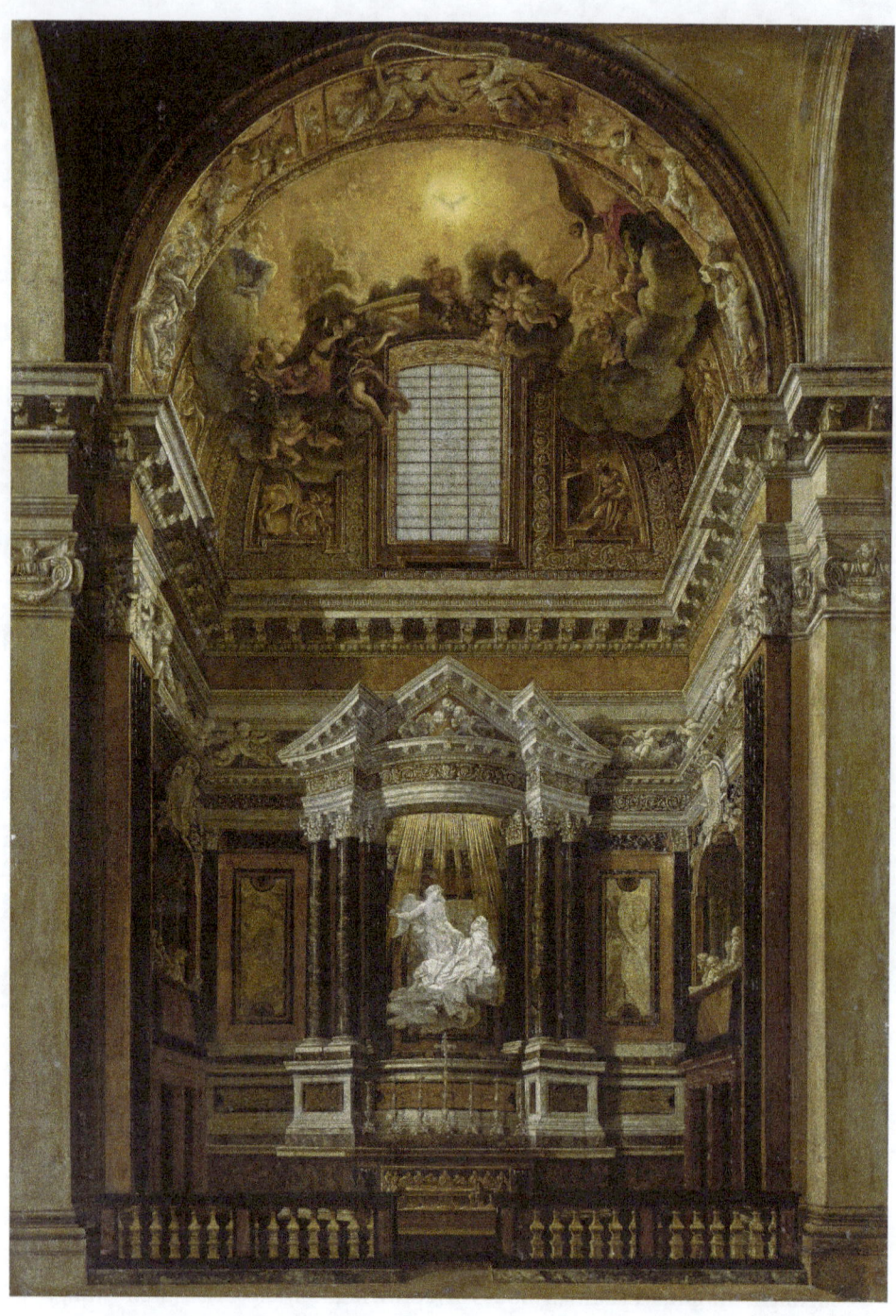

FIG. 1.7 Bernini, Cappella Cornaro in Santa Maria della Vittoria, Rome[19]

Boundlessness

Second, and as a part of this, baroque artworks *undo boundaries*. Think about the division between inside and outside. The painting above appears in most of the commentaries on the sculpture precisely because it is more or less impossible to get a photographic overview of the chapel: you can't get far enough away to see it as a whole, let alone photograph it (Wittkower 1997 [1955]: 158). In practice, then, to see it at all, you are forced to step inside the theatre. But then the question is: where does the spectacle end? Who or what is inside, and who or what is not? The answer is that the boundaries of the spectacle aren't clear – or perhaps it does not end at all. Rudolf Wittkower, historian of Italian baroque art and architecture, argued this is far removed from Renaissance appreciations of art. Rather, the baroque strives for 'the *elimination* of different

spheres for statue and spectator' (Wittkower 1997 [1955]: 15; my emphasis). The same point is made by Genevieve Warwick who notes that baroque theatre deliberately sought to destabilise the distinction between audience and actor (Warwick 2012: 18ff), a description that fits Bernini's chapel, which overflows in multiple and material forms.

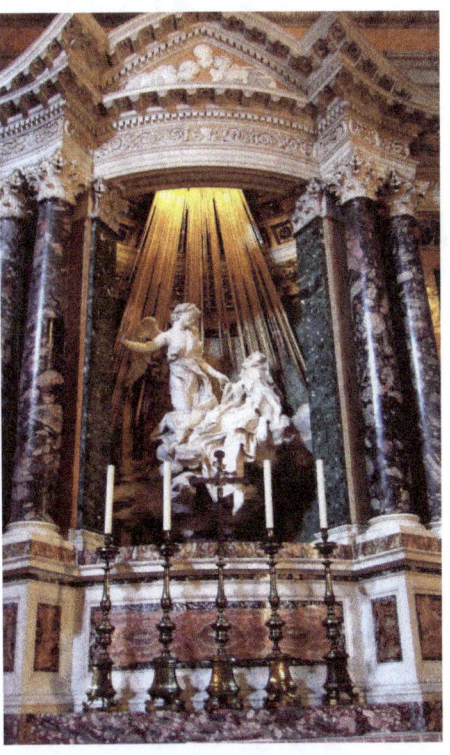

First, Santa Teresa's bare foot hangs below the marble clouds on which she is lying.[21] It escapes the frame.

Second, the golden rays of light behind her burst out from heaven above to illuminate the divine grace being endowed on the saint in her moment of holy but

FIG. 1.8 Bernini, Ecstasy of Santa Teresa d'Ávila[22]

transient irradiation.[23] Third, the pillars and pediment framing the sculpture look as if they are in the process of being blown open by the force of that grace. Look at the ceiling, number four, and the illusion is extended. Up above, and reaching down in a *trompe l'oeil* from far beyond the roof of the chapel, a dove – the Holy Spirit – bursts through billowing clouds that are being blown aside by angels, and (another artifice of boundlessness) those clouds also extend beyond the vault into the nave of the church. And, number five (more boundlessness), the marble spectators in the *prie dieux* are looking in different directions. On the one hand they are part of the spectacle, and on the other hand they are not, since they also seem to be looking *at* it.

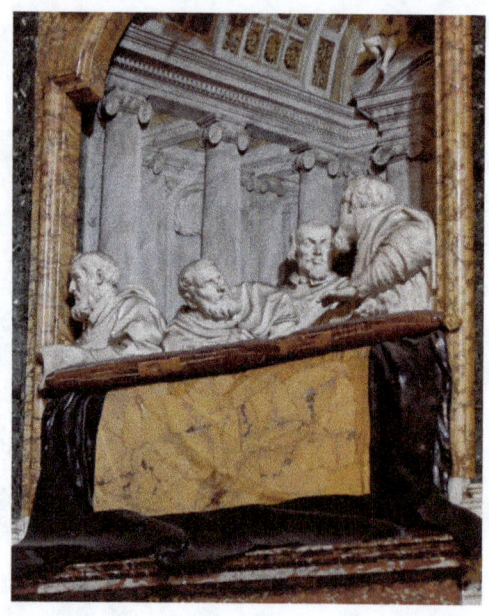

FIG. 1.9 Bernini, Cappella Cornaro in Santa Maria della Vittoria (detail)[24]

And then, six, since one of these spectators is looking out at the visitor, she, the visitor, isn't just looking on from outside either. She's part of the spectacle, too close to detach herself, and is being included in the exchange of gazes the spectacle affords. And finally, seventh, in the floor of the chapel the skeletons of the dead are looking up and gesticulating in hope of the Resurrection. The theatre of the chapel overflows into the groundlings of the underworld as well.

So this is a second stylistic technique of baroque artwork. Its artifices *elide the division between inside and outside.* They resist the perspectival picture framings of the Renaissance and *include* the subject. You never stand outside and watch. If you engage with them at all, you are drawn inside. You cannot do what feminist Donna Haraway calls 'the God trick' of pretending that you can see it all from nowhere in particular. Instead you are entangled. You are *asked to*; you're *required* to submit and to participate.[25]

Heterogeneity

Baroque artworks are *heterogeneous.* They multiply their media. Bernini, we are told, 'gave a public opera wherein he painted the scenes, cut the statues, invented the engines, composed the music, writ the comedy, and built the theatre'.[26] In other contexts Bernini also organised fireworks, and designed carnival floats, squares, and fountains such as the Fontana dei Quattro Fiumi in the Piazza Navona, again in Rome.

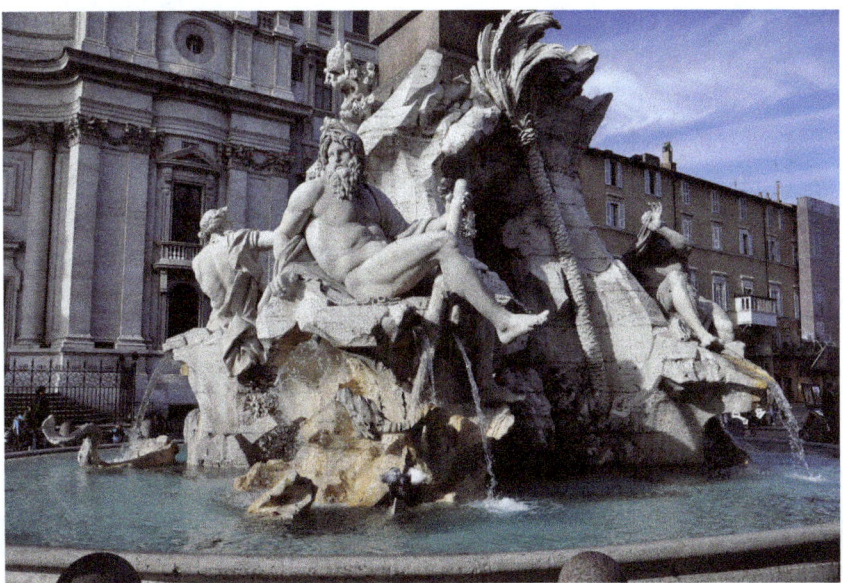

FIG. 1.10 Bernini, Fontana dei Quattro Fiumi, Rome[27]

No doubt he was exceptional, but the baroque pushes towards overlapping art-media – and indeed towards universal art (Deleuze 1993: 123). These media do not collapse into a single art form, but architecture, sculpture, painting, and urban design are all joined together. 'What is the group', asked Wittkower, 'of *St Teresa and the Angel*? Is it sculpture in the round or is it a relief?' (Wittkower 1999 [1958]: 14). His point was that the question cannot be answered in that form.

This expresses itself in material practice in the Santa Teresa chapel. The pillars and the walls are made of rich marbles of different colours. Then there is the highly polished white marble of the statue itself. The ceiling is made of stucco, and is painted, as we have seen, as a *trompe l'oeil*. There are flat reliefs, again made of stucco, at the back of the *prie dieux*, perspectival renderings that meld into and appear to extend the architecture of the church itself (Wittkower 1997 [1955]: 158). The frame for the sculpture is architectural in form. So three-dimensional sculptural work melds into bas relief, which in turn melds into two-dimensional perspectivalism, which is then interwoven with architecture. If we were to go hunting for a contemporary and analogous mode of knowing, we might think of museums, or *son et lumière*, or the digital, or clubbing. We would not be thinking of texts such as the one you are reading now. The challenge, then, is whether we can shift academic media to know and to handle the excessive and the non-coherent – and how we might do this.

Folding: Both One and Two

The question of how to think about boundlessness leads us to a fourth baroque technique: that of the *fold*. For the unboundedness of baroque artwork is not just a matter of the absence of boundaries. Rather it works by pleating insides and outsides together. Think of audiences and actors. On the one hand they are still separate, the outside and in, but on the other hand they are not separate at all.[28] We are in the world of the Möbius strip. The inside becomes the outside, and the outside becomes the inside. Or they are both at the same time.

Look at the folds of Santa Teresa's gown. Yes, in the most obvious way it covers her. We cannot see her body. There is scarcely a hint of its shape. But in another and more important respect it doesn't cover her at all, for the grace of the Christian God stands outside her in angelic form but is also within her, in the form of her ecstasy. We are witnessing spiritual transcendence *and* immanence, two aspects of the same overwhelming force. But – here is the question – how does Bernini *represent* that simultaneous separation and unity? One answer – it comes from Deleuze – is that he does this in the folds of her gown. Like a Möbius band the gown has two sides, but at the same time only one. The fold expresses the single and double grace of the Christian Holy Spirit.[30]

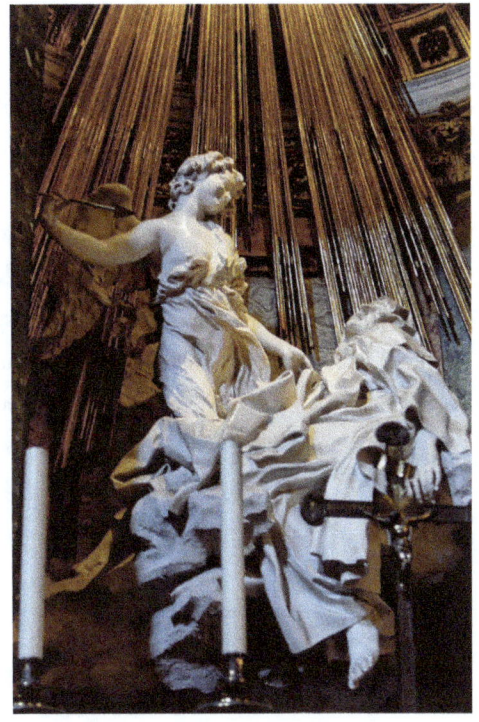

FIG. 1.11 Bernini, Ecstasy of Santa Teresa d'Ávila[29]

Similar artifices are at work elsewhere. Consider again the figures in the boxes. Are they outside? The answer is yes. After all, they are (or perhaps are not) looking on. At any rate they are apart from Santa Teresa and the angel. But at the same time they are not separate, for they are also a *part* of the theatre. And we, the spectators, are in a similar position. We are looking on, so we are outside. At the same time we are also being folded in. Such, at any rate, is the conclusion we might draw if we attend to the figure lurking at the back of the *prie dieu* on the right who is watching not only the figure turned away from us (who seems to be talking to him) but (as we have seen) is also looking at us as well. So we are being included too, pleated into the mixture.

This is the fourth part of Bernini's technique. In this baroque mode of knowing, the artifice of the fold separates inside and outside, but undoes that separation too. It is like a screen, a fabric with two sides that are only one side.[31] To put it differently, it is an artifice that works through tension or, perhaps better, displacement, between within and without. *Within baroque artwork, to experience is to be outside and to be inside at the same time.*

How might this work in contemporary modes of knowing?[32] The answer is complicated, for in this way of thinking knowing necessarily folds the outside in. So as I write this introduction I am folding in artwork from Rome, commentaries on that artwork, plus a dose of social theory. The issue, then, is not so much that there is a *need* to fold but rather *what we make of the continuity between inside and outside* once we start to acknowledge it.

Distribution, Movement and Self-Consciousness

And this moves us to a fifth set of artifices, to do with *distribution* and *movement*. In the artworks of the baroque in Rome, understanding is located in different places. Knowing is a matter of *moving*. So the sculpture of the saint and the angel lie in the spatial centre of the chapel, but for the onlookers it is more complicated. In the *prie dieux* there are conversations (see Fig. 1.12). Someone is reading a text (Santa Teresa's *Life*?) and even those who seem to be looking at her cannot really see her because Teresa is invisible from where these sculptured viewers stand. So what is happening is a *multiplication of viewpoints*. What to make of this?

One message is that there is more than one way of knowing the grace of God or the ecstasy of Santa Teresa. There is *vision*; there are even *visions* in the plural. But such knowing also grows out of the study of *texts*. Through *piety and prayer*. We can see that knowing arises in *discussion*. It may come in the form of *sculpture and artwork*. In all cases the assumption is that human beings are limited. Only God can see the whole truth, while how human beings know is partial, more or less confused.[34] The lesson is that experience is *distributed*, but also that it is important to work at different ways of appreciating or understanding, and to try to hold onto them at the same time. Necessarily what we know is partial, but it is also multiple, allegorical, and mediated. In rejecting the humanist optimism of the Renaissance, the mode of knowing in the baroque rests upon

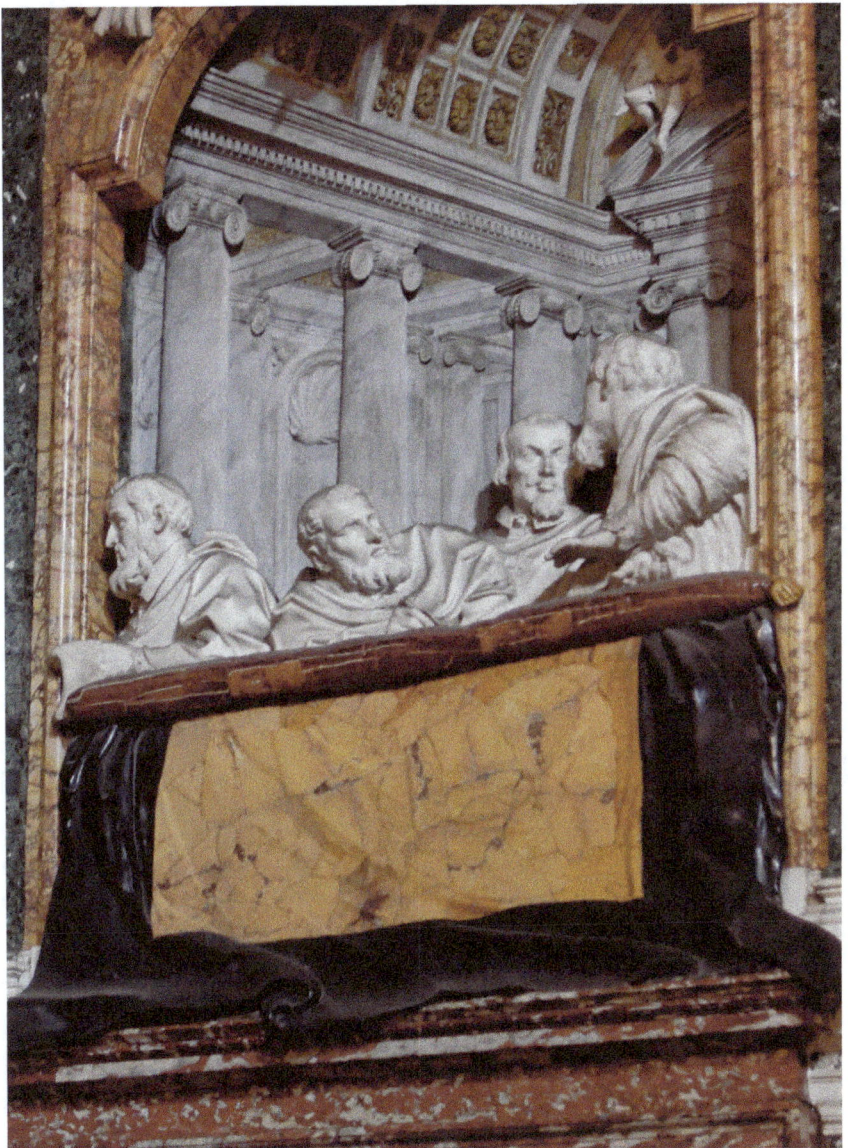

FIG. 1.12 Bernini, Cappella Cornaro in Santa Maria della Vittoria (detail)[33]

multiplication. To experience as best we can is to proliferate media, perspectives, and processes, it is to juxtapose these, and then it is to acknowledge that they cannot be pulled into a humanly coherent whole; to recognise that there is, as it were, an unknowable hole in the middle.[35]

This tells us that baroque artworks are also about *movement*, to be understood as a *process*. The artifices of the baroque are like literal or metaphorical Stations of the Cross; or Teresa's four stages in the ascent of the soul;[36] or indeed the Spiritual Exercises of Saint Ignatius Loyola.[37] But as we've just seen, we are being moved between modes of experiencing within the Cornaro chapel too. So, here is a final twist: as I noted above, knowing in the baroque is also a matter of *self-consciousness*. Its artifices know that they are just *another* form of recognising – though there is nothing ironic or postmodern about this. It is just that that any particular form of experience appreciates that since it is limited it will always be important to move on to another; and then another. All within a particular spiritual or theological hierarchy, a hierarchy exemplified, for instance, by the ceiling by Andra Pozzo in the Jesuit Sant'Ignazio church in Rome, with St Ignatius in the middle on the left, receiving the light from Jesus, and from God the Father in the middle.[38]

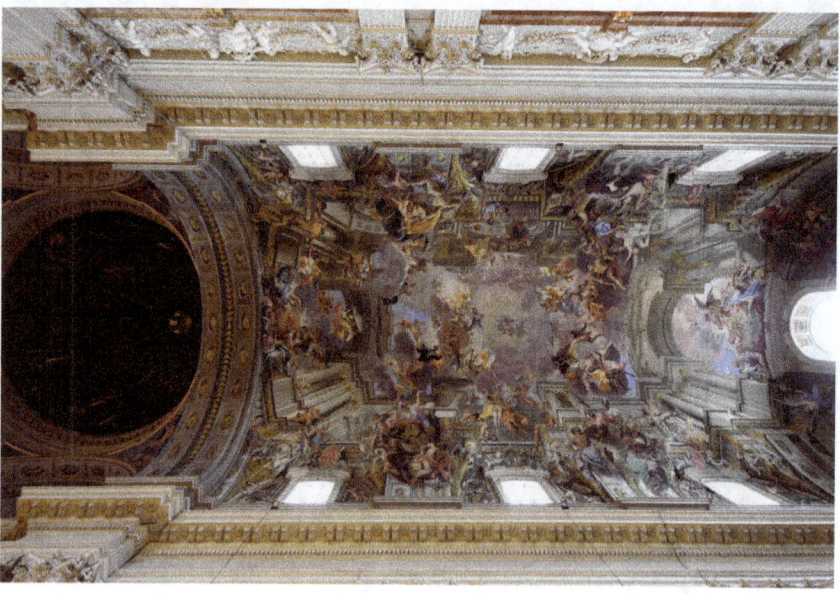

FIG. 1.13 Ceiling by Andra Pozzo, Sant'Ignazio, Rome[39]

These baroque artworks thus cultivate a form of self-consciousness that is also modest because it is inserted low down in a hierarchy of spiritual experience.[40] This is a mode of knowing that is contexted – this is the modesty part – but at the same time is also about the possibility of moving through or rising in that hierarchy. Modesty and a kind of grand ambition are combined together in recognition that the journey to the next Station of the Cross is beckoning and that it may lead to somewhere better through the various worldly intermediaries offered by prayer, study, and devotion. So there is one way in which what is known is almost less important than the *processes of knowing itself*. As intellectual historian Chunglin Kwa observes, disembodied abstraction is foreign to the baroque (Kwa 2002).

Mediation

Finally, I want to say that the baroque knowing becomes sensible to otherness – or the absence of otherness – by working through *mediation*.[41] If understanding is about being seized and transported somewhere else that we cannot really know, then this is how Bernini's Santa Teresa works in a powerful *upward movement* from mundanity to spiritual mystery. Wittkower proposes three levels. There is the human: you, me, and the Cornaros in their boxes, where we are more or less in the dark, both literally and figuratively. Then there is Santa Teresa, in her ecstasy, pierced by the love of God. She is the brilliantly lit *mediator*, human but transported beyond the human. So she is the second level. Then, third, and high above us, there is the *transcendent God* in the form of the *trompe l'oeil* ceiling where we gaze, to quote Wittkower, at 'the unfathomable infinity of the empyrean' (Wittkower (1997 [1955]: 158). 'If', writes Wittkower, '[the viewer] yields entirely to the ingenious and elaborate directions given by the artist, he will step beyond the narrow limits of his own existence and be entranced within the causality of an enchanted world' (1997 [1955]: 158).

So what if we are interested in ways of knowing excess within the contemporary academy? Of recognising the whole that is, at the same time, a hole in our artefacts of knowing or experiencing?[42] The implication is that we need to imagine particular machineries of transport and *mediation*.[43]

ADAPTING THE BAROQUE
Politics

Now I need to call a halt and deal with the fact that the baroque has often been the object of a bad press. Indeed, the word 'baroque' started life in the eighteenth century as a pejorative term to describe the supposedly misshapen and inappropriate exuberance of art of the Catholic Counter Reformation (Maravall 1986: 208). Its politics have always been controversial, for, as Protestants well recognised, it was part of an elaborate and well-developed *strategy of power*. To engage with its artworks was to engage spiritually, emotionally, and physically with a Roman Catholic version of the Christian God. It was also to be embedded in the set of institutions – the papacy, including the worldly power and wealth of popes – that went with Roman Catholicism.[44] So there is a power strategy embedded in the chapel and more generally in the High Baroque. A reaction to the Enlightenment, it is a mode of knowing intended to *shock, to awe, to move,* to *demand participation*, and to *dominate*.

Perhaps, then, to be interpolated is to collude. José Antonio Maravall shows how the Spanish seventeenth-century baroque was an absolutist response to the multiplication of the economic, social, and military crises of that century. The issue was how control might be maintained in a precarious urban world of embryonic mass culture in which material certainties were under threat, but the nascent enquiring individualism and freedoms of the Renaissance could not be pushed back into their box. The answer was the creation of the 'guided culture' of the baroque (Maravall 1986: 73). He argues (we have seen this in the Cornaro chapel) that it worked by turning spectators into accomplices by incorporating them into unfinished scenes and working on their emotions. The lesson here is clear. Unless we're committed to hierarchical social control we need to be cautious of this mode of knowing.

But sometimes the baroque, although potentially authoritarian, does not work out that way. Mario Blaser shows in his chapter in this volume that in many Latin American contexts baroque architecture and art were part of the colonising Spanish culture. Alongside military and political repression, the monarchy and Catholicism moved to metaphorical seduction in the form of elaborate ceremonies, expansive town squares, and ornate baroque churches.[45] But as he also suggests, the techniques of power imported by the Spanish were suborned. They were turned into modes of resistance. The demands for conformity were converted into a resource for other exuberant and non-conformist but equally baroque modes of knowing and being. Bolivar Echeverria draws on that theorist of excess, Georges Bataille, to argue that it was the repression in Latin America that made transgression possible:

> [I]n its theatrical use of the indisputable formal canon, baroque art found the opportunity to animate all its petrified gestures and to revitalize the situation in which it was constituted as a negation and sacrifice of the Other.[46]

In this reading, division and resistance turned around an opposition between formal and informal, and in particular between the rational calculations of the quantitative and the vital energy of the qualitative. To put it simply, the baroque was a culture in tension. It was indeed repressive but it also invited the *transgressions* of lively excess by 'obeying without fulfilling' (Echeverria 2005).

So the baroque isn't necessarily conservative. Walter Benjamin (1985b) suggested this in his rejected *Habilitation* thesis on German tragic drama that foreshadowed his later concern with the possibility of redemption through attention to fragmentation. The simple stories of history and necessity, 'myths' he called them, are fragmented in the desolation and hopelessness of seventeenth-century tragic baroque drama. And the tool is allegory. 'Allegories are', he famously insisted, 'in the realm of thought what ruins are in the realm of things' (Benjamin 1985b). Broken and incomplete, set alongside one another they do not hold together, and offer the basis for resisting the smoothing stories of history that otherwise work to paper over the cracks. They work as mute witnesses to the alternatives that have been written out of the record. This means that it is a task of the baroque scholar to find ways of giving them voice.[47] Benjamin's fragmented – and ambitious – story is thus a parable about the importance of cultivating a baroque sensibility to the alternatives, indeed the ruins, and to the Others that have been lost (Buci-Glucksmann 1994). Allegory becomes a tool for arresting history and recuperating that which has been erased by the storm of progress.[48] And, indeed, this is a sensibility integral to the modern world in its earliest manifestation – the baroque.

Performativity

This brief detour into the politics of the baroque tells us that to experiment with the artifices of the baroque is not necessarily to embrace authoritarianism or conservatism. We do not have to embrace analogues of the hierarchical world of the Counter-Reformation along with the techniques of baroque knowing. But the larger lesson is that such techniques are deliberately *interventionary*. They describe or represent the world, while at the same time they seek to make a difference. Representation and intervention are wilfully bound together. To put it differently, *baroque artifices are explicit about their own performativity*. They seek to shape the world, to operate upon it, formatting it one way or another. In baroque modes of knowing, descriptions are never idle. They are self-consciously normative.[49]

All of which begs the question as to what we should make of the *elasticity* of the category. As I have noted, art historians remind us that 'the baroque' appears in different modes in different parts of the world at different times,[50] and that the label was pasted onto what it describes long after the event. They add that this labelling may itself have had performative effects (Caygill 2011). And indeed the commonalities between (say) Bernini, Caravaggio, Rembrandt, and Rubens (not to mention the eighteenth-century baroque architecture of Latin America) sometimes become hard to discern (DaCosta Kaufmann 2011). But then the meaning of the term has shifted too.[51] As I have just noted, it started as a term of *retrospective disapprobation*, pinned to artwork that was taken to be misshapen, excessive, and exuberant. Then it turned into a *period of artistic production*, one that supposedly followed the Renaissance (perhaps as the Renaissance 'gone wrong') but preceded the constraints of Neo-Classicism. And then it appeared in a third incarnation as an *artistic style*. So Wölfflin treated the baroque as a 'complex of symptoms' (Wölfflin 1984: 17): it was '*painterly*', suggesting displacement and movement by attending to vague forms, for instance in the form of light and shadow; it was *massive, amorphous, and intimidating*, rendering matter supple and turning corners into curves; and then, finally, it worked through the *movement* – especially upward movement – of curves, rhythmic sequences, dissonances, and incompletenesses in which form dissolved fleetingly into light.[52]

So its history covers denunciation, period, and style. And the term is still on the move. More recently the baroque has transformed itself into a set of identifiable *operating principles*, though the character of these principles depends upon who you happen to read. Indeed we've come across such principles in two versions already. Benjamin's move to freeze allegorical ruins and their redemptive juxtapositions is one. And Deleuze's quite different insistence on folds and pleats is a second. '[W]e all', concludes the latter in *Le Pli*, 'remain Leibnizian because what always matters is folding, unfolding, refolding' (Deleuze 1993: 137). And if we are listing operating principles, we need to add Foucault's archaeological analysis of the classical episteme. Here the baroque becomes a table of representations, a linguistic grid preoccupied with the endlessly uncertain classifications and taxonomic orderings of signs, a grid with an absence at its centre (Foucault 1972).[53]

No doubt the list might be further extended. Indeed, to treat 'the baroque' as a mode of knowing is to move the significance of the term yet again. It suggests the need to find ways of thinking about representations, subjectivities, known realities, imaginaries, metaphysical assumptions, im/possibilities, modes of othering, and normativities, simultaneously with architectural and spatial arrangements, institutional forms, economic structures, modes of circulation, and life courses for knowing subjects.

EMPIRICAL WAYS OF KNOWING

The contributions to this book reflect *on* the baroque, on how it works, and how it might be used in a range of different ways. Some more or less implicitly also experiment *with* the baroque. The book chapters fall into two sections. Part 1, *Reflecting on the Baroque*, starts with Mario Blaser, who considers the baroque from a Latin American perspective. Focussing on excess, he explores the ambivalent South American power-saturated history of the baroque that I briefly discussed above, and uses this as a springboard to think about the character of excess in a postcolonial encounter. His focus is that exemplary tool for social and economic development, the community participatory workshop. At stake is a territory, in the past belonging to indigenous Yshiro, which has been substantially deforested and used for ranching, and which is now a designated UNESCO Biosphere Reserve. The Yshiro, under pressure from both the clearing and UNESCO's conservation, participate in this workshop with a range of agendas, but few fit with its ostensible purpose. Some are excessive because they are transgressive: the Yshiro are using the workshop for other political or economic ends: they 'obey without fulfilling'. Others, more 'traditional' in orientation, are excessive in a more radical way: 'territory' implies place-based performative relations with earth-beings, while nature/culture/supernatural divisions have little meaning. To use Viveiros de Castro's language, dialogue takes the form of uncontrolled equivocation. But what is excess? Blaser argues that this is generated in a diffraction between different ways of being which generate what he calls an 'illuminating shadow'. For those involved in development, this is a horror of the unknown. For those embedded in Yshiro performativity, quite differently, it is what might be known-and-done differently. Can the baroque help us to think this? Blaser leaves the question open.

In the next chapter, Antoine Hennion revisits the baroque revival in music and asks about the distinction between the authentic and the fake. In painting this is a distinction that makes some sense, but in musical performance it is much less obvious. Music is performed, so what counts as authentic and what as fake? Exploring this for the revival of ancient and baroque music, Hennion shows that what counts as 'authentic' has changed radically, between the nineteenth-century rediscovery of (say) the music of J. S. Bach and the present day. Rediscovered or at least reinserted into the concert repertoire in the nineteenth century, this music achieved success because it resonated with the expectations and tastes of a nineteenth-century musically 'romantic' public. This double creation of a public and 'the baroque' laid the ground for the contemporary taste for 'authentic' early music – itself a re-creation that tells us more about contemporary taste, aesthetic preferences, programmes, and desires than about the seventeenth century, and creates a vantage point from which what was performed in the nineteenth century and much of the twentieth century as baroque music is now taken to be irredeemably romantic. Hennion's argument is that the notion of the baroque in music has been performative and has led to new and relatively pluralistic modes of empirical sensibility. Rather than there being an authentic and an inauthentic baroque, we are instead in the presence of different versions of what counts as truth. 'Performance', as Hennion puts it, 'is more relevant to music than truth. It is how music is played – and re-played – that is crucial'. Perhaps this is the lesson that we need to carry with us as we think about 'the baroque'.

In the chapter after Hennion's, Adrian Mackenzie notes that big data analytics like those used in President Obama's 2012 re-election campaign focus on individuals rather than populations. But individuals are understood as joint probability distributions within different intersecting populations. But what is a probability? There are two conventional answers. Probabilities may be objective or 'aleatory' frequencies, or they may be Bayesian subjective or 'epistemic' degrees of belief. Created at the time of the historical baroque, these two versions of probability have usually been held apart. However, this separation no longer works. Rather, both are entangled, baroque-like, in what Mackenzie calls a particular contemporary 'mode of computational machinery' which makes it possible to treat individuals as probability distributions. This baroque-inflected machinery includes Markov chain Monte Carlo simulation algorithms for computing multi-dimensional data spaces, in which what is taken as exact has been simulated. In what MacKenzie calls a 'neo-baroque' mode of knowing, objective numbers are being treated as subjective probability distributions. That is, they are folded together. As with Leibniz's monads (as understood by Deleuze), the entire world is being folded inside. The consequence is that truth becomes variation or distributive number and simulation simultaneously builds and maps a distribution. In this distribution (and again following Deleuze) curves become causes. In short, numbers are coming from the world, the subject, and also from places between these two: individuals have become ways of including the world. This, then, is the neo-baroque world of big data.

Evelyn Ruppert reflects on a domain of growing importance, that of sensory sociology, and attends again to 'big data'. Reviewing the state of art in sensory sociology, she argues that this reveals four sensibilities: first, a sensitivity to the specificities of different *media*; second, a concern with *liveliness*, the fleeting, ways of knowing that are distributed, multiple, complex, sensory, emotional, and kinaesthetic; third, an appreciation of their own *performativity*; and finally an openness to inventiveness and what (following Lury and Wakeford) she calls *answerability* to that inventiveness – that is, a concern to detect and explore the social worlds implied and enacted in methods. With this survey as a context, Ruppert turns to 'big data' and explores the performative and political consequences of network diagrams. These, she argues, work by reduction to make excessive data perceptible in ways that are relatively stable, stereotyped, and numbing. But she concludes her chapter by exploring an alternative: Agnes Chavez's (x)trees project. This is a quite different way of re-presenting relations in which those who are researched may become part of what they observe, while it is also inventive, answerable, performative, fleeting. Here data is being made lively, and becomes an encounter that is multiple and in which the self is made active, composed, and recomposed in relation to others.

What happens if we *experiment* with baroque ways of knowing? This question informs all the contributions, but is foregrounded in Part Two of the book. Mattijs van de Port is concerned with a particular disjunction: the observation that the fieldwork realities of anthropologists (or indeed our personally disruptive experiences) do not begin to fit the smooth narrations that we are required to produce as competent academics in seminar rooms or texts. He argues that we frequently experience a world that is in excess of what we make it to be when we bring it home and domesticate it for our audiences. Van de Port finds this disturbing. There must, he believes, be a better way of recognising these excessive realities. With this thought in mind, he turns to the baroque. This, he suggests, seems to be a mode of knowing that appreciates the limits of our representational capacities, and is willing to highlight a radical Otherness – what he calls 'the-rest-of-what-is'. But, he adds, there is a danger. If we subject the baroque to the orderly aesthetics of academia then this may threaten its powers of disruption. No longer a matter of experiencing the sense of being lost, the risk is that it might be domesticated. Perhaps if we ask instead what a baroque register *does* this might help. Taking the baroque of Salvador da Bahia, Brazil, as an empirical starting point, Van de Port takes us into its churches and explores how this aesthetic enters into experience to disrupt the ways in which we usually go about knowing as academics. His object is to thus prepare the ground for a 'baroque anthropology'. This would be a mode of knowing that better recognised the ineradicable tension that underlies all representational practices.

Helen Verran and Brit Ross Winthereik move us to Denmark to compare two visualising devices. Forced into the textual format of a book chapter, they ask the reader to treat this in a baroque 'now you see it, now you don't' mode by imagining their chapter as a performance. The first device comes from the Danish Partnership of Wave Energy and represents five stages of technological innovation as a smooth and single path from an orderly past to an ideal future, even though the participants know reality is more complicated. The other is a 1585 Danish baldachin, or tapestry throne canopy, that visualises and contributes to seventeenth-century innovation in a baroque mode. The authors treat both as visual rhetorics or diagrams in tension with related written texts. Each figures in a collective aspiration to innovate, representing and disciplining a messy present and relating it to an ideal version of the future. But they also work in the excessive here and now as forms of way-finding or pilotage, and Verran and Winthereik argue that they work quite differently. The technoscience wave-energy diagrams enforce non-equivocation and non-contradiction, and render it difficult to manage ambiguities and ambivalences. By contrast, the baroque baldachin offers ways of thinking and living that might make it possible to go on together in difference. The authors argue that learning how to inscribe visualising devices in order to recognise them as offering both representation and pilotage – navigation through the seas of complication without necessarily falling into line – is to nurture a baroque sensibility.

Hugh Raffles tells about the London Stone. What is this? What is its significance? Where does it come from? His chapter is by turns personal (he hunts the stone down in pouring rain on a grey Thatcherite November day to a run-down building near Canon Street); historical (he tells about the building of Roman London, about the revolt of Jack Cade in 1450 against Henry VI); geographical and antiquarian (in William Camden's 1580s encyclopaedia it becomes a rather uninteresting Roman milestone); mythical (a location or a site for Richard

William's nineteenth-century Celtic revival); and geological (an oolitic limestone laid down in the warm Iapetus Ocean around 150 million years ago). So there are different stories, and different times juxtaposed, washing round the London stone, this Ur-stone, lapping up against it, generating it in their different ways: daily minutes and hours, different versions of historical, mythical, symbolic, religious, and geological times. As he tells of this, Raffles cites Walter Benjamin: origin becomes a whirlpool, movement making momentary stability. So there is no priority between the stories. Science, fiction, history, and myth: they are all intertwined. But then, says Raffles, 'One man's hocus pocus is another's religion. One person's religion is another's occult paranoia'. And how are we to judge them? And the baroque? The term itself does not appear in his chapter, except perhaps obliquely via Benjamin. But then again, if we wanted to we could claim the piece for 'the baroque'. Juxtaposition, displacement, incompleteness, multiplication, interruption, a refusal of abstraction, in this experiment all of these are hard at work.

In the final chapter Annemarie Mol talks about clafoutis. Her interest is in using this dish as a way of talking theory and asking questions about coherence, baroque coherence. Her question is: what it is to hang together in the presence of tensions and changes? One part of the answer is composition. A clafoutis is composed of ingredients with different provenances and histories: combining these is an achievement. So agricultural worlds are being combined with techniques, forms of cuisine, the ideas and practices of nutrition, and the sensuous world of taste. As this composition implies a set of tensions and incommensurabilites, the coherence that ensues is baroque. This, however, does not mean that any random composition will do. This needs to be felicitous, to coagulate in a particular way, filled with contrasts internally, but also over time, indeed historically. So, for instance, the way the worlds of agriculture and cuisine came together in nineteenth-century France turned clafoutis into a felicitous possibility. By the mid-twentieth century the dish had spread but also altered and become 'healthy' (less sweet than the alternatives). Whether the worlds of clafoutis will hold together is contingent. Agricultures, modes of eating and cooking, criteria for health, all of these and more may change. And as the conditions of possibility for clafoutis disappear, the composition may fall apart. The lesson – and the fact that we digest clafoutis and excrete the remnants merely underlines this – is that baroque coherence is temporary. To last, a composite has to be done again and again – if necessary in different variants that combine different worlds together in novel ways.

ACKNOWLEDGEMENTS

I am grateful to the participants at the workshop on 'The Baroque as Empirical Sensibility' held from 11 to 13 June 2011 at the Manchester Museum in the University of Manchester, who brought the topic of the baroque in the contemporary humanities and social science to life. This introduction reflects many themes raised at that meeting. The workshop was sponsored by the UK's Economic and Social Research Council (ESRC) Centre for Research in Socio-Cultural Change (CRESC), and I am grateful to CRESC and the ESRC for financial support for the event. I am particularly grateful to Antoine Hennion, Helen Hills, Annemarie Mol, Hugh Raffles, Evelyn Ruppert, Anna Tsing, Mattijs van de Port, and Margaret Weiner, who commented on earlier drafts of this piece.

NOTES

1 Cited in Kerle (1995).
2 See, for instance, Kuhn (1970); Knorr-Cetina (1981); Haraway (1989); and Latour (1998).
3 See, for instance, Haraway (1991a); Staudenmaier sj (1994); Law (2002); and Rose (1994).
4 See *inter alia*, Cole (2002); Gabrys and Yusoff (2011); Guggenheim, Kraeftner, and Kroell (2013); Kraeftner and others (2010); Latour and Weibel (2005); Law (2011b); Myers (2012); Neuenschwander (2008); Shared Inc. (2014).
5 And notably Deleuze and Guattari (1988).
6 See, for instance, Bonelli (2012); de la Cadena (2010); Law (2004)(2011a); Mol (2002); Moser (2008); and Verran (1998).
7 See Mol (1999).
8 See several of the cases assembled by Raffles (2010).

9 See Hall and Ames (1995).

10 See Shapin and Schaffer (1985).

11 Since World War Two, academic knowing has become a factor of economic production, much research has been privatised, knowing has become increasingly functional in character and is shaped by government policy to be applied and instrumental. Perhaps these shifts have started to alter academic modes of knowing (Nowotny, Scott, and Gibbons 2001; Rabinow 1996).

12 <https://upload.wikimedia.org/wikipedia/commons/a/af/Santa_teresa_di_ bernini_04.JPG> [accessed 1 April 2016]

13 <http://commons.wikimedia.org/wiki/File:Santa_Maria_della_Vittoria_-_7.jpg> [accessed 11 July 2015]

14 <http://upload.wikimedia.org/wikipedia/commons/3/3a/Ecstasy_of_St_ Theresa_-_arrow.jpg> [accessed 11 July 2015]

15 In what follows I draw on Wittkower (1997 [1955]; 1999 [1958]); Hibbard (1990); Avery (1997); Toman (1998); and Hills (2007).

16 <https://upload.wikimedia.org/wikipedia/commons/7/7f/Ch%C3%A2teau_de_ Versailles,_salon_de_Diane,_buste_de_Louis_XIV,_Bernin_(1665)_03_black_bg.jpg> [accessed 01 April 2016]

17 <http://en.wikipedia.org/wiki/File:Giovanni_Lorenzo_Bernini-Blessed_Ludovica_ Albertoni-Basilica_of_San_Francesco_a_Ripa.jpg> [accessed 07 July 2015]

18 <https://upload.wikimedia.org/wikipedia/commons/e/e5/The_Incredulity_of_ Saint_Thomas-Caravaggio_(1601-2).jpg> [accessed 07 July 2015]

19 Guido Ubaldo Abbatini: Gian Lorenzo Bernini's Cornaro Chapel (c. 1650), Staatliches Museum, Schwerin. Copyright bpk – used with permission: <www.bpk-images.de> [accessed 25 April 2016].

20 See, for instance, Avery (1997: 144).

21 It's important that her foot is bare: she was the founder of the discalced – the shoeless – Carmelites.

22 <http://upload.wikimedia.org/wikipedia/commons/thumb/3/3e/Estasi_di_Santa_ Teresa.jpg/512px-Estasi_di_Santa_Teresa.jpg> [accessed 02 July 2015]

23 'By contrast to the calm, diffused light of the Renaissance, this directed light [of the baroque] seems fleeting, transient, impermanent' (Wittkower 1999 [1958]: 14).

24 <http://commons.wikimedia.org/wiki/File:Cornaro_SM_della_Vittoria.jpg> [accessed 02 July 2015]

25 This is the topic of considerable discussion in science and technology studies. See Haraway (1991b) and Shapin (1984).

26 John Evelyn, quoted by Wittkower (1997 [1955]: 13).

27 <http://en.wikipedia.org/wiki/File:Rome_Fontana_dei_Quattro_Fiume_10-01- 2011_11-54-14.JPG> [accessed 10 July 2015].

28 The argument comes from Deleuze (1993); see also Hills (2007), who explores Deleuze's argument in part with an account of Bernini's Santa Teresa.

29 <https://upload.wikimedia.org/wikipedia/commons/4/4c/Ecstasy_St_Theresa_ SM_della_Vittoria.jpg> [accessed 1 April 2016].

30 The argument comes from Deleuze. 'And when the folds of clothing spill out of painting, it is Bernini who endows them with sublime form in sculpture, when marble seizes and bears to infinity folds that cannot be explained by the body, but a spiritual adventure that can set the body ablaze' (1993: 121–22). Though Hibbard (1990: 140) offers an alternative reading that deserves serious attention. His suggestion is that it is the angel who is partially clothed in fire, 'a clinging, flame-like drapery'. By contrast, the saint is clothed (he suggests) in a 'coarse cloth' and seems 'almost earthbound, as if dragged down by the weight of material that seems to suffocate her'. The effect, he adds, is a 'poignant contrast between spirit made flesh and flesh made spirit'. Perhaps, then, we need to see the folds of the two gowns themselves as folded. For further commentary see Hills (2011a: 28).

31 I am misquoting Leibniz here. See Leibniz (1998), but of course the point is Deleuze's.

32 There are some responses to this question. Kwa (2002) argues that there is a subordinate but long-term baroque tradition at work in parts of the natural sciences, including meteorology and environmental science, where outsides are found within. Arguably so-called 'actor-network' theory also works in terms of a similar – and monadological – sensibility folding insides and outsides together. See, for instance, Callon and Latour (1981) and Latour (2001). For further commentary see Law (2004).

33 <http://upload.wikimedia.org/wikipedia/commons/a/a0/Cornaro_SM_della_ Vittoria.jpg> [accessed 07 July 2015]

34 I borrow from Leibniz (1998).

35 The incapacity to step outside is also reflected in seventeenth-century Netherlandish artistic practice, with rather different social, religious, and economic effects. See Alpers (1989).

36 These moved through different versions of contemplation, prayer, and ecstatic union with God.

37 These exercises were practised by the devout Bernini for the larger part of his life. Bernini also went to mass daily for forty years (Wittkower 1997 [1955]: 56, 196).

38 I thank Hugh Raffles for discussion on this point.

39 <http://upload.wikimedia.org/wikipedia/commons/3/30/Sant_ignazio_ceiling. jpg> [accessed 10 July 2015]

40 I thank Hugh Raffles for discussion on this point.

41 For the argument that the baroque, as understood by Walter Benjamin, can be treated as an aesthetics of Otherness, see Buci-Glucksmann (1994).

42 I am grateful to Antoine Hennion for discussion on this point, and I am grateful also to Mattijs van de Port for the inspiration of his work on Bahian condomblé. See van de Port (2011).

43 On mediation see Latour (2010a) and Hennion (2015).

44 Include in this pantheon the rich and powerful Cornaro clan, for as we gaze at Santa Teresa the person looking at us is none other than Cardinal Frederico Baldissera

Bartolomeo Cornaro, son of one Venetian Doge and brother of another. So the question is: what are we doing in his family chapel, which is, let's remember, also his sepulchre? The answer is that alongside everything else, we're subjecting ourselves to his scrutiny in addition to that of God.

45 Though he feels uneasy with the term baroque; see DaCosta Kaufmann (2011).

46 Echeverria (2005) in somewhat shaky translation. Echeverria's argument is picked up and explored by Gandolfo (2009).

47 For Benjamin in the form of the card index and the juxtaposed notes that make up the ruins of his unfinished *Arcades Project* (Benjamin 1999). He writes about the card index as 'the conquest of three-dimensional writing' in *One-Way Street* (Benjamin: 1985a: 62). For commentary see Buck-Morss (1989).

48 A misquote from the ninth of Benjamin's *Theses on the Philosophy of History* with its commentary on Paul Klee's *Angelus Novus*. '[The angel's] face is turned towards the past. Where we perceive a chain of events, he sees one single catastrophe which keeps piling wreckage upon wreckage and hurls it in front of his feet. The angel would like to stay, awaken the dead, and make whole what has been smashed. But a storm is blowing from Paradise...' (Benjamin 1992: 249).

49 For this argument applied to the conditions for felicitous speech in religion and developed in a different direction, see Latour (2010b). The argument about performativity has been widely extended to other contemporary forms of knowing, including those of technoscience. See, for instance, Latour and Woolgar (1986).

50 See the essays collected in Hills (2011b) and Hills' introductory essay to that volume (Hills (2011a)), but also Lambert (2004). On art markets and the conditions of art production in the Netherlands in its seventeenth-century 'Golden Age', see Alpers (1988).

51 For accounts of this shift, see Lambert (2004) and Hills (2011a).

52 'The baroque', wrote Wölfflin, 'never offers us perfection and fulfilment, or the static calm of "being", only the unrest of change and the tension of transience' (Wölfflin 1984: 62) and Wölfflin (1984: 64).

53 There's a hole in the middle, a gap, which is the invisible absence of the capacity to represent representation. Such is the point of his deconstruction of Velasquez' Las Meninas.

BIBLIOGRAPHY

Alpers, S., *Rembrandt's Enterprise: The Studio and the Market* (Chicago: Chicago University Press, 1988)

———— *The Art of Describing: Dutch Art in the Seventeenth Century* (London: Penguin, 1989).

Avery, C., *Bernini: Genius of the Baroque* (London: Thames and Hudson, 1997)

Barton, L., ed., *Disability and Society: Emerging Issues and Insights*, Longman Sociology Series (London and New York: Longman, 1996)

Benjamin, W., *One-Way Street and Other Writings* (London: Verso, 1985a)

—— *The Origin of German Tragic Drama*, J. Osborne, trans. (London: Verso, 1985b)

—— 'Theses on the Philosophy of History', in W. Benjamin, *Illuminations* (London: Fontana, 1992), pp. 245–255

—— *The Arcades Project*, H. Zohn, trans. (Cambridge, MA, and London: Harvard University Press, 1999)

Bonelli, C., 'Ontological Disorders: Nightmares, Psychotropic Drugs and Evil Spirits in Southern Chile', *Anthropological Theory*, 12.4 (2012), 407–426

Buci-Glucksmann, C., *Baroque Reason: The Aesthetics of Modernity*, P. Camiller, trans. (London, Thousand Oaks, and New Delhi: Sage, 1994)

Buck-Morss, S., *The Dialectics of Seeing: Walter Benjamin and the Arcades Project* (Cambridge, MA: MIT, 1989)

Callon, M., and B. Latour, 'Unscrewing the Big Leviathan: How Actors Macrostructure Reality and how Sociologists Help them to Do So', in K. Knorr-Cetina, and A. Cicourel, eds., *Advances in Social Theory and Methodology: Toward an Integration of Micro- and Macro-Sociologies* (Boston, MA: Routledge and Kegan Paul, 1981), pp. 277–303

Caygill, H., 'Ottoman Baroque: The Limits of Style', in H. Hills, ed., *Rethinking the Baroque* (Burlington, VT, and Farnham: Ashgate, 2011), pp. 65–79

Cole, P., 'Aboriginalizing Methodology: Considering the Canoe', *International Journal of Qualitative Studies in Education*, 15.4 (2002), 447–459. Also available at: http://dx.doi.org/10.1080/09518390210145516

DaCosta Kaufmann, T., 'Discomfited by the Baroque: A Personal Journey', in H. Hills, ed., *Rethinking the Baroque* (Farnham, UK, and Burlington, VT: Ashgate, 2011), pp. 84–98

de la Cadena, M., 'Indigenous Cosmopolitics in the Andes: Conceptual Reflections Beyond "Politics"', *Cultural Anthropology*, 25.2 (2010), 334–370

Deleuze, G., *The Fold: Leibniz and the Baroque* (London: Athlone Press, 1993)

Deleuze, G., and F. Guattari, *A Thousand Plateaus: Capitalism and Schizophrenia* (London: Athlone Press, 1988)

Despret, V., *Our Emotional Makeup: Ethnopsychology and Selfhood*, M. de Jager, trans. (New York: Other Press, 2004)

Echeverria, B., 'Modernity and Capitalism (15 Theses)', *Revista Theomai/Theomai Journal; Estudios sobre Sociedad, Naturaleza y Desarrollo/Society, Nature and Development Studies*, 11 (2005). Also available at: http://revista-theomai.unq.edu.ar/numero11/artbolivarecheverria11.htm

Foucault, M., *The Archaeology of Knowledge* (London: Tavistock, 1972)

—— *Discipline and Punish: The Birth of the Prison* (Harmondsworth: Penguin, 1979)

Gabrys, J., and K. Yusoff, 'Arts, Sciences and Climate Change: Practices and Politics at the Threshold', *Science as Culture*, 21.1 (2011), 1–24. Also available at: http://dx.doi.org/10.1080/09505431.2010.550139

Gandolfo, D., *The City at its Limits: Taboo, Transgression, and Urban Renewal in Lima* (Chicago and London: University of Chicago Press, 2009)

Guggenheim, M., B. Kraeftner, and J. Kroell, '"I Don't Know Whether I Need a Further Level of Disaster": Shifting Media of Sociology in the Sandbox', *Distinktion: Scandinavian Journal of Social Theory*, 14.3 (2013), 284–304. Also available at http://dx.doi.org/10.1080/1600910X.2013.838977

Hall, D. L., and R. T. Ames, *Anticipating China: Thinking Through the Narratives of Chinese and Western Culture* (Albany: State University of New York, 1995)

Haraway, D. J., *Primate Visions: Gender, Race and Nature in the World of Modern Science* (London: Routledge and Chapman Hall, 1989)

———— 'A Cyborg Manifesto: Science, Technology and Socialist Feminism in the Late Twentieth Century', in D. Haraway, ed., *Simians, Cyborgs and Women: the Reinvention of Nature* (London: Free Association Books, 1991a), pp. 149–181. Also available at http://www.stanford.edu/dept/HPS/Haraway/CyborgManifesto.html

———— 'Situated Knowledges: The Science Question in Feminism and the Privilege of Partial Perspective', in D. Haraway, ed., *Simians, Cyborgs and Women: the Reinvention of Nature* (London: Free Association Books, 1991b), pp. 183–201. Also available at http://www.staff.amu.edu.pl/~ewa/Haraway,%20Situated%20Knowledges.pdf

Hennion, A., *The Passion for Music: A Sociology of Mediation* (Farnham: Ashgate, 2015)

Hibbard, H., *Bernini* (London: Penguin, 1990)

Hills, H., 'The Baroque: Beads in a Rosary or Folds in Time', *Fabrications: The Journal of the Society of Architectural Historians, Australia and New Zealand*, 17.2 (2007), 48–71

———— 'The Baroque: Grit in the Oyster of Art History', in H. Hills, ed., *Rethinking the Baroque* (Burlington, VT, and Farnham: Ashgate, 2011a), pp. 11–36

———— ed., *Rethinking the Baroque* (Burlington, VT, and Farnham: Ashgate, 2011b)

Kerle, A., *Uluru, Kata Tjuta & Watarrka: Ayers Rock/the Olgas & Kings Canyon, Northern Territory* (Sydney: University of New South Wales Press, 1995)

Knorr-Cetina, K., *The Manufacture of Knowledge: An Essay on the Constructivist and Contextual Nature of Science* (Oxford: Pergamon Press, 1981)

Kraeftner, B. et al., 'A Pillow Squirrel and its Habitat: Patients, a Syndrome, and their Dwelling(s)', in M. Schillmeier, and M. Domenech, eds., *New Technologies and Emerging Spaces of Care* (Burlington: Ashgate, 2010), pp. 169–195)

Kuhn, T. S., *The Structure of Scientific Revolutions* (Chicago: Chicago University Press, 1970)

Kwa, C., 'Romantic and Baroque Conceptions of Complex Wholes in the Sciences', in J. Law, and A. Mol, eds., *Complexities: Social Studies of Knowledge Practices* (Durham, NC, and London: Duke University Press, 2002), pp. 23–52

Lambert, G., *Return of the Baroque: Art, Theory and Culture in the Modern Age* (London: Continuum, 2004)

Latour, B., 'Circulating Reference: Sampling the Soil in the Amazon Forest', in B. Latour, ed., *Pandora's Hope: Essays on the Reality of Science Studies* (Cambridge, MA: Harvard University Press, 1998), pp. 24–79

———— 'Gabriel Tarde and the End of the Social', in P. Joyce, ed., *The Social in Question. New*

Bearings in History and the Social Sciences (London: Routledge, 2001), pp. 117–132. Also available at http://www.ensmp.fr/~latour/articles/article/082.html

———— *On the Modern Cult of the Factish Gods* (Durham, NC, and London: Duke, 2010a)

———— '"Thou Shalt Not Freeze Frame", Or How Not to Misunderstand the Science and Religion Debate', in B. Latour, *On the Modern Cult of the Factish Gods* (Durham, NC, and London: Duke, 2010b), pp. 99–123

———— *An Inquiry into Modes of Existence: An Anthropology of the Moderns* (Cambridge, MA and London: Harvard University Press, 2013)

Latour, B., and P. Weibel, *Making Things Public: Atmospheres of Democracy* (Karlsruhe and Cambridge, MA: ZKM and MIT Press, 2005)

Latour, B., and S. Woolgar, *Laboratory Life: The Construction of Scientific Facts*, 2nd edn (Princeton, NJ: Princeton University Press, 1986)

Law, J., *Aircraft Stories: Decentering the Object in Technoscience* (Durham, NC: Duke University Press, 2002)

———— *After Method: Mess in Social Science Research* (London: Routledge, 2004)

———— 'Collateral Realities', in F. Domínguez Rubio, and P. Baert, eds., *The Politics of Knowledge* (London: Routledge, 2011a), pp. 156–178

———— 'The Explanatory Burden: An Essay on Hugh Raffles' *Insectopedia*', *Cultural Anthropology*, 26.3 (2011b), 485–510

Leibniz, G. W., 'Monadology', in R. S. Woodhouse and R. Franks, eds., *G.W. Leibniz: Philosophical Texts* (Oxford and New York: Oxford University Press, 1998), pp. 268–281

Lin, W., and J. Law, 'A Correlative STS? Lessons from a Chinese Medical Practice', *Social Studies of Science*, 44.6 (2014), 801–824. Also available at doi:10.1177/0306312714531325

Maravall, J. A., *Culture of the Baroque: Analysis of a Historical Structure* (Manchester: Manchester Univerisity Press, 1986)

Mol, A., 'Ontological Politics: A Word and Some Questions', in J. Law, and J. Hassard, eds., *Actor Network Theory and After* (Oxford and Keele: Blackwell and the Sociological Review, 1999), pp. 74–89

———— *The Body Multiple: Ontology in Medical Practice* (Durham, NC, and London: Duke University Press, 2002)

Mol, A., I. Moser, and J. Pols (eds), *Care in Practice: On Tinkering in Clinics, Homes and Farms* (Bielefeld: Transcript Publishers, 2010)

Moser, I., 'Making Alzheimer's Disease Matter: Enacting, Interfering and Doing Politics of Nature', *Geoforum*, 39 (2008), 98–110

Myers, N., 'Dance Your PhD: Embodied Animations, Body Experiments, and the Affective Entanglements of Life Science Research', *Body & Society*, 18.1 (2012), 151–189

Neuenschwander, R., *Contingent*, [artwork] (2008). Available at <https://www.youtube.com/watch?v=gurlpLOyubA>

Nowotny, H., P. Scott, and M. Gibbons, *Re-Thinking Science: Knowledge and the Public in an Age of Uncertainty* (Cambridge: Polity Press, 2001)

Polanyi, M., *Personal Knowledge: Towards a Post-Critical Philosophy* (London: Routledge and Kegan Paul, 1958)

Rabinow, P., *Making PCR: A Story of Biotechnology* (Chicago and London: Chicago University Press, 1996)

Raffles, H., *Insectopedia* (New York: Pantheon Books, 2010)

Rose, H., *Love, Power and Knowledge: Towards a Feminist Tranformation of the Sciences* (Cambridge: Polity, 1994)

Serres, M., *Biogea* (Minneapolis: Univocal, 2012)

Shapin, S., 'Pump and Circumstance: Robert Boyle's Literary Technology', *Social Studies of Science*, 14 (1984), 481–520

Shapin, S., and S. Schaffer, *Leviathan and the Air-Pump: Hobbes, Boyle and the Experimental Life* (Princeton, NJ: Princeton University Press, 1985)

Shared Inc., 'Pillow Research', in *Truth Is Concrete: A Handbook for Artistic Strategies in Real Politics* (Berlin and Graz: Sternberg Press, 2014)

Staudenmaier sj, J., 'To Fall in Love with the World: Individualism and Self-Transcendence in American Life', *Studies in the Spirituality of Jesuits*, 26 (1994), 1–28

Teresa of Àvila, *The Life of Teresa of Jesus* (Image Books, 1964)

Toman, R., ed., *Baroque: Architecture, Scultpure, Painting* (Cologne: Könemann Verlagsgesellschaft mbH, 1998)

Ufan, L., *Marking Infinity* (New York: Guggenheim Museum Publications, 2011)

van de Port, M., *Ecstatic Encounters: Bahian Condomblé and the Quest for the Really Real* (Amsterdam: Amsterdam University Press, 2011)

Verran, H., 'Re-Imagining Land Ownership in Australia', *Postcolonial Studies*, 1.2 (1998), 237–254

——— *Science and an African Logic* (Chicago and London: Chicago University Press, 2001)

Warwick, G., *Bernini: Art as Theatre* (New Haven, CT, and London: Yale University Press, 2012)

Wittkower, R., *Bernini: The Sculptor of the Roman Baroque* (London and New York: Phaidon, 1997 [1955])

——— *Art and Architecture in Italy 1600–1750: II High Baroque*, J. Connors, and J. Montague, rev (New Haven, CT, and London: Yale University Press, (1999 [1958]))

Wölfflin, H., *Renaissance and Baroque* (London: Collins, 1984)

REFLECTION ON THE BAROQUE

2

ON EXCEEDING BAROQUE EXCESS: AN EXPLORATION THROUGH A PARTICIPATORY COMMUNITY WORKSHOP

Mario Blaser

'TO PUT IT SIMPLY, THE BAROQUE WAS A CULTURE IN TENSION. IT WAS indeed repressive but it was also (and therefore) about the *transgressions* of lively excess, about "obeying without fulfilling"'. This thought (which I take from John Law's introduction to this volume) is attractive because it is, or so we have been told, constitutive of a mythical place I feel I belong to – that of Latin America. Walter Mignolo has argued that Latin America is an idea that emerged 'in the process of the transformation of the colonial Creole baroque ethos into the postcolonial Creole "Latin ethos"' (2005: 65).

The short version of the story goes like this: in Europe the baroque emerged as a response to the Protestant reformation; when it came to the Spanish colonies the baroque took two different forms. On the one hand, there was a version of the baroque that expressed the distinct aesthetics of the *peninsulares* (the expatriate European elites at the top of the colonial administration), but it also operated as an instrument of empire geared to awe the Indians. On the other hand, there was a 'civil society' form that expressed the emerging 'critical consciousness' of the Creoles of Spanish descent, who were socially and economically subordinate to those European expatriates.

Mignolo bases his notion of a 'civil society' baroque on Bolivar Echevarria, from whom he translates the following passage:

> There were the Creoles from low social levels, the Indian and Afro-Mestizos, those whom, without knowing it, would end up doing what Bernini did with the classical canon of painting: these mixed groups of lower social strata endeavored to reestablish the most viable civilization, which was the dominant one, the European. They intended to wake it up and then to restore its original vitality. In doing so, in invigorating the European code over the ruins of the pre-Spanish code (and with the remainders of the African slaves' codes brought by force into the picture), they would find themselves building something different from their original intention; they would find themselves raising up a Europe that never existed before them, a different Europe, a 'Latin American' Europe (Bolivar Echevarria, in Mignolo 2005: 63).

Commenting on this passage, Mignolo points out that not only is 'Latin America' an anachronism (this entity would not exist until the nineteenth century) but also that 'this political project in practice as well as in consciousness was still defined by the Spanish and Portuguese Creole elites, who kept their backs to the Indian and African populations co-existing among them' (2005: 63). In effect, after the independence wars in the nineteenth century, these Creole elites displaced the peninsular elites and set themselves the task of building polities that had Europe as model and vector. Though the identity of the postcolonial nation was imagined on the basis of the Creole baroque (that is, a hybrid Latin America), the project was about 'the restoration of the most viable civilization (said Echevarría) – the European, and not the Indigenous or African' (Mignolo 2005: 64).

Mignolo's take on the Creole baroque and its relation to Latin America foregrounds two points I engage with in this chapter. The first is that a baroque sensibility is inherently neither dominatory nor transgressive. Which of these forms it takes depends on specifically situated relations. In Europe, and in relation to the Reformation, the baroque was intended to sustain the status quo. In the New World, but only in the relations between creoles and 'peninsulares', the baroque exceeded and transgressed its original conservative intent, becoming a vehicle that articulated the aspirations of the former. The second and connected point is that transgressive excess can *also* be exceeded. The realisation of the Creoles' aspirations implied a shift in, but not an end to, the subordinate positions of Indigenous and Afro-descendants, whose aspirations exceeded what was articulated through the Creole baroque.

This suggests the potential fruitfulness of exploring the character of excess carefully and empirically to see how it gets composed as transgressive or otherwise. What I seek to do in this chapter is recount a 'community participatory workshop' that took place in an Yshiro Indigenous community in Paraguay.[1] In what follows I do not experiment with style. I do not seek to perform a baroque way of knowing. Rather, and like some of the other contributors to this volume, my concern is with excess – and the *uses of excess*. Nonetheless, at the end of the chapter I hope that I have something to say about the baroque or at least that I have raised some questions which may be pertinent to our understanding of its uses.

SETTING THE STAGE

Over the last two decades or so, the geographical area where the Yshiro live has endured an aggressive advance of cattle-ranching enterprises that have clear-cut forests and built fences that parcel up the land. The process has been rather dramatic. Indeed, the region is close to the top in the world's ranking of forest loss (Coca and Reymondin 2012). As a consequence, the region has also become the target of a range of public and private initiatives aimed at curbing the loss of 'biodiversity' associated with this process. The main initiative has been the establishment of a Biosphere Reserve that, under the umbrella of UNESCO's Man and Biosphere Programme, encompasses over 7 million hectares. Over 1 million hectares of this Reserve are in protected areas designated as National Parks (UNESCO 2006). One of these, the Rio Negro National Park, is located right in Yshiro traditional territory.

On the ground, the existence of these programmes and initiatives translates in a range of ways which include restrictions on access to the natural resources still available. Being directly or indirectly dependent on the forest, the Yshiro have found themselves caught between a staggeringly fast process of deforestation and increasing restrictions on access to whatever is left. By 2005 it had become evident to them that their future capacity to live in and from their territory was under severe threat.[2] This triggered a series of discussions among the Yshiro leadership in search of a joint response. In my role as an advisor and researcher with *Unión de las Comunidades Indígenas de la Nación Yshir* (UCINY) – the organisation that federates the Yshiro leaders – I was tasked with setting up and garnering resources for a process of internal discussion and consultation within the communities.

I had been working with the Yshiro communities since 1991, and in 1999 I collaborated with them in the creation of UCINY as part of a very similar process to the one the Yshiro leaders were seeking in this case. This meant that I was not surprised to find the work arduous, as the creation of a common strategy had to overcome important internal differences of a kind that I had experienced before (see Blaser 2010). Indeed, the Yshiro communities are far from being homogeneous. Thus, though this is simplistic, to get the idea across quickly, one way of talking about this is in terms of a continuum between traditionalists and non-traditionalists. The terms are variably used by the Yshiro themselves and point to a cluster of characteristics which tend to be associated – although not as consistently as the labels would make it appear. Thus, traditionalists are likely to be illiterate, know little or no Spanish, be heavily dependent on direct use of natural resources for subsistence, and participate in practices that involve earth-beings. In the present context it will suffice to say that this term seeks to capture two main points: the existence of entities that do not fit modern distinctions between cultural, natural, and super-natural domains; and the degree to which these entities are thoroughly imbricated with particular places.[3] Non-traditionalists, in contrast, would more likely have some degree of literacy, be relatively more fluent in Spanish, more likely to be in some form of permanent or seasonal wage-labour, and either be committed Christians who reject anything associated with 'cultura' (a term that glosses relations with earth-beings), or at least be quite sceptical with regard to the validity of traditionalists' values and understandings.

These differences suggest that what went under the label of 'territory' was not exactly the same for different groups in the communities. Consequently, different people conceived the processes affecting this entity – and how to respond to them – in different and not necessarily compatible ways. For example, at one end of the spectrum there were a few non-traditionalists for whom 'territory' meant little more than having a little bit of land to build up an economic base for family-based farming mixed with waged jobs. For these people the key solution to the threat posed by a disappearing forest was to secure jobs. At other end of the spectrum there were knowledgeable traditionalists for whom access to the entire territory was crucial not only for the Yshiro's 'economic' survival, but also to avert the ongoing disappearance of the *yrmo*. For the moment, let me just indicate that the *yrmo* connotes a localised symbiopoietic tangle of relations in which practices such as hunting, visiting places, initiation rituals, and careful protocols in relation to earth-beings are crucial.[4] In this sense, while in some contexts the term *yrmo* can be legitimately understood as equivalent to 'traditional territory', this would only be a superficial rendering of it. I will return to the point later. For the moment I focus on the community discussions.

Since most people expressed views that fell somewhere between the two ends of the spectrum described above, it became evident that for the majority, securing the territory was a basic condition for their survival, regardless of whether one conceived of this in its extensive or restricted meaning. Thus, the result of the process of community discussions was a simple yet ambitious mandate for the Yshiro leaders and UCINY: to recover and secure control of the Yshiro traditional territory by any possible means.

After considering several options, the leaders finally decided that the best initial strategy was to attack the Paraguayan government's lack of consultation in setting up conservation programmes in the area, and to see if UCINY could win a 'seat' among the partners running the conservation programmes. From that position, the leaders anticipated, UCINY could pursue several lines of action, such as persuading the government to buy and/or expropriate private ranches and restore the property to the Yshiro; enticing environmental NGOs that had been promoting carbon-offset programmes to partner with UCINY to buy lands in a consortium; and progressively gaining de facto if not *de jure* control over the management of the Rio Negro National Park that was the nucleus of the protected area in Yshiro territory. The strategy gravitated around the fact that institutions like the Global Environmental Facility (GEF) and the United Nations Development Program (UNDP) were financing several conservation projects in the protected areas. These institutions require project proponents (in this case the Paraguayan government) to consult with the local peoples affected by the projects they finance. In 2007, the Yshiro leaders sent a letter to the Paraguayan Secretariat of the Environment making clear that they would tell the funders that the agency had lied when it asserted that the National Park was being established with the agreement of the local population, and that in fact the local population still had no participation in what was taking place in their traditional territories. The participatory workshop I discuss here was part of the Paraguayan government's response to the Yshiro claim.[5]

The stated aim of the workshop was to 'harmonise' the 'development' needs of the Yshiro with the conservation plans underway in the area. Between 45 and 50 people attended, including a team of technicians from an NGO carrying out the exercise (including a participatory methods facilitator), male and female leaders from the various Yshiro communities, a large group of community members who had heeded the call to participate in the participatory workshop, and me in my role as advisor to the leaders. The reader should bear in mind that at least a third of the participants had little to no knowledge of Spanish (the language used by the facilitator), for another additional third many of the words and concepts being used were rather foreign, and the Yshiro assistant in charge of translating himself struggled to find appropriate words in Yshiro to convey what the facilitator intended.

CREATING ACCOMPLICES

Participatory methods like those deployed in the workshop are fundamentally instruments of planning. What distinguishes them is that they are staged in such a way as to evoke a feeling of involvement in the 'target population'; or such, at least, is the expectation. In fact, many 'practitioner manuals' stress the ludic, aesthetic, and theatrical aspects of the methodology as crucial to attracting participants and developing in them a sense of ownership of the results (Steyaert and Lisoir 2005; Chevalier and Buckles 2011). In contrast with the austere setting of a pedagogical (or top-down) intervention, where people usually play the role of audience to an expert, the participatory workshop is full of movement as people group and regroup, conversational circles are formed, furniture is moved around, role-play is enacted, floors and walls are used as drawing boards, and colourful sticky notes are fixed all over the place.

The workshop followed this pattern. The activities took place in the school of the largest and (for outsiders) most accessible Yshiro community. We occupied a large room and formed a series of concentric semicircles facing a wall where graphics, large sheets of paper, and sticky notes were progressively pinned up as the activities advanced. During the day and a half of the workshop, the facilitator deployed at least six different 'techniques' displaying an abundance of forms and elements. The workshop began with the facilitator pinning a large white card on the wall with the words 'desired scenarios' written in red and inviting participants to think collectively about it. He explained what he meant by this: 'think for a moment what you would need for the community to be satisfied and happy'. Then he explained how the exercise would proceed: people would form groups of four individuals that would discuss the topic and designate a spokesperson who would report verbally to the rest of the groups after ten or fifteen minutes.

I approached one of the groups to listen in on the discussion. The four people in the group very quickly started talking about the mandate the communities had given to UCINY, that is, the recovery of territory. Something similar may have happened in the other groups, for when other spokespersons reported back to the whole meeting the message was quite consistent: what was important was access and free movement within an extended territory.[6] The facilitator wrote the words 'general goal = recovery of territory' on a large sheet of paper. And with this he started another exercise aimed at answering the question 'why is territory important?' Again participants were divided, but this time into pairs.

The aim was to pair someone who could write and speak Spanish with someone who could not, since the result of the discussion had to be written on a card. Each pair had to discuss and note down five reasons why territory was important, and each reason should be expressed in no more than a brief line. When they read from their cards each pair would have an opportunity to expand on what they had written.

Once everyone was ready the facilitator started to invite spokespersons to present and discuss the reasons they had come up with, and as people were talking he wrote new labels on the large sheet of paper. At the end, three labels ('economic', 'cultural', and 'environmental') ended up as the main reasons for 'why is territory important?' Although at this point we took a break, through subsequent exercises the labels were used as domains containing 'specific problems' and their potential solutions expressed as goals. In the rest of the workshop, exercises further subdivided these specific goals into smaller objectives to be achieved through specific tasks.

In each instance, the same pattern was repeated. The facilitator would pose an 'issue'. He would provide a specific procedure to think about that issue (e.g. think of an individual response, discuss in a small group, open general discussion); a specific form to express the thought (verbally, written, or drawn); and a specific form to inscribe it (cards, large sheets of paper, or inserted into pre-formatted graphics). These inscriptions would then be 'summarised' as labels or bullet points at the end of each exercise, and they would in turn, provide the starting point for the next exercise. In this way the workshop moved sequentially from establishing a set of 'desired scenarios' for the communities, to breaking down the scenarios into a number of domains within which specific objectives had to be established, to a definition of conditions needed and obstacles to be sorted to achieve the objectives, and finally to drafting a road map of actions (including the distribution of individual or institutional tasks and responsibilities).

At first sight this might look like a simple movement from the general to the specific, but on a closer look it is clear that at each step, through translation and inscription, the desires, visions, and values of participants were being guided in specific directions. For instance, during the exercise to define the reasons that made territory important, participants expressed concern about increasing obstacles to hunting and fishing as a way of subsistence. Translated into a 'problem', the concern ended up within the domain of economics. The corresponding solution/objective teased out of the discussion was (again) inscribed as a written label that read as 'generating economic alternatives'. The subsequent exercises in this 'domain' were geared to breaking down this 'large objective' into smaller ones that could be tackled through specific tasks. In a similar way, concerns with access to places of 'ritual' importance were translated and inscribed as another large objective: 'protecting cultural heritage' and its associated smaller objectives and tasks. And again the same happened with concerns expressed by some Yshiro as 'the animals are being left without a house', that were translated and inscribed into the objective 'protecting natural resources'. I will return later to what was 'lost in translation' through this process. First, however, I would like to point out a few resonances I find between the workshop as an artefact and the baroque.

For a casual observer not familiar with the Yshiro communities and their language, the workshop would have seemed highly successful, at least in engaging participants. And indeed, the abundance of forms and elements in the staging of the workshop did facilitate participants' engagement. Almost everybody actively took part and the atmosphere was largely relaxed and fun, in part because participatory techniques are designed in a game-like fashion, but also because for many Yshiro the prompts from the facilitator were somehow perplexing or confusing, which led to much teasing among them (in their own language). In any case, people's participation lent plausibility to the facilitator's claim that the workshop had helped to generate a plan based on the community's desires, visions, and values, even though the process of translating and inscribing what participants expressed also implied guiding them in specific directions. This recalls Maravall's comment, mentioned in the introduction to this volume, that the baroque was in part a 'guided culture' created in the face of an enquiring individualism and its freedoms, which responded not by simply imposing silence but also by guiding and turning spectators into accomplices.

But, if the baroque was intended to control and guide an emerging culture of individualism and freedom, what was this workshop trying to guide as it harnessed participation? And why, in this case, did guidance require participation?

COMMANDING WITHOUT REPELLING

The history and the value of 'participation in development' planning are large and contested topics (see Cooke and Kothari 2001; Hickey and Mohan 2004). The practices associated with the concept have many roots, and the paths that led to its mainstreaming as a tool of governance are also multiple. However, in relation to indigenous peoples, it is clear that 'participation' did not become a central concern for governmental and other agents of 'development' until the mid-1980s when these groups' political mobilisation and increasing visibility on the international stage began to render moot the expectation that they were either 'absent' (i.e. extinct as viable societies) or on the way to becoming so (see Blaser 2010). Here there were peoples with relatively increasing political clout claiming the right to self-determination and to being different. What could possibly be the content of such claim of difference? And what implications could it have for the political economy of the nation state?

At this point the concept of 'ethnodevelopment' came to do several forms of conceptual work. First, it indexed the end of the assumption that 'Indians' were an absence (actual or future) embedded in more or less tempered Rostownian notions of development as modernisation (i.e. the unilinear trajectory to be followed by everyone and leading to the status of 'developed' society). Secondly, it provided a workable placeholder for the 'unknown' inherent in indigenous peoples' claims to self-determination. In the mid-1980s, Rodolfo Stavenhagen (1986), one of the earlier proponents of the concept, pointed out that claims to self-determination, and more generally claims articulated in terms of ethnic identity, certainly implied demands for a better life. However, the argument followed that these demands could not be simply equated to a claim for development understood as economic growth and modernisation. Rather, they implied a diversity of visions as to what a good life would consist of and how to achieve it (Stavenhagen 1986). Thus, ethnodevelopment was proposed as a term to account for this diversity and as a practice to be fostered in contradistinction to the ethnocidal practices implied by development as modernisation.

Ethnodevelopment went on to have a successful career in development circles, particularly as it eventually found comfortable accommodation within the panoply of neoliberal reforms being rolled out across the world after the collapse of the Soviet bloc (see Andolina, Laurie, and Radcliffe 2009). In this space, ethnodevelopment and participatory methods quickly became entangled. In effect, participatory methodologies promised to turn the 'unknown' content of notions of a good life implicit in indigenous claims for self-determination into something knowable and amenable to governmental intervention. It is precisely at this point that the idea of ethnodevelopment showed its workability; as long as it required governmental intervention for its realisation, a door remained open for participatory methodologies to guide the 'unknown' into acceptable forms. This does not imply a malevolent intent. Quite the contrary – in many cases guidance was and is conceived as helping indigenous communities and organisations to gain a 'realistic understanding' of the context in which their impetus for self-determination, or whatever demands they have, must unfold. Significantly, however, this 'guidance' moves away from open coercion, and thus from repelling those being guided, by folding the coercive character of the enterprise into a sort of external and mute 'reality' – or 'reality principle'. In other words, there is an implicit claim that the direction given by those 'guiding' participation is not an arbitrary imposition but a response to 'reality'. All of this was quite evident in the Yshiro workshop.

The NGO that ran it was tasked with helping the Yshiro come out with a 'development' plan that would be in synergy with the ongoing conservation projects and policies promoted in the area. As is usually the case, the NGO's mandate had a number of unspoken constraints. These were 'issues' that, while central to the topic of the workshop, had to remain out of bounds. For instance, it went without saying that an expanding cattle-ranching industry was an unshakable fact and would remain such. Similarly, it went without saying that different governmental schemes for the protection of natural resources were there to stay. Neither of these issues was up for discussion. Thus whatever came out of the workshop had to be something that could stand between these two 'elephants in the room'. It is not that the NGO staff running the workshop or the Yshiro participants could not see how central these issues were to the whole discussion. The point is that as soon as there was any sign that these issues might be brought to the fore, their scope and their assumed 'scale' pulled them into the background again. When a few Yshiro started to vent their frustration as to why the government was just creating protected areas instead of stopping cattle ranchers from clear-cutting the forest in their properties, the facilitator pulled the discussion back 'on track'.

> Guys, guys, let's keep on topic. Yes, it is true the ranchers keep cutting down trees, but we cannot do anything about this here in this workshop. You have to petition the government, speak with the *diputados* [parliamentary representatives] to modify the laws. In the meantime we have to be realistic and work with what we have.

The magnitude of the work required to 'tame the elephants in the room' was used to indicate that the 'site' to address such issues was elsewhere and not in the workshop. By pleading the need to keep on topic the facilitator was implicitly imparting a command to the workshop participants: 'help us stage a credible participatory process from which "we" (you and us) can draft a *realistic* development plan'. It does not take much to see how in one event a participatory workshop mimics the overall form of engagement that is commanded from indigenous peoples in a liberal multicultural society: express your vision/difference in a way that we can work with, or, to use Povinelli's words, make yourself doable for us (Povinelli 2001). But as has been noted before, the baroque makes it possible to obey without fulfilling, so let us explore how participants in our workshop did this.

OBEYING WITHOUT FULFILLING: TRANSGRESSIONS, DIGRESSIONS, AND EQUIVOCATIONS

The community mandate to recover control over the territory was important for leaders and community members engaged in the participatory workshop, but many were also clearly aware of the bounded kind of 'participation' that the event would offer. Indeed, participatory methods have been deployed regularly in the Yshiro communities at least since the late 1990s (see Blaser 2010). Thus, some of the participants – especially former and current leaders – engaged in the theatrics of the process not primarily for the overt aim of generating a development plan, but as a way of gaining a foothold to pursue more ambitious goals. Insofar as these goals run counter to the mandate to remain 'realistic' (i.e. not seeking to counter the double process of destruction and protection of 'natural resources'), a transgressive element was present in the staging of the participation.

But alongside transgression, there were also digressions. Thus without running directly against the grain of the workshop, many were involved as a way of positioning themselves to better tap into the material resources that would likely be made available through an ethnodevelopment plan. So for those for whom a lot of what was being done in the workshop made little sense or for those who were sceptical about the lofty, if reduced, goals that the plan might actually achieve, it was still worthwhile helping to stage 'participation'. Later they could demand reciprocity from the NGO and the leaders, for example through temporary paid jobs on 'the project'. And again, in some cases digressions were also part of the transgressions. For example, as with other projects, the leaders were expecting to use travel expenses paid for by this project to meet lawyers who would help them make their land claims.

Interestingly, neither the transgressions nor the digressions went undetected by the NGO team, although they dealt with them in different ways. The primary importance that the control of territory had for the Yshiro was openly expressed in the first exercise, where people were invited to imagine the best possible future scenario for the communities. As we have seen, the facilitator managed the potential for transgression implicit in this 'vision' by progressively translating this desired scenario into (apparently) more specific objectives, all the while guiding the translation into conformity with a 'reality' that was not up for discussion. The NGO team was also not oblivious to the 'narrow interests' (i.e. digressions) that drove many to participate. Apart from the facilitator, the rest of the team consisted of veterans of 'development work' in the countryside. One was quite candid about his scepticism, commenting privately about the number of participatory projects he had seen to come to a halt as soon as resources to keep people interested were withdrawn. As an example, he mentioned a 'herbal medicine garden project' he had run years before in one of the Yshiro communities:

> We supported a few families with food and equipment for a while so they could dedicate themselves to the task. But as soon as the aid was finished, they left the crops to die. Pulled out the wires in the fences and sold them. Supposedly they were interested in doing it for themselves, but I now realise that they were only interested in the food and equipment we gave them.

For seasoned development workers such as the team members, it was obviously that these kinds of interests were driving a good proportion of the non-leadership participants. Yet they had no other choice but to turn a blind eye to it, for otherwise they would not have the participatory process and plan that was expected up the chain of command by the Paraguayan government and financial institutions. In short, there was a convergence of interests on both sides to keep staging participation.

'Commanding without repelling' and 'obeying without fulfilling' were possible because almost everyone understood what the game was about. Ironically, the few Yshiro that participated without intending to transgress or digress were those that could not understand the game, and were thus 'unworkable', not only because what they said could not be translated into a 'realistic plan', but also because it just did not make sense.

There were a couple of traditionalist elders who had felt quite mobilised by the months of discussions about recovering control of the territory and who eagerly participated in the workshop. It is very common that from the perspective of non-indigenous peoples, a traditionalist elder appears as the epitome of 'cultural difference'. A sense of reverence and awe is displayed in the face of their utterances. It was no different in the workshop. Every time one of these elders intervened the NGO team paid full attention, took notes, and filmed, following the translation as if they had received ultimate words of wisdom, even if they could make little sense of what was being said! Let us take a look at one of these interventions during the exercise I mentioned above, when the facilitator had asked why it was important to have a territory.

As I noted above, the facilitator had invited people to form pairs, matching a person who could not write with one who could. The card of a pair formed by a traditionalist elder and a young man read: 'Cannot sing; *el monte* (the bush) is being destroyed; cannot hunt, no food'. The pair was invited to explain. The young man said he could not explain. He had just jotted down a translation of what the elder had said, but he did not understand what he meant very well. The elder, Don Ramon Zeballos Bibi, started to speak, and the young fellow translated:

> I am a shaman. All those animals that are there are my children. I am their child as well. If I sing, those animals come out [come into being]. If I do not sing there are no animals. When I was a child I ate *pitino* [anteater]. I was not supposed to eat it. Prohibited!! But I ate anyway. I was hard-headed. Then I got sick. And that guy came. The owner of the *pitino*. 'You are very hard-headed, you will not withstand my power. You will die now'. But I spoke to him. That guy has a daughter, she was fat, beautiful girl. I spoke to that guy to let me marry his daughter. Then I married her [...]

At this point one of the leaders, an individual fitting the 'non-traditionalist' description mentioned earlier, interjected with 'this is not the place for *monexne* [traditional stories]'. Don Ramon gave him a mean look as he continued,

> Then, that *pitino* owner let me go. Now he is my father-in-law. He gives me his song, to bring about the *pitino*. If I don't sing, there are no more [anteaters]. Nobody will eat *pitino*. Nobody will be able to hunt it. Then that owner gets mad. There, around nepurich [a place within the Yshiro territory] I have to go. But now there is a *patron* [cattle rancher] that does not allow anyone to pass [through his property]. He is destroying the *yrmo* [the word was translated into Spanish as *monte* (bush) by the young fellow]. I have nothing for [i.e. materials to make] *peyta* [maracas]. How can I sing? All those animals are not coming out any more, they no longer have their house, because nobody take cares of the *yrmo* [monte].

For a brief moment after the elder finished, the facilitator looked disconcerted, glancing at his Yshiro assistant as if expecting an explanation. But none was forthcoming. Then he picked up the card that the young fellow had written and his face looked as if he had found a life raft in the middle of the ocean. He started to talk as he moved towards the large sheet paper with the heading 'Why is territory important?' 'So, what Don Ramon is reminding us is how important the cultural traditions of the Yshiro are, and how this will get lost if the forest is destroyed. So it is not only the food that gets lost', he said as he underlined the words 'economic reasons' that had been written before, 'but also the culture', and below the previous label he wrote 'cultural reasons'. He turned around, smiling, and called the next pair of participants to discuss their card.

I will return to the leader's comment shortly, but now, and in order to illustrate the magnitude of what got lost in this translation, I want to offer an alternative, a translation as 'controlled equivocation' – that is, a translation that is keenly aware that we are mostly forcing Yshiro concepts into the straightjacket of our own conceptual toolbox even as we try to make the latter hospitable to the former (see Viveriros de Castro 2004).[7] The key terms on which my translation hinges upon are the words *yrmo* and *monte*. When Don Ramon spoke he used the word *yrmo*, which the young man translated into Spanish as *monte*, and I translate into English as bush. Bush and *monte* share a similar semantic cloud. But this is not the case with *yrmo*. When used to indicate the thick of the forest in contrast with the edge of the river, the term means something like the Spanish and English words. But that is as far as equivalence goes; for, as I earlier noted, the *yrmo* more precisely refers to the symbiopoietic tangle of relations and practices that constitute the Yshiro world. In effect, Don Ramon first speaks of a relation that carries with it obligations (to sing) so that *pitino* (anteaters) come into being and people can eat them. Then he says that he can no longer go to a place where he can get the material to make maracas to play along with his singing because the *patron* (cattle rancher) doesn't let him pass. So he cannot sing any longer, and the animals are not coming out. And it is precisely because the cattle rancher is interrupting these *yrmo*-making practices that he is destroying it.

The translation of Don Ramon's intervention into 'cultural reasons' was certainly crude and partly obeyed the need for planning clear cut and workable categories, but it also conformed to a common equivocation – and one used by the facilitator. This was to assume that one aspect of Don Ramon's speech spoke of culture (the references to the animal owner and the singing) and another about nature (the destruction of *monte*). Evidently he could not immediately figure out how the two parts connected *for* Don Ramon, and thus he offered a somewhat flimsy explanation: if one was destroyed the other would disappear too. But this make-do explanation aside, the facilitator just followed the beaten conceptual track. Whatever connection he was trying to illustrate, what Don Ramon said would surely somehow fit the nature/culture divide. This is certainly an uncontrolled equivocation.

Now, it is important to stress the nature and scope of the difference between obeying without fulfilling through transgression and digression, on the one hand, and obeying without fulfilling through equivocation, on the other. While the first two exceed what is expected by commanding without repelling, they sustain a relation of mutual intelligibility with it. In effect, transgressing or digressing were perfectly intelligible to the NGO team: the implicit command to be 'doable' was a way of recovering territory and tapping into resources. Likewise, most Yshiro participants understood perfectly what they needed to do to keep this form of commanding going and to avert the alternative based on open coercion; they know how to make themselves minimally workable.

Yet, notwithstanding their intelligibility, transgressions and digressions also carry the shadow of equivocation. While the NGO team can understand the aim of recovering territory as part of Paraguay's political economy (and even as part of the politics of culture), for many Yshiro the significance of this aim exceeds what political economy and the politics of culture can encompass. It means something that can only approximately be conveyed as enhancing the symbiopoietic capacity of the *Yrmo*. But this excess remains very much muted, almost undetected, not least because those who transgress or digress want it that way. The point becomes clearer if we look at the incident involving Don Ramon and the leader who interrupted him.

Notwithstanding the facilitator's attempt to capture it, Don Ramon's intervention clearly exceeded the partial two-way intelligibility of transgression and digression; it was rather evidently unworkable for the NGO and the development network. For some leaders, making this unworkability evident raised the spectre of open coercion. In effect, it is this to which the leader responded. I have seen reactions such as that of the leader in many settings where governmental and development agents come into contact with community members. As soon as someone starts to make references to the *yrmo* in ways that clearly indicate that it is something else than 'the bush', some leaders become very fidgety and uncomfortable. In this case the leader was particularly rude, showing a lack of respect towards traditionalist understandings. But the concern expressed is more general and has to do with leaders having learnt to expect the consequences of giving the impression that the Yshiro are 'unreasonable' people who cannot speak about 'reasonable' things, and thus do not deserve a seat in the 'participation game'.

There are some Yshiro, however, who stand on the other side. For instance, Don Veneto Vera, another respected shaman and a good friend of mine, did not waste time with euphemisms to explain to me why he never takes part in these kinds of events:

> These people [those organising workshops in the communities] cannot know the *yrmo*. You tell them about the *tobich*[8] but they do not change and then they fuck up everything. They are different. Their work is different. It's better to stay here in the *yrmo* working with the *weterak* [initiated youth] and they stay there in the school working with the teachers on their project.

Brief though it is, the commentary is extremely thick in implications that I can only skim over at the cost of substantial simplification. The quickest way is starting with the reference to the *weterak*. These are young males who are initiated into the *tobich*. Among other things, the initiation involves a substantial amount of instruction conveyed through stories not very different from the kind Don Ramon shared in the workshop.[9] It is expected that the initiation and the instruction will produce a transformation of the individuals being initiated, increasing and developing their *eiwo*, a fine-tuned capacity to discern what needs to be done in particular circumstances. I will expand a little more on this later, but for now let me just point out that developing *eiwo* is itself very important to the sustenance of the *yrmo*, as the latter's status or quality partly depends on how the Yshiro conduct themselves.

This helps us to better understand Don Veneto's comment on the impossibility of the NGO staff knowing the *yrmo*. It is not simply that they misunderstand what is said. They are different kinds of people because they are not transformed by being exposed to the *tobich* and thus they cannot behave in a way that contributes to the sustenance of the *yrmo*. Instead they 'fuck it up'! What is the best course of action in this case? The answer is to leave them alone to do their 'project' with the Yshiro who understand them (i.e. the teachers); keep them away as far as possible from meddling with that which they cannot know (i.e. the *yrmo*); and keep working with those who can do it (i.e. the initiated men). In short, for people like Don Veneto the command to participate poses a risk for the *yrmo*, and so, having decided to disobey and ignore it, they keep playing their own game; a game whose exact rules and stakes we do not know – and perhaps *should* not know.

KNOWING EXCESS?

In his introductory chapter, John Law suggests that baroque as a mode of knowing seems to offer a set of techniques 'for recognising and relating to absence or Otherness', and asks whether it offers 'ways of knowing excess within the contemporary academy? Of recognising the whole that is, at the same time, a hole in our artefacts of knowing or experiencing?' Engaging these questions diffractively with the help of my previous discussion I see two 'patterns' and a connection between them that might be worthwhile pursuing.[10]

Let me call the first pattern 'excess as an illuminating shadow'. To a large extent, the 'excesses' manifested in my discussion can be conceived as the shadow cast by the 'thing' that is known and serves as the 'measure' to determine what falls beyond it (i.e. the excess). For example, the 'recovery of traditional territory' sought by UCINY only becomes recognisable and say-able as excess in relation to the realistic 'development project' sought by the NGO. The latter constitutes the 'measure'. Of course, the 'standpoint' is crucial in defining 'the measure' of excess. In effect, the 'recovery of traditional territory' sought by UCINY and the realistic 'development project' sought by the NGO exceeded each other. Which one was the measure and which was in excess of the measure depends on whose standpoint we consider. In a similar fashion, I could make the excess implicit in equivocation manifest for the reader only in relation to the 'measure' I sought to build, that is the interplay between commanding without repelling and obeying without fulfilling. To put it in other terms, the *yrmo* can be grasped as excess only in relation to something else (the measure), which in this particular case I provided in the form of a relation of mutual intelligibility between commanding without repelling and obeying without fulfilling. This relation, that I made known for the reader, is the 'measure' that casts an illuminating shadow into that which was not included, the excess. Excess then emerges as co-constituted and co-constitutive of a standpoint and a 'measure', that which is known.

I will call the second pattern that my little diffraction generates *horror ignotum*. To see this, I begin with the promise held by participatory methods in relation to ethnodevelopment. As it might be recalled, this promise consisted in turning the unknown content of indigenous visions of a good life into something knowable and amenable to governmental intervention. Of course the way of knowing implicit here is in many senses closer to the standard academic styles that stand in contrast to the baroque. However, I feel in the imperative of participatory methods to know the unknown something similar to the *horror vacui* to which Carlos Fuentes referred; it is worthwhile quoting him at length:

> The Baroque [...] is the language of peoples who, not knowing what is true, desperately seek it [...] Góngora, like Picasso, Buñuel, Carpentier or Faulkner did not know; they discovered. The Baroque, language of abundance, is also the language of insufficiency. Only those who possess nothing can include everything. The *horror vacui* of the Baroque is not gratuitous – it is because the vacuum exists that nothing is certain. The verbal abundance of [Carpetier] or [Faulkner] represents a desperate invocation of language to fill the absence left by the banishment of reason and faith. In this way post-Renaissance Baroque art began to fill the abyss left by the Copernican Revolution (cited in Parkinson Zamora and Kaup 2009: 25).

In this passage, Fuentes is trying to characterise a source of the baroque's drive towards 'abundance' of forms, and finds it in the horror of the vacuum, the vacuum being the absence produced by the Copernican Revolution. Yet, as Parkinson Zamora and Kaup point out, in his own works Fuentes uses the 'abundance' of baroque language to interrogate another 'absence', the one created by the European invasion of the New World, the absence of the Natives. Along similar lines, we can see participatory methodologies as an abundant 'form' that interrogates a similar absence, or better an absence that has turned into a presence – the Natives that would not go away but rather stake a claim to remain and be different. As an abundant form, participatory methodologies spring from horror, but in this case *horror ignotum* (horror of the unknown). *Horror ignotum* grows from the impossibility of accepting the presence of things, such as Indigenous visions of a good life that cannot really be known, and with which, nevertheless, one has to live with. And here we come to the connection between the 'diffraction patterns' that might raise questions for the baroque as a way of knowing excess.

If we accept that excess is more properly conceived as a relation that also involves a standpoint and a measure, we may ask about the standpoint and the measure that co-constitute the excess that the baroque promises to help us know. Perhaps an answer might be gleaned from the equivalence suggested in the introduction between knowing excess and 'recognising the whole that is, at the same time, a hole in our artefacts of knowing or experiencing'. Might it be the knowledge that there is 'a whole that is a hole' that operates here as the measure co-constituted with the excess? And might it be representation itself that operates as the standpoint co-constituted with the measure and the excess? Van der Port (this volume) refers to this whole that is a hole as 'the-rest-of-what is', a term to conceptualise a 'vacancy, [a] "beyond" all representation'. Representation is crucial here, for it is the impossibility of representing it that throws 'the whole' into sharp relief as excess. But the idea of a whole that is somehow external and exceeds it is as crucial to representation as the other way around. Hence we see how representation, the lack and the whole as excess, co-constitute each other.

The baroque as a set of techniques holds the promise of helping us know (grasp, acutely experience, and so on) this whole that manifests as the excess illuminated by the lack of representation. But then, and to paraphrase Carlos Fuentes, is the baroque the way of knowing of people who, not having knowledge of 'the-rest-of-what is', desperately seek it? Is *horror ignotum* driving this pursuit? If this is the case it might be appropriate to ponder the consequences of this drive. The full weight of the point can better be conveyed through a contrast.

When Don Veneto says of the NGO staff that they cannot know the *yrmo*, he is not referring to an incapacity to represent it accurately in their minds. In fact, as with other (so-called) indigenous 'epistemologies', knowing is not here conceived as involving representation. Rather, it is always already performative of what is there to be known (see Burkhart 2001). Deploying the institution of the *tobich*, Don Veneto and other initiated older men change young men in ways that enable them to know/do the *yrmo*. This is why developing *eiwo* is crucial to the sustenance of the yrmo. The NGO staff are different. They do not change so they cannot know/do the *yrmo*. But notice that the NGO staff's inability to know/do the *yrmo* does not translate for Don Veneto into the attribution of total ineptitude. They are perfectly capable of doing 'their project'. How these different knowings/doings might intersect with each other down the road is an open-ended question that occupies many of the conversations that the Yshiro individuals I most respect have among themselves and with me. But what is certainly clear is that there is a difference between these knowings/doings. And this is not a difference between one being 'real' and the other a 'mistake about the real'. Rather, these doings/knowings stand in the presence of each other as real performed worlds.

Adopting a 'standpoint' which is not that of representation but that of performativity casts a different light (or illuminating shadow) on 'the-rest-of-what-is', and what knowing it might imply. Let me put it this way, 'the whole' in this case is nothing other than a multiplicity of ongoing knowings/doings, for properly speaking, if some-thing is not being done there is no-thing. This means that what occupies the role of excess here (without being exactly the same) is not some-thing that escapes knowledge (as is the case with 'the whole' in representation) but rather the possibility of knowing/doing some-thing differently or newly. Some consequences follow from these points.

Horror ignotum, or the unrestricted drive towards knowing the whole, is seen, if not with alarm, at least with the suspicion a foolish pursuit deserves. It always implies consequential interference between different knowings/doings. For Don Veneto, NGO staff members have shown that they cannot know the *yrmo* as they know 'their projects', and conversely he does not feel he can do the *yrmo* by doing their projects. It is better that each stay on their own. While many of my Yshiro friends consider that these interferences might be necessary or inevitable, they also agree that they need to be carefully staged. Finally, the positive value of knowing/doing 'excess' (i.e. some-thing that is not being done) is not a foregone conclusion. In contrast to the scenario proposed by representation, where (by definition) lack postulates the drive to incorporate excess as a good, the scenario proposed here suggests a sort of precautionary principle. This is that some-things are better left unknown/undone or at least un-interfered with. This precautionary principle is hard to digest for 'academic knowledge' and kindred practices like 'participatory methods', for which more knowledge is always better. The consequences of this expanding reach on other ways of knowing/doing worlds are plain to see, at least in the Yshiro territory. Then the question that comes to mind, and with which I conclude, is this. Does a baroque way of knowing have something different to offer in this regard? Could it take on this precautionary principle? Or might it actually just end up adding more techniques to escape the ghost of *horror ignotum*?

NOTES

1 A contribution by Penny Harvey in the seminar that originated this volume inspired me to see the possible connections that could be established between the Baroque and the participatory workshop.

2 For a short documentary illustrating this process, see Blaser (2013).

3 The term 'earth-beings' was first advanced by Marisol de la Cadena (2010).

4 Helmreich (2011) proposes the term to stress the centrality of relations rather than unity to the processes Francisco Varela labeled 'autopoiesis'. These are processes through which living things call forth the conditions of their own existence through 'interactions and transformations [that] continuously regenerate and realize the network of processes (relations) that produced them; and ... constitute ... [them] as ... concrete unit[ies] in the space in which they exist' (Varela, cited in Helmreich 2011: 688).

5 Since 2007 there have been numerous consultations and workshops involving the Yshiro communities and a myriad environmental NGOs that are the actual on-the-ground managers of conservation programmes in Paraguay. Although UCINY has sustained ambivalent relations with these NGOs, at times collaborative and at times confrontational, the general consensus among the leaders is that the relations have to be sustained. In this context, and given my involvement with UCINY, I have taken measures to avoid creating unnecessary resentments among these circumstantial partners. Thus, I have changed details or remained deliberately vague about some of them to conceal which organisation and fieldworkers conducted this particular workshop for informed readers. This does not affect the core of the argument.

6 The consistency is not surprising if we consider that the topics had been discussed for several months in the communities before the workshop.

7 Equivocations imply the use of the same concept to refer to things that are not the same. An equivocation takes place when there is a failure to understand that, while using the same term, interlocutors are referring to different things.

8 Tobich is a place, a clearing in the forest where young males are initiated.

9 For a more detailed (yet still simplified) rendering of what is implied in the initiation ritual, see Blaser (2010).

10 I take from Karen Barad (2007) the idea of 'reading' something (in this case the Baroque as a way of knowing) diffractively. What this entails is to create interferences through contrast in such a way that new, potentially illuminating questions can emerge.

BIBLIOGRAPHY

Andolina, R., N. Laurie, and S. Radcliffe, *Indigenous Development in the Andes: Culture, Power and Transnationalism* (Durham, NC: Duke University Press, 2009)

Barad, K., *Meeting the Universe Halfway: Quantum Physics and the Entanglement of Matter and Meaning* (Durham, NC: Duke University Press, 2007)

Blaser, M., *Storytelling Globalization from the Chaco and Beyond* (Durham, NC: Duke University Press, 2010)

———— 'Biodiversity Conservation: For Whom?' [documentary film, directed by M. Blaser, 2013] <http://www.lifeprovida.net/index.php?option=com_content&view=article&id=11231%3Ax&catid=16%3Amultimedia&Itemid=6&lang=en>

Burkhart, B., 'What Coyote and Thales can Teach us: An Outline of American Indian Epistemology', in A. Waters, ed., *American Indian Thought: Philosophical Essays* (Malden, MA: Blackwell, 2001), pp. 26–36

Chevalier, J., and D. Buckles, *A Handbook of Participatory Action Research, Planning and Evaluation* (Ottawa, Canada: SAS2 Dialogue, 2011)

Coca, A., and L. Reymodin, 'Is the Paraguayan Chaco at Risk from Extreme Habitat Destruction?', *Terr-I*, (2012) < http://www.terra-i.org/terra-i/news/news-Is-the-

Paraguayan-Gran-Chaco-at-risk-for-extreme-habitat-destruction.html> [accessed 28 April 2014]

Cooke, B., and U. Kothari, *Participation: The New Tyranny?* (London: Zed Books, 2001)

De la Cadena, M., 'Indigenous Cosmopolitics in the Andes: Conceptual Reflections beyond "Politics"', *Cultural Anthropology*, 25 (2010), pp. 334–70

Helmreich, S., 'What was Life? Answers from Three Limit Biologies', *Critical Inquiry*, 37.4 (2011), 671–96

Hickey, S., and G. Mohan, *Participation: From Tyranny to Transformation? Exploring New Approaches to Participation in Development* (London: Zed Books, 2004)

Law, J. 'Modes of Knowing: Resources from the Baroque', this volume

Mignolo, W. D., *The Idea of Latin America* (Hoboken, NJ: John Wiley & Sons, 2009)

Povinelli, E. A., 'Radical Worlds: The Anthropology of Incommensurability and Inconceivability', *Annual Review of Anthropology*, 30 (2001), 319–334

Parkinson Z., L. and M. Kaup, eds., *Baroque New Worlds: Representation, Transculturation, Counterconquest* (Durham, NC: Duke University Press, 2009)

Stavenhagen, R., 'Ethnodevelopment: A Neglected Dimension in Development Thinking', in R. J. Apthorpe, and A. Kráhl, eds., *Development Studies: Critique and Renewal* (1986), 71–94

Steyaert, S., and L. Herve, *Participatory Methods Toolkit: A Practitioner's Manual* (Belgium: King Baudouin Foundation and the Flemish Institute for Science and Technology Assessment, 2005)

UNESCO, 'MAB Biosphere Reserves Directory Paraguay-El Chaco', 2006 <http://www.unesco.org/mabdb/br/brdir/directory/biores.asp?code=PAR+02&mode=all> [accessed 28 April 2014]

Viveiros de Castro, E., 'Perspectival Anthropology and the Method of Controlled Equivocation', *Tipití Journal of the Society for the Anthropology of Lowland South America*, 2 (2004), 3–22

3

FALLACY OF THE WORK, TRUTH OF THE PERFORMANCE: WHAT MAKES MUSIC BAROQUE: HISTORICAL AUTHENTICITY OR ONTOLOGICAL PLURALITY?

Antoine Hennion[1]

BAROQUE MUSIC HAS ENJOYED A REVIVAL OVER THE LAST HALF-CENTURY centred around the idea of a more authentic interpretation. Does this mean playing it '*as it was played at the time*', rediscovering *the* truth of an interpretation? Or does it mean the opposite, finally accepting the irreducible plurality of music as performance (Hennion 2014)?

Music is a good place to think about how we might reformulate the question of authenticity.[2] In the history of art the issue turns around the problem of forgery. But what counts as a fake in music? A piece has to be replayed each time anyway. 'Falsification' does not really arise. It is 'allographic' (Goodman 1976): the binary true/false division relevant in literature or with the original in the visual arts turns into something different in music – a wide range of interpretations that are *more or less* authentic. Is there any room then, for musical forgery? Conversely, if the fake is impossible, what is authenticity in music? We

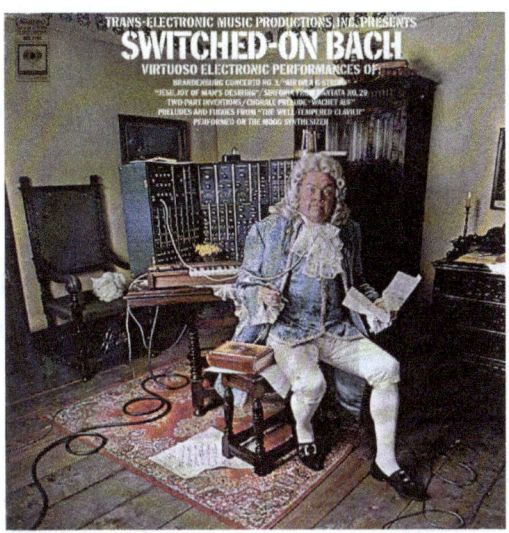

FIG. 3.1 Bach, horrified on the Wendy Carlos Synthesised-Bach disc

will indulgently look at baroque 'modernised' versions from the nineteenth or twentieth centuries; in doing so are we simply in the business of making provocative worldly paradoxes? Or may we redefine the true as variation itself? As the mobility, the fragility, the irreducible incompleteness of work that has always 'to be done'? And then, do we need to distinguish between the 'true fake' and the 'pretend fake' in music, or not? These are the questions I explore in this chapter.

ARE THERE FAKES IN MUSIC?

In the visual arts the question of fakery cannot be avoided. The physical materiality of the object imposes a radical distinction between original and copy. This generates confusion between the aesthetic truth of a work and the erudite determination of its historical origins. The latter may take on almost judicial or police-like definitions of authenticity. Indeed, the process may end up in court. By contrast, pieces of music do not sell themselves as unique-and-original. The fraudster cannot work here. S/he lacks the support afforded by confusion between the original work and its cloaked copies. Instead of the difficulty for an expert faced with an original that s/he doubts (Bessy and Chateauraynaud

1995), music substitutes the continuous succession of different *versions* of 'the same' work. Critics, scholars, and aesthetes endlessly evaluate and re-evaluate. Through its limitless interpretations music offers a continual unfolding of variations rather than the rigidity of marble.

At the same time, however, neither should we exaggerate the opposition between these forms of art. Rather than radical differences, their medium-related contrasts instead suggest unevenly tangible properties that are common to them both. Aesthetics engages 'the work of the art', and not 'works-of-art', as Gérard Genette very nicely puts it (1994). As he argues, there is no stabilised ontology. Instead there are 'works' in the etymological sense of communal work between objects and their readers, their spectators, their listeners. There is interplay between them, through a long series of mediations, captures, and input screens. It is this interplay which enables them to stand the test of time (Hennion 2015). Pictures push us to dissociate a work of art 'itself' from its 'reception'. Art theory strives to reconnect them. The need to keep music updated (in the case of ancient music under the aegis of ever more 'faithful' interpretation) works in the other direction: the continuous co-production of the work and its public is made tangible (or perhaps, to put it more precisely, the public and 'its' works). If the question of forgery is posed in art, for instance as de-attribution,[3] then music offers an analytical advantage by highlighting the paradoxes of aesthetic truth. It helps to bring these centre stage for the 'work' of art, and not as a 'yes or no' issue.

Music extract no. 1: Albinoni's Adagio by Karajan[4]

Here is a famous tune: Albinoni's *Adagio*, a classical music hit. I have not used quotation marks, but this is because I would need to put them round every word including 'Albinoni's'! Indeed, for once we are in the presence of a pretend musical, of a 'real' fake, as it were. For reasons that we have already seen, this is not so common in music. Musical forgeries do indeed exist, not because they lack authenticity but because the intention is to deceive. However, they are more a product of hoaxes, provocations, or sometimes commercial stunts. The intentions may be good (as is partially the case with Albinoni's *Adagio*). They may

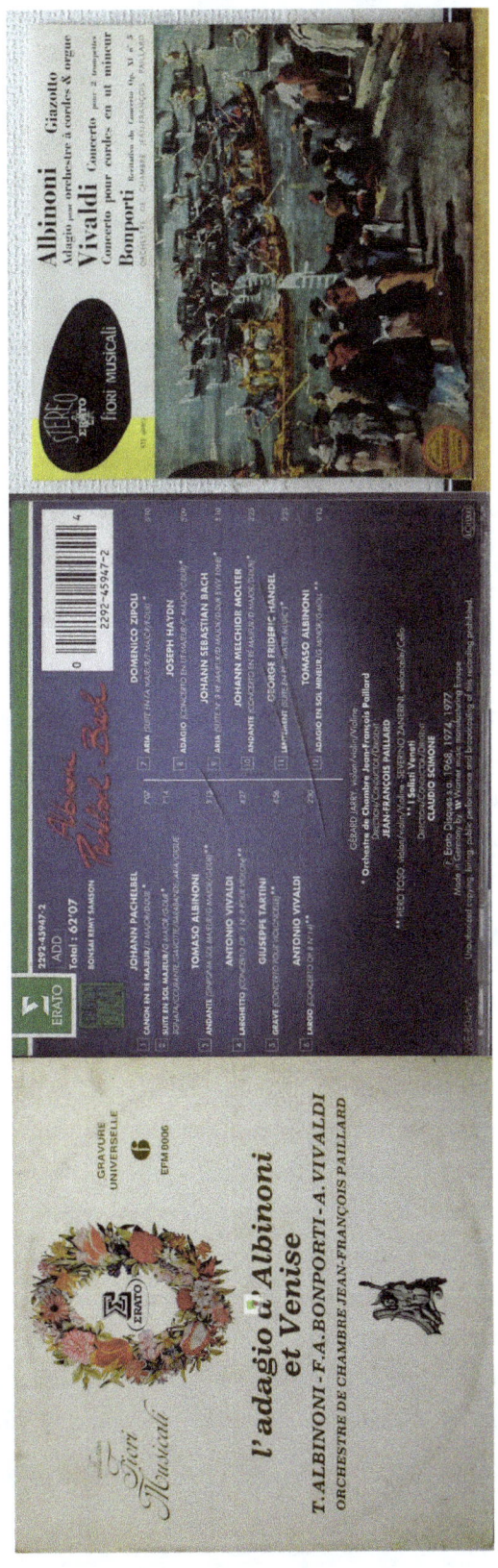

FIG. 3.2 Covers of Erato LP, including Albinoni's *Adagio* by Jean-François Paillard[5]

have nothing to do with forgery in the more restrictive, analytical sense used by art historians which couples deceivers and deceived, such as counterfeiters and buyers, collectors or curators.[6]

Let us start as factually as possible with our *Adagio*. It was Remo Giazotto who wrote this slow languid movement in 1957. What is interesting here is that Giazotto was neither a prankster nor a con artist. Instead he was an expert pushed by 'his' composer, whom he sought to elevate to the heights of Corelli, Vivaldi, or Torelli. Giazotto, who published *Tomaso Albinoni* in Milan in 1945, was *the* Venetian composer's musicologist. He identified so narrowly and with such more or less good intentions with Albinoni, that when knowledgeable reconstitution of the sheet music was not enough to produce a playable piece, he ended up writing one instead.

The record industry is not quite so candid. It knows well how to lie by omission. The proven Albinoni fake (certified, factual) turns into a much more clearly intentional falsification. Trickery, linked as is often the case to commercial interests, is added to the mix. Here is an example from the recording of Erato's *Adagio*. Following the CD cover biography of Albinoni and the caption 'arrangement/Bearbeitung: Giazotto' we read the following:

> The adagio in G minor, recently discovered by an Italian, Giazotto, which he had published in 1948 in Milan, is part of a sonata for trios in G minor, without an opus number and for which Giazotto realized the figured bass.

This, to put it mildly, is a somewhat modest account of Giazotto's intervention. Though perhaps more surprisingly, musical dictionaries and histories often have difficulty situating themselves on these matters. It is as if they were reluctant to openly offend music lovers, preferring to leave everyone free to keep their illusions. So while the Laffont dictionary for musicians does not underplay Giazotto's role to the extent of the Erato booklet, it also seems to shy away from completely denouncing its authenticity: 'The famous Adagio for strings and organ is almost entirely the work of musicologist R. Giazotto'. In the same collection, the erudite *New Oxford Companion to Music* loses little sleep over such diplomatic concerns:

By peculiar coincidence, the sheet music which contributed to his recent celebrity is apocryphal: the adagio in G minor, in all its romance and sentimentality, is in fact the sole work of musicologist Remi [*sic*] Giazotto.[7]

The former convenient omissions are reminiscent of the artistic blur with which publisher Buchet/Chastel envelops *The Chronicle of Anna Magdalena Bach*, a book in which Magdalena speaks in the first person. The origin of the text is explained, somewhat Jesuitically, in this 'editor's note':

> This book, published anonymously in England and Germany, translated into almost every language, enjoyed considerable success everywhere. It must be attributed not only to the often passionate interest that the person and the music of J.-S. Bach never fails to arouse, but above all due to the fact that this little book, at once moving and precise, is inspired by the most beautiful love that ever existed.

Does this tell us that Magdalena is not the author? If so, then this is the only occasion in the book when this happens – unlike the first Buchet/Chastel edition, which noted that the author was an early twentieth-century Englishwoman (since identified as Esther H. Meynell, the original dating to 1925). But the advantage of ambiguity is that it can be implied without saying that the text *still* comes[8] more or less directly from Bach's second wife – as with the *Notebook for Anna Magdalena Bach*. In this collection of music, which of course provided a guide for Meynell, Magdalena noted her husband's, children's, and their loved ones' favourite songs. There are advantages to omission and imprecision.

THE BIGGEST PRETENDERS: THE PUBLIC

Let's come back to Albinoni. The *Adagio* has been an enormous success. It is a 'hit'. This time I put 'hit' in quotation marks because the *Adagio* belongs more to the world of recording, media, and modern taste than to its supposed century of origin. 'Classical-Music', hyphenated and in quotation marks

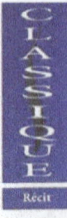

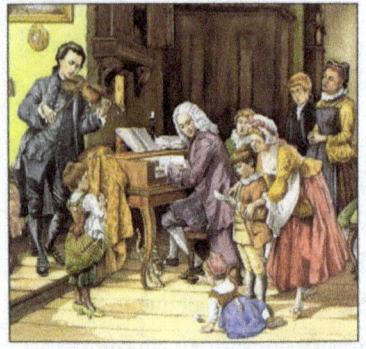

CLASSIQUE
Récit

La petite chronique
d'Anna Magdalena Bach

BUCHET/CHASTEL

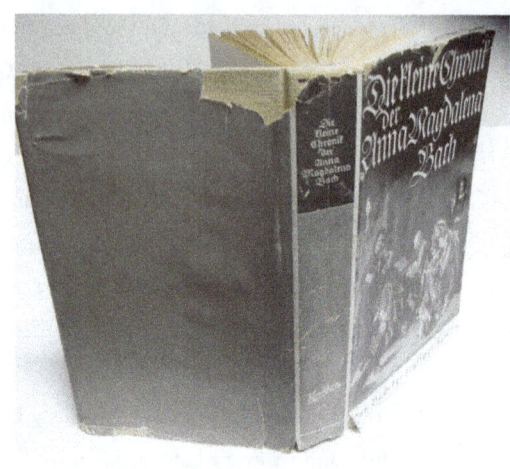

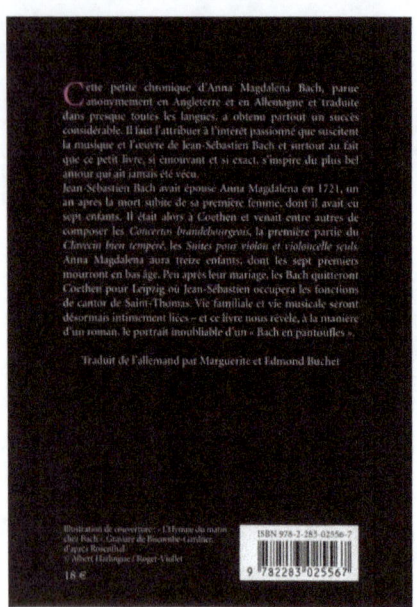

Cette petite chronique d'Anna Magdalena Bach, parue anonymement en Angleterre et en Allemagne et traduite dans presque toutes les langues, a obtenu partout un succès considérable. Il faut l'attribuer à l'intérêt passionné que suscitent la musique et l'œuvre de Jean-Sébastien Bach et surtout au fait que ce petit livre, si émouvant et si exact, s'inspire du plus bel amour qui ait jamais été vécu.

Jean-Sébastien Bach avait épousé Anna Magdalena en 1721, un an après la mort subite de sa première femme, dont il avait eu sept enfants. Il était alors à Coethen et venait entre autres de composer les *Concertos brandebourgeois*, la première partie du *Clavecin bien tempéré*, les *Suites pour violon et violoncelle seuls*. Anna Magdalena aura treize enfants, dont les sept premiers mourront en bas âge. Peu après leur mariage, les Bach quitteront Coethen pour Leipzig où Jean-Sébastien occupera les fonctions de cantor de Saint-Thomas. Vie familiale et vie musicale seront désormais intimement liées – et ce livre nous révèle, à la manière d'un roman, le portrait inoubliable d'un « Bach en pantoufles ».

Traduit de l'allemand par Marguerite et Edmond Buchet

Illustration de couverture : L'Hymne du matin
chez Bach / Gravure de Boissoube-Gravelier,
d'après Rosenthal
© Albert Harlingue/Roger-Viollet

ISBN 978-2-283-02556-7

18 €

COLLECTION MUSIQUE

ESTHER MEYNELL
La Petite chronique
d'Anna Magdalena Bach

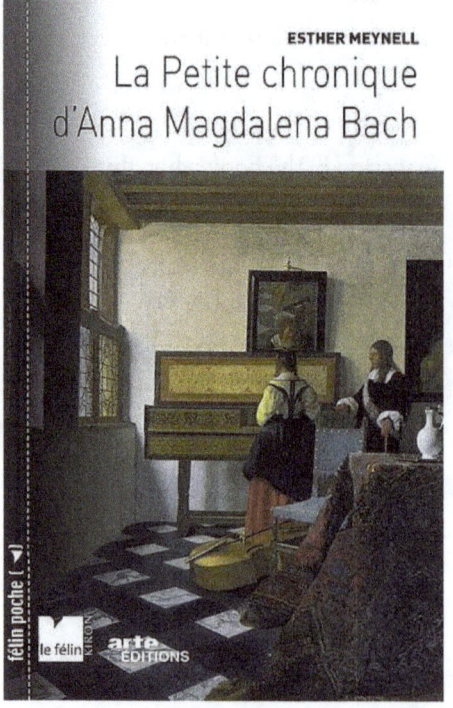

le félin   arte
EDITIONS

FIG. 3.3 Front and back covers of the book, in French and German. See, in particular, the more recent 2012 version from Buchet-Chastel, which mentions 'translated from German'

as well,[9] points to a body of work that is shared by musicology, the music industry, and the taste of the listening public, a well signposted ensemble of pieces of music from the past. This 'Classical-Music' has transformed the past into chronological and alphabetical shelves, ensembles of composers, and styles in which difference becomes a bonus within a homogenised, reconstituted space. As with 'brands', periods and styles increase product differentiation, as they would say in marketing. They are no longer fragile and evanescent traces of irretrievably lost listenings. Nothing is less historical than the histories of music played on a small scale in listeners' homes, the classics categorised on the shelves of record stores (including specific places for 'anonymous' pieces, opera, or potpourris). 'Historical' recording does not necessarily have anything to do with history. It presents the past; it does not present it as passed.[10]

The advantage of the *Adagio* is that it is so excessive that from its first phrase it reveals the key to its success in its time. It must be said that since then the renewal of the repertoire of the baroque and its fans have given us the tools to understand how un-'baroque' the *Adagio* really sounded. It has been said of the great modern art forgers that a successful fake depends on a gap, an expectation, a desire that the imitated work could fill (Grafton 1990; see also Laclotte, or Rowland, in Lista 2009.). The fake is so anticipated; it fits so well into place that one hardly even wants to smell a rat. The desire for baroque both in its twentieth-century and its current form are an effect. Both have been the product of perfect marketing, not as intentional manipulation but rather as a response to the expectations of its publics: a modern public, and an 'old' product, by which I mean a product that was made to seem old.[11]

Once again, nothing is more modern than the old, and nothing evolves faster. The accents of the *Adagio* ring out all the more romantically to our ears because they were trying to express in caricatural form the mid-twentieth-century sense of baroque feeling. A little like the style of Victor Hugo for the Middle Ages, the more they wanted to make it baroque, the more they made it romantic! What best characterised a piece as baroque in 1957 is what betrays it today, what most clearly 'dates' it, as we very nicely put it. It brings us a faithful version of the desire for ancient music in the 1950s. It is a 'true' fake, this time in the sense that it contains its share of truth. And a truth that gives way to something different is always stronger than the one that seeks to display itself.

There are other well-known cases of musical fakes. They may be innocent in intention. Sometimes it is simply the effect that is surprising. Conceived as a challenge or a joke, a pastiche may work so well that it gets fused to the work of the composer being imitated. This is more or less what happened with Mozart's *Adélaïde* concerto in D major for violin. Violinist and conductor Marius Casadesus (1892–1981) said he found sketches and presented it as an early work written by a ten-year-old Mozart for the daughter of Louis XV, Princess Adélaïde. Casadesus had it edited in 1930 by Schott in Mainz.[12] With his friend Yehudi Menuhin, he 'created' it in 1931 in Paris with the Lamoureux Orchestra. Amused by their slick move, the two accomplices recorded it with EMI, and the joke took off. Frequently performed by the two musicians, it became a hallmark of their collaboration. It was widely appreciated, played by other violinists, and became well-known. In 1964, it was given a Köchel number (the catalogue of Mozart's work, reviewed by Alfred Einstein, 6th edition), K Anh. 294a. It was only in 1977, following a dispute about the copyright of its orchestration, that Casadesus admitted the deception: he had composed it in the style of the composer himself, for fun, and to benefit his violinist friend.

Music extract no. 2: The concerto played by Menuhin[13]

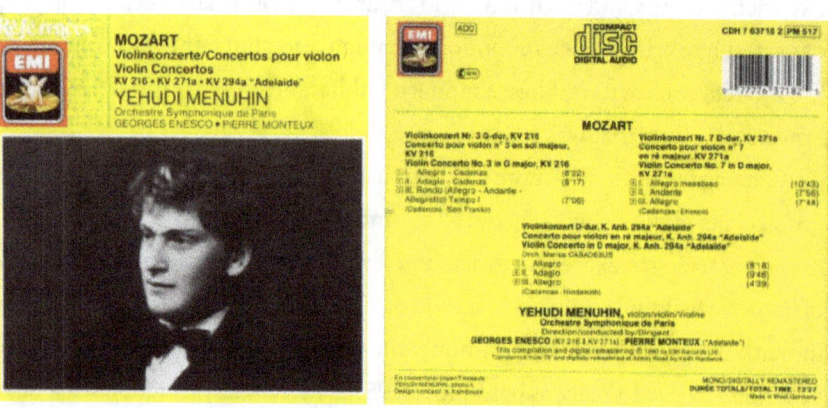

FIG. 3.4 Sleeve of Menuhin's recording: no mention that the score was not written by Mozart[14]

But history does not stop there: even catalogued as spurious or a fake as it now is (Anh 294a/C 14.05), the concerto continues to flourish as though nothing had happened. Its popularity reflects on our problem in an interesting way, for since the admission was made, it has been the taste of the public rather than commercial interests which have prolonged the fakery. There has been no faker apart from the public itself, and this does not want to inhibit its enjoyment, or let 'its' Mozart Concerto be taken away. The contrast with museums or gallery de-attributions is stark: here the truth does not seem to matter much.

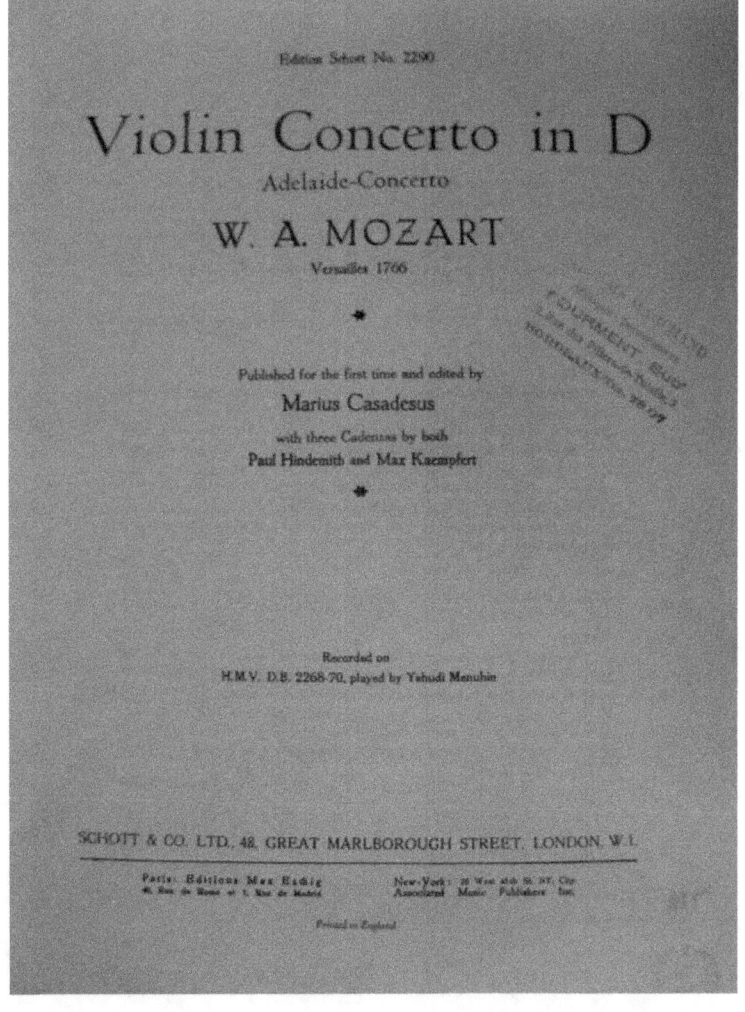

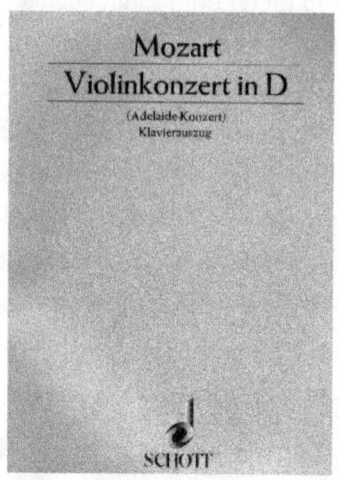

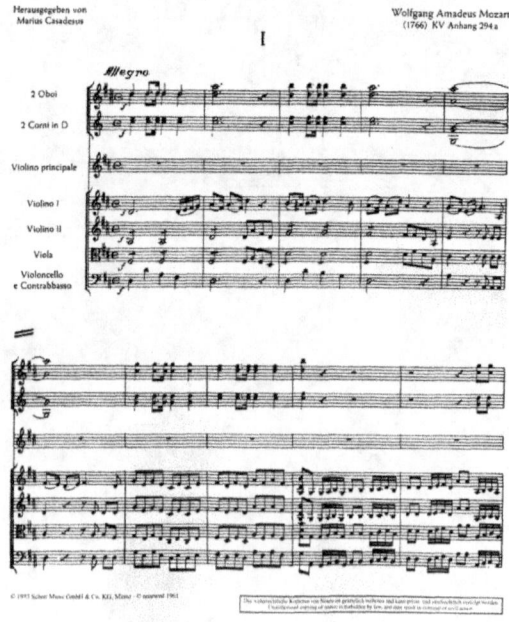

FIG. 3.5 The first two images are fly-leaves of the score, published before and after Casadesus' confession, without any change. The third is from a website which still sells it as a piece by Mozart, mentioning only that it was 'edited' (*herausgegeben*) by Casadesus

Pieces that are Larger than Life

In other instances deception has a more direct, polemical, and aesthetic purpose. When it goes beyond notes it becomes a matter of discovering a style, a spirit. For instance, it was Berlioz who signed the choral piece *L'Adieu des bergers* as Pierre Ducré in 1850.[15] He wanted this (from which *L'Enfance du Christ* would originate) to pass as older music in order to garner admiration for its fervour, its 'sweet', 'naïve' simplicity,[16] for, in short, its authenticity. Nothing is more true than the false – this is normal. It is so well made to be true.

Music extract no. 3:
L'Adieu des bergers/The Shepherds' Farewell, by Cluytens[17]

Father Émile Martin (1914–89), with his own *Messe pour le Sacre des Rois de France*, that he performed in 1949 as a work by Étienne Moulinié (1599–1676), and the musicologist Jacques Chailley made similar moves, but these were less for musical and more for religious or political traditionalist reasons. Father Martin, for example, was a strong advocate of a return to religious choral art. But whatever the motive, when the work lacks context it can be tailor-made. Whether as romantic provocation or traditionalist protest, the gestures of the faker express taste. In one way, indeed, they express it better because they are more radical and explicit. They respond to the desire for an object with a fake that is larger than life. A forgery expresses more raw desire than authentic objects. The latter, caught up in their historical precedence, have to fashion the taste that targets them – and in doing so, they partially mask this taste.[18] The moulding action of the forger is exactly the opposite: it fills the empty space that is a public's possible taste (or a public's *impossible* taste – which is to say almost the same thing).

A HISTORICAL FAKERY OR A NEW LISTENING?

Music extract no. 4: Gounod's Ave Maria, by Pavarotti[19]

On hearing Gounod's no less famous *Ave Maria* (or Bach's, Gounod-Bach's, or Bach-Gounod's, the attributions keep changing), it appears we are swimming in the same water. This becomes a successful wedding tune, a standby for an international star, a Christmas album. The caricature classic becomes a variety hit. And it is a caricature marked from birth by its dubious authenticity, since it is a melody that Gounod added to the first prelude of Bach's *Well-Tempered Clavier*. With this music, in short, one bathes in arrangements from the beginning. In its present-day and aggressively commercial character it simply replaces the romanticism and the veiled manoeuvrings of the nineteenth century with contemporary tastes.

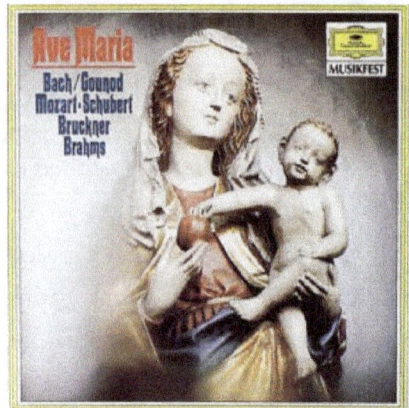 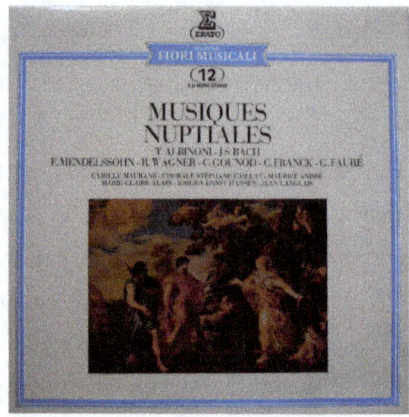

FIG. 3.6 Gounod's *Ave Maria* on a 33 potpourri of Ave Maria (by Bach/ Gounod), and one from the Marriage Airs (by C. Gounod alone)

Yet it would be a grave error to call this piece a fake. Or, more precisely, what it perfectly illustrates is that nothing is more historical than the notion of fakery itself. Indeed, from a strictly analytical point of view Gounod's *Ave Maria* is exactly the opposite of Giazotto's *Adagio*. For the latter a composer tried to imitate this style to meet a modern desire for old masters. At the same time, despite himself he betrayed it in favour of the romantic vision of the past then preferred by the contemporary public: the 'forger' modelled his work on this to a much larger extent than he himself believed he was doing. Nineteenth-century Gounod was a Bach lover, sad that Bach was not better known. He sought to make a public with no real desire to listen to Bach come to appreciate his work. He was interested neither in being musicologically faithful, nor in passing off

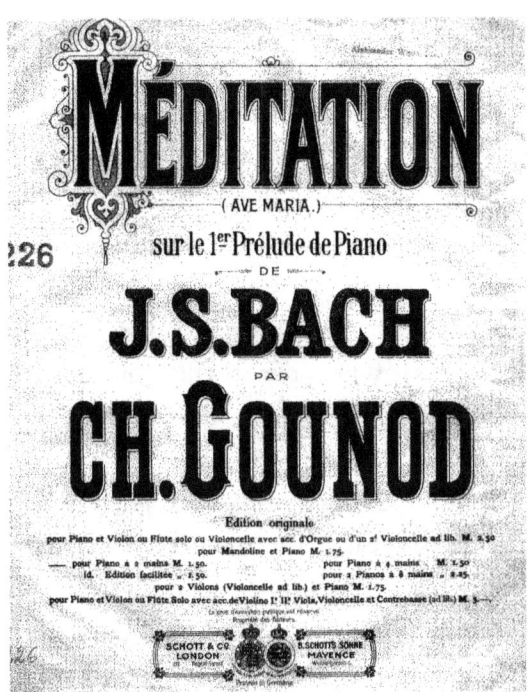

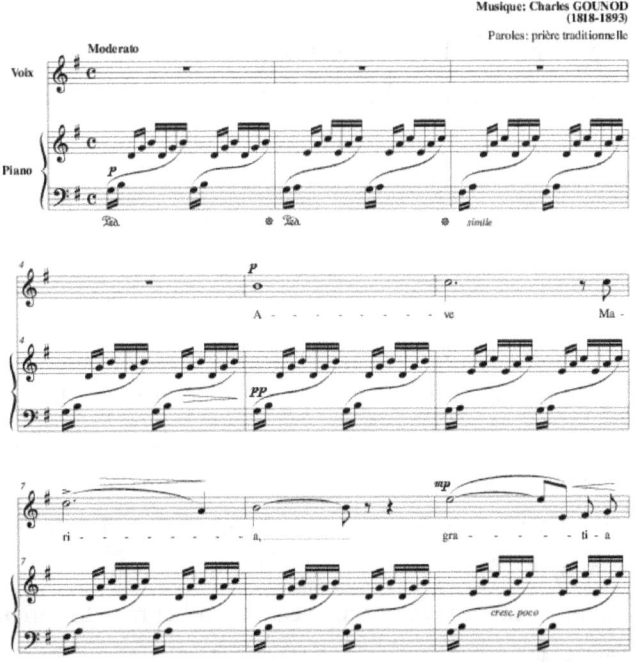

FIG. 3.7 The first page of the original sheet music
by Gounod, and a modern score

his own work as that of a more important composer. Even less was he looking to follow fashion: there was no passion for the baroque. Above all, he was not seeking to 'imitate' Bach, but rather to turn the work of the latter back into music.[20] He didn't seek to mimic Bach's style but to retrieve what it is in Bach's music that transcends his own era. He believed that Bach's music is eternal in what it reveals and can produce in its listeners. Correspondingly, it was not the note-by-note detail of its past performances that counted for him. This meant it was appropriate to add a melody to what he conceived of as a harmonic pattern: his object was to show its strength by 'realising' it. He made music using what he read as a starting point, a little like a saxophonist in a present-day jazz improvisation. This is how he used Bach's chorales in a similar fashion to teach harmony and counterpoint at the Conservatoire.

A few others including Boëly, Chopin, Liszt, and Saint-Saens also sought to extract music that an 1850s listener could appreciate from Bach. And the result of this love and dedication was the slow creation of a new taste for Bach in France. First he became the absolute master, the father of music, and a source of inspiration. Soon, in what was quite unusual at a time when people only listened to contemporary work, he became a composer whose work could be listened to live – provided, of course, that it was adapted to the orchestras of the time, to concert habits, and to the contemporary ear. The need, in short, was to amputate what only had meaning for an eighteenth-century audience. And this was Gounod's most explicit aesthetic aim: to be selective and eliminate what appear to have been concessions made by Bach to the tastes of his time. Bach is cleaned up to become universal – or, more realistically, brought into conformity with present tastes.

The work of adaptation, transcription, and arrangement was huge in scope. From Bach's music it was necessary to make a sort of modern-day music, arranged so that the contemporaries of Gounod or Saint-Saens could hear its eternal elements. Far from being a betrayal, these arrangements were the necessary translations of their time.[21] They would gradually familiarise listeners with older styles and, more simply, to the idea that listening to music written one hundred and fifty years ago can bring meanings other than the archaeological or the pedagogical.

A Story of Desire for History

But the more their work succeeded, the more these tireless adapters came to seem to feed parasitically off the tastes that they themselves had created, and to obscure the great ancestors they believed they were serving. Their very success is what would gradually downgrade their transcriptions by instilling a desire to return to the original sources.[22] This desire is indeed a paradoxical figure hiding behind fidelity to the original whilst doing the exact opposite. It is nothing less than the historical production of an unprecedented desire for authenticity, and even of the very invention of an 'original' to be respected.[23] Listening to these old masters as a result of the work of their nineteenth-century transcribers, twentieth-century Bach lovers would come to despise those transcribers, couching their feelings of superiority in the musicological and aesthetic authenticity.

The very notion of authenticity that leads us to despise Gounod-Bach's *Ave Maria* today therefore has a story. The first early music lovers were reinventing music from the classics (and especially Bach). This was music that was only being studied – and studied selectively – at the time. It was like learning Latin or Greek. Nineteenth-century musicians who loved their music made space to perform these old masters who were otherwise only known and respected for their knowledge of the science of music. The result was the creation of a new space for the love of music and production of a repertoire free from the tastes of the day which lay the foundations for our modern taste for classical music. This new conception of music and its recasting of the tastes of music amateurs and how they relate to the past would gradually include an increasing requirement for fidelity to the original by tearing composers out of history and integrating them into modern taste. There again, the more they are historicised, the less historical they are. The more they become present in our modern world of music, the more we want them to belong to the 'past', to be carriers of traces, remnants. But as we do this we integrate them into this new, homogeneous, musical taste.[24] If we call this 'the history of music' this is antiphrasis. Today's 'baroque music' became so only when it turned into a genre and was labelled in catalogues for its present-day enthusiasts. It belongs resolutely to modern times rather than to history.

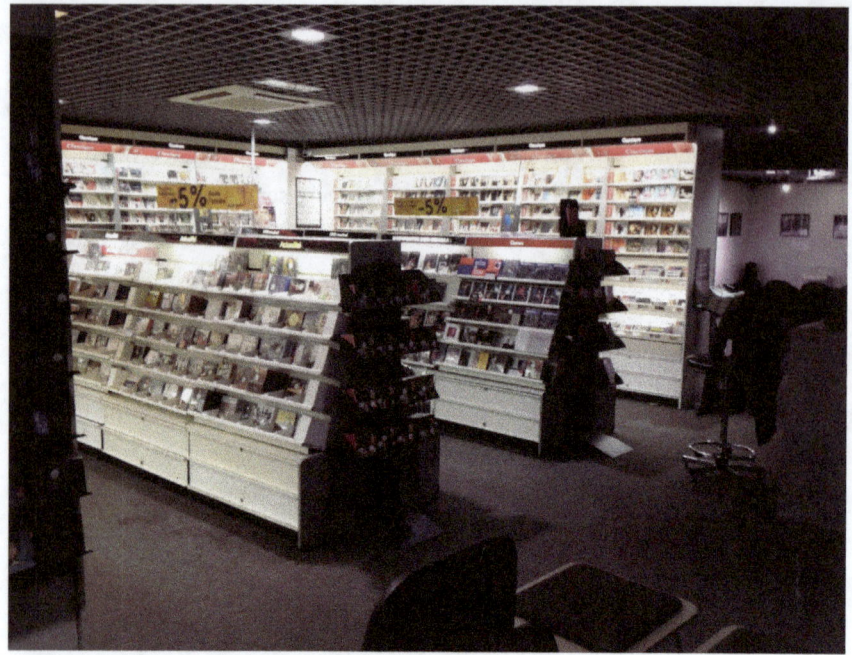

FIG. 3.8 Photograph of a 'Baroque Music' section
from an outlet like Fnac or Virgin

In other words, what we are observing is not the authentic versus the inauthentic. Rather, it is two competing conceptions of truth. The transcriptions and arrangements of the nineteenth century and modern musicology's concern to relieve Bach of his romantic burden and play his music as it was played in his era simply point to different versions of truth. The nineteenth century draws from classicism – as did Gounod himself, who wrote some sublime passages on the capacity of some works to contain all music, serving as both a guide and inspiration in infinite musical re-creation. And he made us share his opinion.

Which is the More Baroque?

Let us close with a final experiment that straddles two time periods.[25] We are in the spring of 1974. Within an interval of a few weeks, two complete versions of Jean-Philippe Rameau's (1735) heroic ballet *Les Indes Galantes* have come out on LP. The event will trigger yet another vicious quarrel between the ancients and the moderns! The very name of the protagonists poses a problem: our newcomers are modern precisely because they are playing on period instruments, while the old ones become old because they insist on playing on modern instruments. In France, the term 'baroqueux', derogatorily derided or proudly claimed, will come to bridge this terminological vacuum for ten years. Only in the 1990s will

FIG. 3.9 The cover of the sheet music for *Les Indes galantes*

we return to 'baroque' or the traditional terminology of 'early music'. The difference is important. With the slip from naming the performers to naming their repertoire, these words denote the victory of the 'baroqueux'. It is now the music that has *become baroque*, and not just its interpretation. And from now on, 'baroque' music may only be played in one way.

These memorable disputes deserve closer study. Their vigour is poorly understood once they have passed, but these are very rich moments. They give rise to new ways of feeling, of valuing, and loving things, and of defining the self. Taste is not a passive reservoir of prejudice. It is a capacity to be captured, transported, and converted. Quarrels are creative: the fight between camps redraws both parties.

CBS Versus Erato

The dispute centred around *Les Indes galantes*. Not Rameau's *Indes*, but those 'of' Jean-Claude Malgoire and Jean-François Paillard – or (to put it differently) those of CBS and Erato. In 1974, everything is at stake in the tense competition between these two labels.

Up until that moment the CBS catalogue had favoured the big soloists and it had issued little music predating Mozart. Its manager in France, Georges Kadar, in betting on Malgoire, a thirty-four-year-old oboist, is hoping to make it into the big league with an outsider.[26] CBS France is pushing the development of a French interpretation for a repertoire which, having long been the preserve of British performers, is being reborn. The company senses this rise, but also notes that its main defenders, the Dutch, Belgians, or Germans, after starting on small labels, have mostly already signed up to specialist labels belonging to major companies: Teldec, Archiv, Seon.

By contrast, for Paillard there is continuity. The 'baroque' in the modern sense, as it will gradually bloom, does not yet exist in France: the quarrel of *Les Indes* will be one of its founding events. Far from being 'baroque' in the histori- cal sense, the catalogue promoted by Paillard is called 'French classical music'. This is the title of a *Que sais-je?*[27] that he publishes in 1970, and it is in line with the analyses of musicologist Norbert Dufourcq (who had been the professor of Erato's Artistic Director Michel Garcin). Dufourcq had always insisted on the opposition between the great music of Versailles and currents of baroque in Southern and Central Europe.

In 1974, Paillard, who is fifty-six years old, has been issuing seventeenth- and eighteenth-century French music with Erato for twenty years. Though he sometimes uses singers and choirs, he mostly works with small string ensem- bles, which he has gradually adapted to mainly instrumental repertoires from France, Italy, and Germany, without differentiating greatly between their national styles.[28] The numbers of instrumentalists are small. The soloists, mostly French performers, are more varied than in the romantic concerto repertoire and create a lively and rhythmic music that contrasts well with the regular slow movements. In all this Erato is a precursor, and the label has effectively used

Paillard to create a strong image and find a new, younger, and more popular audience than those for classical and romantic music. Concerns with style and instruments do not take centre stage, and for Paillard himself, the publication of *Les Indes* in a four-disc box set is the crowning moment of a long recording career entirely with Erato.

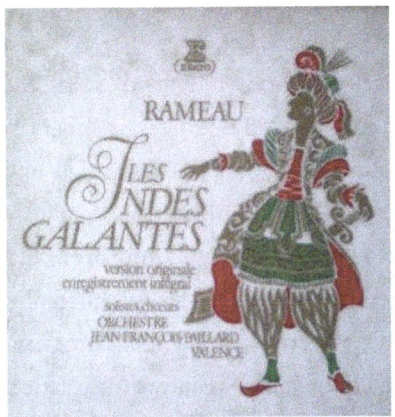 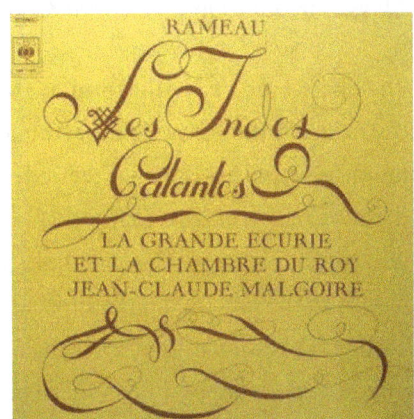

FIG. 3.10 Covers of *Les Indes galantes* by Paillard at Erato, and by Malgoire at CBS

The card CBS plays with Malgoire is quite different. In 1974, this instrumentalist, having trained at the Conservatoire and worked at the Orchestre de Paris, is far from bathing in everything that would give 1980s baroqueux recordings a flavour all of their own and ensure the triumph of Harnoncourt, Savall, Jacobs, and Herreweghe.[29] He does not use very low pitches,[30] the voices of children or counter-tenors, dance phrasing, rhythmic inequality, forgotten ornamentation, or the touching accents of the lute or viola. But Malgoire shares an interest in the more varied and slightly acidic tones of these older instruments and he collaborates with instrument makers. Indeed, he is one of the first to speak of 'authenticity' in this field. A first record in 1967 has already caused a stir, and it is this emerging taste which brought Malgoire (himself influenced by Dufourcq) closer to the French music of the seventeenth century. 'La Grande Écurie et la Chambre du Roy' (The Great Stable and the King's Chambers) is the name of the ensemble that he establishes in 1966, and that title represents the banner of Versailles music's revival. It is forged on the model of the woodwind ensemble playing in the court of Louis XIV, though in reality in Malgoire's ensemble only the flutes, a few oboes, and a 'natural baroque' trumpet (as noted on the cover of the box) are ancient.

Classic or Baroque – Is it that Clear?

The quarrel soon takes the form of a war between two well-defined camps: the classical and the baroque. Everything is about opposites. Voices, numbers of performers, old instruments, revised or original score, pitch – it is like night and day. Over the years that follow the conflict only grows – though it also quickly leads to the victory of the *baroqueux*, who oust most of the traditional ensembles from the pre-1800 repertoire. No question: with all his flaws, Malgoire is part of the baroque camp, and anyone who subscribes to the new 'baroquist' mindset must support him; with all his qualities, Paillard is part of the classical camp and this is doomed to disappear – the case is open and shut. Here is an example, a critical 1994 review of *Les Indes* by Paillard (disdainfully specified as 'Paul Dukas' version'), twenty years after the release of the LP – in French, its tone is so arrogant and definitive that it even sounds vulgar:

> *Opéra international*-November 1994-evaluation 1/5
>
> Clearly, Jean-Français [*sic*] Paillard has in no way understood that a heroic-ballet [the subtitle given by Rameau to his *Indes*] is a form of entertainment. His only concern seems to be to turn the music into a simplified film soundtrack, so that we can taste the intrigue, but strictly in the first degree, factually. What we hear is simply boulevard theatre – not even boulevard opera, because the music is absent. The ear has nothing to savour. Not to mention the fat, sluggish string section, an elephantine choir and a very weak cast of singers: Gerda Hartman too tight, Louis Devos screaming his highs, with his voice often remaining caught in his throat, Philippe Huttenlocher short-winded as usual. Fortunately, Jennifer Smith and John Elwes have the good merit to keep their heads under water [*sic*, obviously for 'above'] in such a shipwreck.

The story has been settled, and long ago! However, is the evidence of the ear so clear? To test this we carried out an experiment[31] gathering all the material of the dispute (works, reviews, excerpts of broadcasts from *France Musique*, the French national radio station, booklets, and CD cases, etc.). This shows that radical opposition between the two versions can be traced in a careful, discographic staging (booklet, illustrations, list of instruments, facsimile, interviews, and so on) which contrasted completeness with authenticity and the fame of the pieces against their historically informed performance. But things are not so obvious when we switch from marketing to actual performance. Here the opposition is much less clear cut. Indeed, sometimes the *baroquisants* features are even inverted (in addition, both recordings were done very quickly in an atmosphere of enthusiastic improvisation). Malgoire insists on the reduced number of his ensemble, but despite the talk Paillard's is nearly as small.[32] The 440 Hz pitch in the CBS recording is barely any lower than the 445 Hz of the 'modern' Erato version. Both conductors have resorted to large, amateur choirs. But what is least in accordance with the texts and pronouncements is the cast of singers. The Malgoire version was saved *in extremis* by Janine Micheau, veteran of French opera, who had already sung in Hans Rosbaud and Maurice Lehmann's 1952 production at the Opéra de Paris. Another veteran, Jean-Christophe Benoît, rubs shoulders with Anne-Marie Rodde and Bruce Brewer, theatre singers experienced in this repertoire and ornamental know-how, as well as some very young artists, most of whom, Rachel Yakar aside, would not continue in baroque singing. It is quite different for Paillard. In the years that followed, his soloists would emerge as baroque singers at various levels: Gerda Hartman, Philippe Huttenlocher, Louis Devos, and especially Jennifer Smith (who would sing in a *Les Indes* concert in London under the baton of Malgoire, a year later!) and John Elwes, who would later be one of the favourite tenors for Bach's complete cantatas by Harnoncourt and Leonhardt.

The critics at the time did not hear any of this. All their comments contrast the two versions. *Harmonie* (6–7–8, 1974) runs a contrast 'for' and an 'against' Malgoire 'to better understand the debate'. Does this clarify it, or simply sustain it? What both critics definitely agree on is the certainty of their disagreement: '*The fact that* these two versions of *Les Indes* are so clearly dissimilar…',

'*Obviously*, for Paillard, Rameau does not cover the same things as Malgoire. It is not within the same universe' (our emphasis). The 'evidence' is the same in another music journal, *Lyrica* (I, 8–9, 1974): '*What really stands out* is that right down to the smallest detail their interpretations are the reflection of two personalities which could not be more different'. *Diapason* helpfully brings this opposition back to 'the conceptual differences between the two conductors [...] *as they themselves explain*': the intensive orchestration of their rivalry in the advertising by their record labels meant that nobody dared to disagree. This collective coaching effect no doubt echoed the expectations of the public. The latter was starting to divide between traditional versions and the 'neo-old'. The only question was which camp to choose: in a time of religious wars, it is not good to be stuck in the middle.

The Les Indes Dispute: Forty Years On...

The object is not to mock the blindness of the past with advantage of the illusory benefits of hindsight. On the contrary, it is to extend respect to a way of listening that is *other* to our own: to analyse rather than to sneer. However, listening again to these recordings, Joël-Marie Fauquet and I (both witnesses, if not insiders, to the 1974 event) were surprised to find that our impressions or sensations have changed. Everything that had made us pick sides with such fervour at the time has been diluted. Indeed, during this seminar both of us even felt that, more than Malgoire, Paillard is the one who sounds more like a precursor to William Christie, or to any other big name among the 'baroqueux'.

Music extracts nos. 5–6: 'Forêts paisibles' from Les Indes in each version[33]

It was the same for the heterogeneous audience at the seminar. Radical differences that scarred the adversaries fade before glaring similarities whose features are obvious to us now, though they seem to have been inaudible to listeners back then. What happened between 'baroque' and 'classical' advocates in 1974 is happening again now, but between these two – and us. And, far from overlapping, these two sets of opposing judgements, then and now, barely even recognise one another. So much for the 'evidence' derived from listening!

Are we simply reverting back to the idea that taste is arbitrary? Do we simply like what we like as a function of identity? Does the music have nothing to do with it? Though now we are submerged in a sea of sociologism which claims a certain quality of scientific proof for these previously iconoclastic claims, the answers are not obvious. After all, who should we believe? Why would we favour our modern-day ears? They may simply be too distant to detect the relevant differences. The witnesses to this 1974 story felt that the versions presented to them were different. Is there any point in judging the effects of music if it is not at the time and place of their reception? The situations that enable us to compare the 1974 listener with one today are itself an artefact of the disc. But there is more. Engraving music onto a durable material accentuates the tendency to attribute the effect of the music to the music itself alone. Everything else that made us listen and love stays in the shadows. Places, moments, and dispositions that made us sensitive, habits, the music that we play in our heads, our systems of reference which rendered certain things significant and others insignificant, all of these disappear (Hennion 2015). Vanished, then, is the collective ear; the contexts of our expectations; the conflicts; whatever it is that makes us desire music even if that music does not yet exist; and *then* what leads us to appreciate it or not.

And here we are back with the original question. What is it that makes musical estimation possible and updates this as time passes? The answer has nothing to do with fixed 'recordings' that simply need to be broadcast. It has nothing to do with isolated sounds. Rather it is music as a collective, sensorial event made – and absorbed – by particular tastes. Listeners were not simply embracing isolated sounds but aesthetic programmes, emerging movements, sonorous desires, and attitudes towards tradition.[34] To hear a piece of music from afar is to hear nothing at all. What now appears to us as secondary may have been crucial back then. The clumsiness of the baroque instrumentalist to which we pay little attention or which brings a smile to our lips may have been most striking back then in its novelty and tonic, colourful, provocation.

The desire for the work precedes and 'creates' it. This does not mean that the work is nothing, or that any other piece would have been judged apt for consumption in its place. However, it is this condition that enables the pieces to be read and loaded with meaning. It is this that makes them eligible as possible pieces even before they are desired. Taste is a music-maker, not an opus consumer. There is an invisible mask of input in music. It is what the story makes perceptible. We see this at work at the time of the moderns versus the 'neo-ancients', but also as the period's most seemingly steadfast traits got inexorably lost. The passage of time has prioritised what was common to them – and this is precisely why a 1970s 'sound', a way of playing and singing, was less noticeable at the time. It reveals the historic character of taste in an exemplary fashion. The baroque game made the object of its historical concerns visible and official in an entirely new way ('play in the old way'). Desire for baroque music was more important than sticking to the old treatises. In particular, it raised a desire that was completely of the moment, to challenge the classical mould. With hindsight this is seen most clearly than at the time, when it had achieved only partial success. The taste for 'baroque' was a product of its time to such a degree that it quickly became dated and now it tells us more about the 1970s than it does about the eighteenth century.

CONCLUSION: MUSIC AS 'DESIRE FOR MUSIC'

So what have we learnt? The answer is that performance is more relevant to music than truth. It is how music is played – and replayed – that is crucial.[35] Those variations which characterise ways of playing make the 'authentic' baroque of the first *baroqueux* sound very ''70s' – that is, very *1970s*. Our Harnoncourt and Leonhardt, too, are already '*Viollet-le-Ducquised*'.[36] Fidelity to source 'dates' – this marks a performance with the seal of the period in which it is made rather than the period it aims to cover. Art specialists know this well. There it takes the form of controversies about restoration.[37] But for paintings and statues, it is relegated to the sidelines: 'present-ation' is effaced in the mounting of an exhibition, a museum, a gallery, or when a painting is hung at home. In music, on the contrary, it is centre stage. Music is an art form where the presence of the living bodies is paramount. Performers, singers, and the instruments are in action. Objects are set in motion, not showcased behind glass. Music is to be made and done. It is to be played. It is not to be contemplated.

Between the two poles of the object and the subject, the score that comes to us from the past and modern taste that we very selectively bring to these vanished repertoires, is a third term, that of interpretation. This is present in all the arts, but especially in music. Here we are helped by a double entendre. 'Interpretation' in music is about both understanding and playing. Michael Baxandall (1972) wrote of the 'eye' of the time in painting. In music we might talk about the 'ear' of the century. As time passes, such sensibilities to listening and hearing become more difficult to identify and document as the objects and writings themselves become more present and pervasive. However, the need to replay the music, and not just to hang it on a picture rail, necessarily highlights the communal work of musicians and audiences needed to hear works written in other eras than our own. The interpretation of a piece of music enables a modern ear to penetrate work from the past, turns it into something else, and enables it to enter the repertoire of available authors. Composition: this is precisely *le mot juste* for musical things, not only for the composer but also *from the point of view of the listener*. Listening to a work is a composition between what it attempts to 'reach' and what the listener makes of it. And the latter depends on all the modern prostheses and the work carried out by bringing together generations of 'interpreters' in both senses of the word. It is this which separates and connects the modern-day-listener to the old work.

So what have we done here? Have we talked of 'baroque music'? If we stick to a textbook definition of the history of art or music, discussing the historical features of a style, then undoubtedly we have not! Yet we have been looking at the specific characteristics of music associated with origins in the 'baroque'.[38] These traits are by no means arbitrary. If Giazotto lends his quill to Albinoni, two centuries after his death, it is to be more baroque than baroque itself, even if it only means projecting the 1950s romantic image of the Italian baroque onto his favourite author. These are some qualities specific to Bach that Gounod wants to revalorise in the composition of present-day music – even and especially if his concern is universality rather than the baroque from which he tries to rid Bach. And it was from all the wonderful trappings of seventeenth-century opera that two competing conductors drew the weapons with which they chose to work. In this way, drawing on the forgotten inflections of what was *classical* French music, they together contributed to the reincorporation into the repertoire of what has now become twentieth-century 'baroque'.

In a strange ballet, intersecting, composite fragments pass between centuries and customs foreign to one another, relying on each other for expression and transformation. Revisions, loans, projections, annexations – none of these refer to the historical relevance of a repertoire. Nor do they point to the arbitrary gestures of a contemporary producer or the appropriation of a fickle and fleeting public fancy. These variations are neither true nor false: they are what make music.[39] Far from a fidelity frozen in deference to the objects of the past, the work of taste forms ears and trains bodies, invents devices and scenes, and mobilises collectives. On each occasion that the music is remade, its arrangement is unprecedented. If we think of sculptural movements that have continued to surprise the very stones from which they grow, what is ultimately more baroque than these perpetual musical impulses which, without ever resting on the objects of the past, bring them back to life indefinitely?

NOTES

1 Translation by James O'Hagan and John Law.

2 The baroque case in music has often been used to defend or criticise conceptions of authenticity, e.g. Adorno (1967); Taruskin (1991); Hennion (2015, ch. 6).

3 If a de-attribution or evidence of forgery causes the price of the 'same' painting to drop, is it not the price tag alone which affords value? Svetlana Alpers opposes a magisterial response to the false evidence of this cynical (or sociological) thesis formulated, for example, by Alsop (1982). By inverting the argument, she shows Rembrandt carefully installing the authority of the artist-creator: even the possibility of copying his paintings is part of his own work (Alpers 1988). On this slow historical production of the notion of the original, see the beautifully deployed analysis of Haskell and Penny, about Roman statues (1982).

4 This chapter includes a number of music extracts, which can be listened to online. Readers are encouraged to follow the relevant hyperlinks, as in this case to Albinoni's *Adagio in G Minor* (Karajan) <https://archive.org/details/HennionAuthenticOrTrueA lbinoniAdagio>[accessed 06 February 2016]

5 Giazotto is credited as editor in the second album.

6 See, for example, Dutton (1983), or *De main de maître* (Lista 2009), the proceedings of a 2004 Louvre conference on forgery in art.

7 On p. 48, in the conclusion of the Albinoni section (Arnold 1983).

8 One thinks of the brilliant analysis proposed by O. Mannoni (1969) of this adverbial phrase as a marker of denial: 'I know, but still…'

9 The art of the social sciences is one of quotation marks, while that of the counterfeiter is doubtless that of omitting them at the right time.

10 See Hennion et al. (2000), and on history and 'history', Hennion (2011).

11 … 'il a été fait pour faire vieux': French says it better, by using the verb *faire*, between 'to seem' and 'to be'. This taste for the old has a long history and its continuous extension of the classical repertoire can be traced back to the mid-nineteenth century. On music, see Fauquet and Hennion (2000), or Campos (2003), and on other forms of arts, see again Haskell and his work on the taste variations (1980; 1987; Haskell and Penny 1982).

12 I owe the details of these cases to J.-M. Fauquet, as well as many other precisions, arguments, and elements of discussion on the idea of the fake in music.

13 *Adelaïde*: Orchestre Symphonique de Paris, conductor Pierre Monteux, violin Yehudi Menuhin, recorded in 1934 <https://archive.org/details/HennionAuthenticOrTrueMenuhinAdelaideMozart> [accessed 06 February 2016]

14 On the back of the sleeves, Casadesus is mentioned as the 'orchestrator'.

15 An invented name inspired by Joseph-Louis Duc, his friend since their stay in the Medici Villa.

16 See his *Mémoires*' Post-Scriptum (1991: 556). After its success, Berlioz was prompt to reattribute the choir to himself when it would be integrated into his oratorio.

17 Hector Berlioz (1803–69), *L'Adieu des bergers, de L'Enfance du Christ*, Chœurs René Duclos/Orchestre de la Société des Concerts du Conservatoire/André Cluytens <https://archive.org/details/HennionAuthenticOrTrueBerliozAdieuDesBergers> [accessed 06 February 2016]

18 The expert's gesture mirrors the 'faker'. The former looks with uncertainty at an object of unknown provenance, and evaluates whether it is authentic or false by using multiple signs, takes, clues. As s/he gradually 'feels' it out, this is a real test involving body senses. The 'obvious' character, the clarity of the final verdict, is quite unlike the uncertain states that lead to this. See the striking developments of this expert's paradoxical judgement in Bessy and Chateauraynaud's book (1995), precisely entitled 'Experts and Fakers'.

19 *Ave Maria* by Charles Gounod, Pavarotti <https://archive.org/details/HennionAuthenticOrTrueGounodAveMaria>[accessed 06 February 2016]

20 For the complete analysis, see Fauquet and Hennion (2000: 161 *sqq*).

21 On musical mores in the nineteenth century, see Fauquet, dir. (2003).

22 See M. de Certeau, in *The Writing of History* (1988: 136), about our relation to the past: 'the "Return to origins" is always a modernism as well'.

23 If we think of Rameau's opera which he reforms every time he performs, or Bach's cantatas brimming with borrowed tunes from instrumental works and vice versa, what is the sense in the idea that one of these versions is an original and others are deformations? The production principle moves towards the live performance, rather than being centred around one author's work in the modern sense: the retro-projection of this repertoire on the idea of originality is an anachronism dressed up as fidelity to origins.

24 Haskell and Penny (1982) note that in the early nineteenth century Roman statues that had come in great number to fill the French museums and to decorate English gardens were abundantly restored. By the end of the same century, whatever signalled their antiquity was generously highlighted, even if it meant damaging them on purpose.

25 See a detailed account of the case in Hennion and Fauquet (2004).

26 The large body of work that he entrusted to someone who is still a beginner bears witness to this: Lully's *Alceste* in 1975, Rameau's *Hippolyte et Aricie* in 1978 that followed, and after them Vivaldi, Haendel, Monteverdi, Mozart...

27 A famous series of pedagogic handbooks published by the Presses Universitaires de France.

28 He sold more than 100,000 records of a compilation including Pachelbel's *Canon*, Albinoni's *Adagio*, Bach's *Aria* from the Suite in D major etc. (see fig. 1).

29 Also, due to their real concern about research on the repertoire and the updating of the public's taste for unknown names must be highlighted: *Tous les matins du monde*, a film by Alain Corneau, whose stars were Monsieur de Sainte-Colombe and Marin Marais, would crown the success of this restoration process in 1991.

30 Ancient pitches were much lower than modern ones – it is said around 415 Hz instead of 450, but it is not the right way to put it: first and foremost, they changed in time and from one place to another.

31 Experimental seminar 'Aimer la musique (To Love Music)' on listening, amateurs (music lovers), and taste, organised at the CSI by A. Hennion and J.-M. Fauquet.

32 *Diapason*, a music journal, no. 187, May 1974: 'The two "great machine" scenes from the score [...] for my tastes, are undoubtedly better off being played by Jean-François Paillard's larger orchestra than by Jean-Claude Malgoire's over-minimalist one': 24 musicians on the first, 23 on the second!

33 Two bitterly disputed versions of Rameau's *Indes Galantes* both out in 1974, by Paillard (Erato) and Malgoire (CBS): 'Forêts paisibles', with the famous Danse des sauvages <https://archive.org/details/RameauSauvagesPaillard>[accessed 06 February 2016]

34 This partially explains the very unequal commercial careers of both versions. Paillard was re-edited for CD, whereas Malgoire's sales dropped quickly: it is Malgoire, which a direct competition with new Baroque versions before the same public has outdated, particularly Christie's *Indes* in 1991.

35 For even the first time round it is played in relation to the 'intentions' of the composer.

36 Reference to Eugène Viollet-Le-Duc, famed for his interpretive restorations of medieval cathedrals [translator's note].

37 Restoration is a work that evokes both forgers through technique, and music, through its link between interpretation, and today's ways of showing: *re-presentations*, indeed, in the strongest sense of the word. See Étienne and Hénaut (2012).

38 We re-adorn the word with quotation marks to reinforce that it is a 'performative', not a 'constative': it makes baroque, it does not observe it as a fact.

39 See Kopytoff (1986) on the careers of objects.

BIBLIOGRAPHY

Adorno, T. W., 'Bach Defended Against his Devotees', in *Prisms* (Cambridge, MA: MIT Press, 1983 [1967]), pp. 133–46

Alpers, S., *Rembrandt's Enterprise* (Chicago, IL: University of Chicago Press, 1988)

Alsop, J. W., *The Rare Art Traditions: The History of Art Collecting and its Linked Phenomena Wherever They Have Appeared* (New York: Harper & Row, 1982)

Arnold, D., *The New Oxford Companion to Music* (Oxford: Oxford University Press, 1983)

Baxandall, M., *Painting and Experience in Fifteenth-Century Italy* (Oxford: Oxford University Press, 1972)

Berlioz, H., *Mémoires*, P. Citron, ed. (Paris: Flammarion, 1991)

Bessy, C., and F. Chateauraynaud, *Experts et faussaires. Pour une sociologie de la perception* (Paris: Métailié, 1995)

Campos, R., *La Renaissance introuvable? Entre curiosité et militantisme: la Société des concerts de musique vocale, religieuse et classique du prince de La Moskowa (1843–1847)* (Paris: Klincksieck, 2000)

de Certeau, M., *The Writing of History* (New York: Columbia University Press, 1988)

Dutton, D., ed., *The Forger's Art: Forgery and the Philosophy of Art* (Berkeley: University of California Press, 1983)

Étienne, N., and L. Hénaut, dir., *L'Histoire à l'atelier: restaurer les œuvres d'art (XVIIIe-XXIe siècles)* (Lyon: Presses Universitaires de Lyon, 2012)

Fauquet, J.-M., and A. Hennion, *La Grandeur de Bach: l'amour de la musique en France au XIXe siècle* (Paris: Fayard, 2000)

Fauquet, J.-M., *Dictionnaire de la musique en France au XIXe siècle* (Paris: Fayard, 2003)

Genette, G., *L'Œuvre de l'art. Immanence et transcendance* (Paris: Le Seuil, 1994)

Goodman, N., *Languages of Art* (Indianapolis: Hackett Publishing Company, 1976)

Grafton, A., *Forgers and Critics: Creativity and Duplicity in Western Scholarship* (Princeton, NJ: Princeton University Press, 1990)

Haskell, F., *Rediscoveries in Art: Some Aspects of Taste, Collecting, and Fashion in England and France* (Ithaca, NY: Cornell University Press, 1980)

——— *Past and Present in Art and Taste* (New Haven, CT: Yale University Press, 1987)

Haskell, F., and N. Penny, *Taste and the Antique: The Lure of Classical Sculpture, 1500–1900* (New Haven, CT: Yale University Press, 1982)

Hennion, A., 'Présences du passé: le renouveau des musiques "anciennes". Sources et retours aux sources', *Temporalités* [online] 14 (2011), <http://temporalites.revues.org/1836> [accessed 15 May 2014]

———'Playing, Performing, Listening. Making Music – or Making Music Act?', in L. Marshall, and D. Laing, eds., *Popular Music Matters: Essays in Honour of Simon Frith*, (Farnham: Ashgate, 2014), pp. 165–180

——— *The Passion for Music: A Sociology of Mediation* (Farnham: Ashgate, 2015)

Hennion, A., S. Maisonneuve, and É. Gomart, *Figures de l'amateur. Formes, objets, pratiques de l'amour de la musique aujourd'hui* (Paris: La Documentation française/DEP-Ministère de la Culture, 2000)

Hennion, A., and B. Latour, 'How To Make Mistakes on So Many Things at Once – and Become Famous for it', in H. U. Gumbrecht, and M. Marrinan, eds., *Mapping Benjamin: The Work of Art in the Digital Age* (Stanford, CA: Stanford University Press, 2003), pp. 91–97

Hennion, A., and J.-M. Fauquet, 'Le Baroque en stéréo: la querelle des Indes galantes', *Cahiers de médiologie* 18 (2004), 79–89

Kopytoff, I., 'The Cultural Biography of Things: Commoditization as Process', in A. Appadurai, ed., *The Social Life of Things* (Cambridge: Cambridge University Press, 1986), pp. 64–91

Lista, M., ed., *De main de maître. L'Artiste et le faux* (*actes du colloque du Louvre en 2004*) (Paris: Hazan/Musée du Louvre Éditions, 2009), pp. 13–24; 207–236

Mannoni, O., 'Je sais bien, mais quand même…', in *Clefs pour l'imaginaire* (Paris: Le Seuil, 1969), pp. 9–33

Taruskin, R., 'L'ancienneté du présent et la présence du passé', *Harmoniques*, 7 (1991), pp. 69–102

4

DISTRIBUTIVE NUMBERS: A POST-DEMOGRAPHIC PERSPECTIVE ON PROBABILITY

Adrian Mackenzie

'We ran the election 66,000 times every night', said a senior official, describing the computer simulations the campaign ran to figure out Obama's odds of winning each swing state. 'And every morning we got the spit-out – here are your chances of winning these states. And that is how we allocated resources' (Scherer 2012).

IN THE US PRESIDENTIAL ELECTIONS OF NOVEMBER 2012, THE DATA ANALYSIS team supporting the re-election of Barack Obama were said to be running a statistical model of the election 66,000 times every night (Scherer 2012). Their model, relying on polling data, records of past voting behaviour, and many other databases, was guiding tactical decisions about everything from where the presidential candidate would speak, where advertising money would be spent, to the telephone calls that targeted individual citizens (for donations or their vote). Widely reported in television news and internationally in print media (*Time, New York Times, The Observer*), the outstanding feature of Obama's re-election seems to me to be the figure of 66,000 nightly model runs. Why so many thousand runs? This question was addressed neither in the media reports nor, surprisingly, in the online discussion on blogs and other online forums that followed. A glimmering of an answer appears in more extended accounts of the Obama data analytics efforts (Issenberg 2012) that describe how, in contrast to the much smaller and traditional market research-based targeting of demographic groups used by the Republican campaign for Mitt Romney, the Obama re-election campaign focused on knowing, analysing, and predicting what *individuals* would do in the election. We should note that the Obama data team's efforts are not unique or singular. In very many settings – online gaming, epidemiology, fisheries management, and asthma management (Simpson, Tan, Winn, et al. 2010), similar conjunctions appear. In post-demographic understandings of data, individuals appear not simply as members of a population (although they certainly do that), but themselves as a kind of joint probability distribution at the conjunction of many different numbering practices. If individuals were once collected, grouped, ranked, and trained in populations characterised by disparate attributes (life expectancies, socio-economic variables, educational development, and so on), today we might say that they are distributed across populations of different kinds that intersect through them. Individuals become more like populations or crowds. This chapter seeks to describe, therefore, a shift in what numbers do in their post-demographic modes of existence.

$PR(A)$: EVENTS AND BELIEFS IN THE WORLD

How can individuals appear as populations? A standard textbook of statistics introduces the idea of probability as event-related numbers in this way:

> We will assign a real number $Pr(A)$ to every event A, called the *probability* of A (Wasserman 2003: 3).

Note that this number is 'real' so it can take infinitely many values between 0 and 1. The number concerns 'events', where events are understood as subsets of all the possible outcomes in a given 'sample space' ('the *sample space* Ω is the set of possible outcomes of an experiment. [...] Subsets of Ω are called *Events*'

(Wasserman 2003: 3)). The number assigned to events can be understood in two main ways. Wasserman goes on:

> There are many interpretations of $Pr(A)$. The common interpretations are frequencies and degrees of belief. [...] The difference in interpretation will not matter much until we deal with statistical inference. There the differing interpretations lead to two schools of inference: the frequentists and Bayesian schools (Wasserman 2003: 6).

The difference will only matter, suggests Wasserman, in relation to the style of statistical inference. Even apart from these relatively well-known alternative interpretations of probability, the practice of assigning numbers to events in Ω does not, I will suggest, remain stable. If we keep an eye on the machinery that assigns numbers, then we might have a better sense of how events and beliefs themselves might change shape.

Summarising his own account of the emergence of probability, the philosopher and historian Ian Hacking highlights the long-standing interplay of the two common interpretations of probability as frequencies and degrees of belief:

> I claimed in *The Emergence of Probability* that our idea of probability is a Janus-faced mid-seventeenth-century mutation in the Renaissance idea of signs. It came into being with a frequency aspect and a degree-of-belief aspect (Hacking 1990: 96).

In this work from 1975, Hacking, writing largely ahead of the marked shifts in probability practice I discuss, claims that there was no probability prior to 1660 (Hacking 1975). As we can verify in the statistics textbooks, there is nothing controversial in Hacking's claim that probability is Janus-faced. Historians of statistics and statisticians themselves regularly describe probability as bifurcated in the same way. Statisticians commonly contrast the frequentist and degree-of-belief, the *aleatory* and the *epistemic*, views of probability. Although the history of statistics shows various distributions and permutations of emphasis on the subjective and objective versions of probability, statisticians are now relatively happily normalised around a divided view of probability.

Contemporary probability, however, has become entwined with a particular mode of computational machinery – and here we might think of machinery as something like baroque theatre machinery, with its interest in the production of effects and appearances that are never fully naturalised – that deeply convolutes the difference between the epistemic and aleatory faces of probability. Not only is probability a baroque invention, but the fundamental instability that permits recent mutations in probability practice has a distinctively baroque flavour in the way that it combines something happening in the world with something that pertains to subjects. The techniques involved here include the bootstrap (Efron 1975), expectation-maximisation (Dempster, Laird, and Rubin 1977), and Markov-Chain Monte Carlo (Gelfand and Smith 1990). These techniques support increasingly post-demographic treatments of individuals, in which, for instance, individuals progressively attract probability distributions, as in Obama's data-intensive re-election campaign.[1] In examining a salient contemporary treatment of probability, my concern is the problem of invention of forms of thought able to critically affirm mutations in probability today. I suggest that these mutations arise in many, perhaps all, contemporary settings where populations, events, individuals, numbers, and calculation are to be found. In such settings, a baroque sense of the enfolding of inside and outside, of belief and events, of approximation and exactitudes, offers at least tentative pointers to a different way of describing what is happening as the aleatory and epistemic senses of probability find themselves redistributed.

EXACT MEANS SIMULATED

The contour plot in Fig. 4.1 was generated by the widely used statistical simulation technique called MCMC (Markov Chain Monte Carlo simulation). MCMC has greatly transformed many statistical practices since the early 1990s. The diagram shows the contours of a distribution (a bivariate normal distribution in

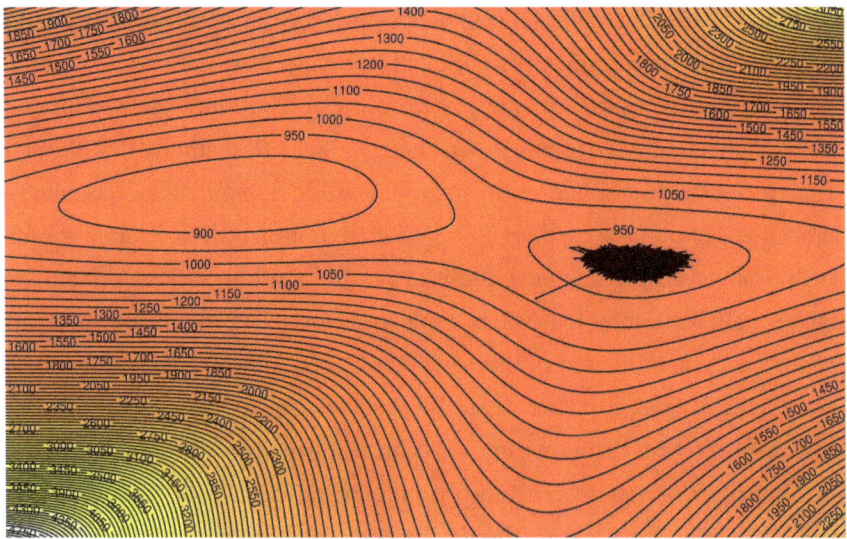

FIG. 4.1 Bivariate normal distribution produced by Gibbs sampling

this case) generated by MCMC that fits a mixture of two normally distributed sets of numbers to some data. The topography of this diagram is the product of a simulation of specific kinds of numbers, in this case the mean values of two normal distributions. The contour lines trace the different values of the means (μ_1, μ_2) of the variables. For the time being, we need to know nothing about what such peaks refer to, apart from the fact they are something to do with probability, with assigning numbers to events. A set of connected points starting on the side of the one of the peaks and clustering on the peak marks the traces of the itinerary of the MCMC algorithm as it explores the topography in search of peaks that represent more likely events or beliefs. Importantly for present purposes, this path comprises 60,000 steps (that is, around the same number mentioned by Obama's data team).

When 'Sampling-Based Approaches to Calculating Marginal Densities', the article that first announced the arrival of MCMC in statistical practice (Robert and Casella 2010: 9), appeared in the *Journal of the American Statistical Association* (Gelfand and Smith 1990), the statisticians Alan Gelfand and Adrian Smith (subsequently Director General of Science and Research in the UK government's Department for Innovation, Universities and Skills) stated that the problem they were addressing was how 'to obtain numerical estimates of non-analytically available marginal densities of some or all [the collection of random variables] simply by means of simulated samples from available conditional distributions, and without recourse to sophisticated numerical analytic methods' (1990: 398). Their formulation emphasises the mixture of using things that are accessible – simulated samples – to explore things that are not directly accessible – 'non-analytically available marginal densities [...] of random variables' (some of this probability terminology will be explored below). For present purposes, the important point is that a newly non-analytical probability is in formation here. It lies at some distance from the classical probability calculus first developed in the seventeenth century around games of chance, mortality statistics, and the like.

Note that these statisticians are not announcing the invention of a new technique. They explicitly take up the already existing Gibbs sampler algorithm for image-processing, as described in Geman and Geman (1984), investigate some of its formal properties (convergence), and then set out a number of mainstream statistical problems that could be done differently using MCMC and the Gibbs sampler in particular. They show how MCMC facilitates Bayesian statistical inference – the approach to statistics that shapes basic parameters in the light of previous experience – by reconfiguring six illustrative mainstream statistical examples: multinomial models, hierarchical models, multivariate normal sampling, variance components, and the k-group normal means model. The illustrations in the paper suggest how previously difficult problems of statistical inference can be carried out by sampling simulations. As they state in another paper from the same year, 'the potential of the methodology is enormous, rendering straightforward the analysis of a number of problems hitherto regarded as intractable' (Gelfand and Smith 1990: 984).[2]

Note too that while the MCMC technique has become important in contemporary statistics, and especially in Bayesian statistics (Gelman, Carlin, Stern, et al. 2003), it plays significant roles in applications such as image, speech and audio processing, computer vision, computer graphics, molecular biology and genomics, robotics, decision theory, and information retrieval (Andrieu, De Freitas, Doucet, et al. 2003: 37–38). Usually called an *algorithm* – a series of precise operations that transform or reshape data – MCMC has been voted one of 'the ten most influential algorithms' in twentieth-century science and engineering (Andrieu, De Freitas, Doucet, et al. 2003: 5).[3] But MCMC is not really an algorithm, or at least, if it is, it is an algorithm subject to substantially different implementations (for instance, Metropolis-Hastings and Gibbs Sampler are two popular implementations). In all of these settings, MCMC is a way of simulating a sample of points distributed on a complicated curve or surface (see Fig. 4.1). The MCMC technique addresses the problem of how to explore and map very uneven or folded distributions of numbers. It is a way of navigating areas or volumes whose curves, convolutions, and hidden recesses elude geometrical spaces and perspectival vision. Accounts of MCMC emphasise the 'high-dimensional' spaces in which the algorithm works: 'there are several high-dimensional problems, such as computing the volume of a convex body in d dimensions, for which MCMC simulation is the only known general approach for providing a solution within a reasonable time' (Andrieu, De Freitas, Doucet, et al. 2003: 5). We might say that MCMC, alongside other statistical algorithms such as the bootstrap or EM, increasingly facilitates the envisioning of high-dimensional, convoluted data spaces. Simulating the distribution of numbers over folded surfaces, MCMC renders the areas and volumes of folds more amenable to calculation.

What MCMC adds to the world is subtle yet indicative. In their history of the technique, Christian Robert and George Casella, two leading statisticians specialising in MCMC, write that 'Markov chain Monte Carlo changed our emphasis from "closed form" solutions to algorithms, expanded our impact to solving "real" applied problems and to improving numerical algorithms using statistical ideas, and led us into a world where "exact" now means "simulated"' (Robert and Casella 2008: 18). This shift from 'closed form' solution to algorithms and to a world where 'exact means simulated' might be all too easily framed by a postmodern sensibility as another example of the primacy of the simulacra over the original. But here, a baroque sensibility, awake to the convolution of objective-event and subjective belief senses of probability, might allow us to approach MCMC less in terms of a crisis of referentiality and more in terms of the emergence of a new form of distributive number.

How so? The contours of Fig. 4.1 define a volume. In its typical usages, the somewhat complicated shape of this volume typically equates to the joint probability of multiple random variables. MCMC, put in terms of the minimal formal textbook definition of probability, is a way of assigning real numbers to events, but according to a mapping shaped by the convoluted volumes created by joint probability distributions. The identification of $Pr(A)$ with a convoluted volume offers great potential to statistics. For instance, political scientists regularly use MCMC in their work because their research terrain – elections, opinions, voting patterns – little resembles the image of events projected by mainstream statistics: independent, identically distributed ('iid') events staged in experiments. MCMC allows, as the political scientist Jeff Gill observes, all unknown quantities to be 'treated probabilistically' (Gill 2011: 1). We can begin to glimpse why the Obama re-election team might have been running their model 66,000 times each night. In short, MCMC allows, at least in principle, *every* number to be treated as a probability distribution.

1/∞: DISTRIBUTED INDIVIDUALS AS RANDOM VARIABLES

Let us return to the typical problem of the individual voters modelled by the Obama re-election team. Treating every number as a probability distribution involves exteriorising numbers in the service of an interiorising of probability. Techniques of statistical simulation multiply numbers in the world and assign numbers to events, but largely in the service of modifying, limiting, and quantifying uncertainties associated with belief. This folding together of subjective and objective, of epistemic and aleatory senses of probability, can be thought as a neo-baroque mode of probability. The baroque sense of probability, especially as articulated by G. W. Leibniz, the 'first philosopher of probability' (Hacking 1975: 57), is helpful in holding together these contrapuntal movements. Leibniz's famously impossible claim that each monad *includes* the whole world is, according to Gilles Deleuze, actually a claim about numbers in variation. Through numbers, understood in a somewhat unorthodox way, monads – the parts of the world – can include the whole world. Deleuze says, 'for Leibniz, the monad is clearly the most "simple" number, that is, the inverse, reciprocal, harmonic number' (Deleuze 1993: 129).

Having a world – for the monad is a mode of having a world by including it – as a number entails a very different notion of *having* and a somewhat different notion of number. The symbolic expression of this inclusion is, according to Deleuze: $1/\infty$. The numerator 1 points to the singular individual (remember that for Leibniz, every monad is individual): the denominator, ∞, includes a world. The fraction or ratio of 1 to ∞ tends towards a vanishingly small difference (zero), yet one whose division passes through all numbers (the whole world). In what sense is this fraction, in its convergence towards zero, including a world? Deleuze writes that for in the baroque, 'the painting-window [of Renaissance perspective] is replaced by tabulation, the grid on which lines, numbers and changing characters are inscribed. [...] Leibniz's monad would be just a such grid' (1993: 27). This suggests a different notion of the subject, no longer the subject of the world view who sees along straight lines that converge at an infinite distance (the subject as locus of reason, experience, or intentionality), but as 'the truth of a variation' (Ibid: 20) played out in numbers and characters tabulated on gridded screens. The monad is a grid of numbers and characters in variation.

How could we concretise this? Alongside the individual voters modelled by the Obama re-election team, we might think of border control officers viewing numerical predictions of whether a particular passenger arriving on a flight is likely to present a security risk (Amoore 2009), financial traders viewing changing prices for a currency or financial derivative on their screens (Knorr-Cetina and Bruegger 2002), a genomic researcher deciding whether the alignment scores between two different DNA sequences suggest a phylogenetic relationship, or a player in a large online multiplayer game such as World of Warcraft quickly checking the fatigue levels of their character before deciding what to do: these are all typical cases where numbers in long chains of converging variation populate the monadic grid. $1/\infty$ entails a significant shift in the understanding of number. Deleuze writes that 'the inverse number has special traits: [...] by opposition to the natural number, which is collective, it is individual and distributive' (1993: 129). If numbers become 'individual and distributive', then the calculations that produce them might be important to map in the specificity of their transformations.

Earlier we saw the flat operational definition of probability as assigning real numbers between 0 and 1 to events. By contrast, a random variable 'is a mapping that assigns a real number to each outcome' (Wasserman 2003: 19), but this number can vary. If events have probabilities, random variables comprehend a range of outcomes that are mapped to numbers in the form of probability distributions. The practical reality of random variables is variation, variations that usually take the visual forms of the curves of the probability distributions shown in Fig. 4.2. These distributions each have their own history (see Stigler (1986) for a detailed historical account of key developments), but for our purposes the important points are both historical and philosophical. On the one hand, the historical development of probability distributions, particularly the Gaussian or normal distribution, but also lesser known Chi-square, Beta or hypergeometric distributions, displays powerful inversions in which the mapping of numbers to events becomes a mapping of events to numbers. Hacking, for instance, describes how the nineteenth-century statistician Adolphe Quetelet began to treat populations. The normal distribution 'became a reality underneath the phenomena of consciousness' (Hacking 1990: 205). A whole set of normalisations, often with

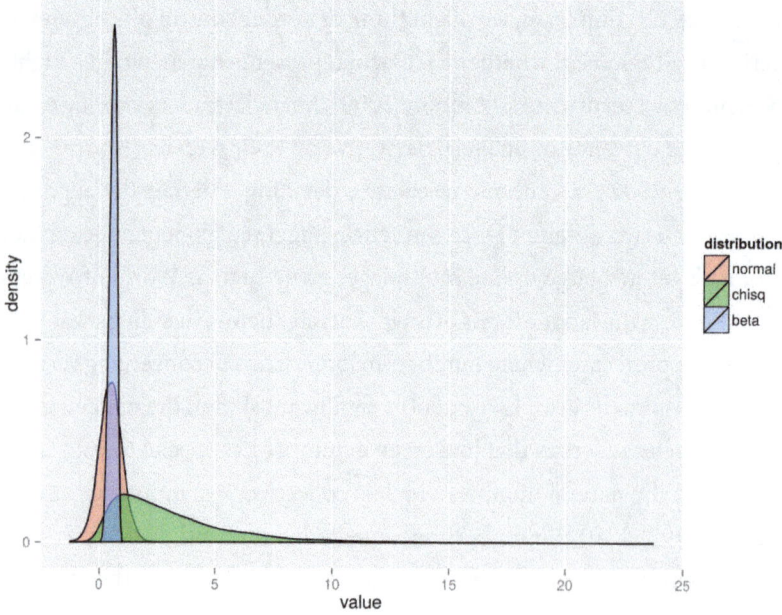

FIG. 4.2 A variety of distributions

strongly biopolitical dynamics, hinges on this inversion of the relation between numbers and events in nineteenth-century probability practice.

On the other hand, the regularity, symmetry, and above all mathematical expression of these functions in equations, such as the one shown in equation 4.1, more or less delimited statistical practice. Such expressions offer great tractability since their shape, area, or volume can all be expressed in terms of key tendencies such as μ, the mean, and σ, the variance. The eighteenth and nineteenth-century development of statistical practice pivots on manipulations that combine or generalise such expressions to an increasing variety of situations. For instance, in Fig. 4.2, the normal distribution shown in Equation 4.1 for one variable x becomes a bvariate normal distribution for two variables x_1 and x_2. Nevertheless, these equations also limit the range of shapes, areas, and volumes that statistical practice could map onto events. When statisticians speak of 'fitting a density' (a probability distribution) to data, they affirm their commitment to the regular forms of probability distributions.

$$f(x;\mu,\sigma^2) = \frac{1}{\sigma\sqrt{2\pi}} e^{-\frac{1}{2}(\frac{x-\mu}{\sigma})^2}$$

EQU. 4.1 Gaussian probability density function

THE ENDLESS FLOW OF RANDOM VARIABLES

Both aspects of this commitment – the curve as underlying reality of events, and the normalised expression of curves in functions whose parameters shape the curve – begin to shift in techniques such as MCMC. In particular, following Deleuze's discussion of the monad as distributive number, we might say that the probability distributions now function less as the collective form of individuals, and more as the distributive form of individuals across increasingly complex and folded surfaces. We saw above that MCMC inaugurates 'a world where "exact" now means "simulated"' (Robert and Casella 2008: 18). This comment links an analytical quality – exactitude – with a calculative, modelling process – simulation. But rather than attesting to the pre-eminence of simulation, we should see techniques such as MCMC as ways of exploring the concavities and convexities, the surfaces and volumes generated by random variables. Put more statistically, MCMC maps the contoured and folded surfaces that arise as flows of data or random variables come together in one joint probability distribution. These surfaces, generated by the combinations of mathematical functions or probability distributions, are not easy to see or explore, except in the exceptional cases where calculus can deliver a deductive analytical 'closed form' solution to the problems of integration: finding the area and thereby estimating the distribution function for one variable. By contrast, MCMC effectively simulates some important parts of the surface, and in simulating convoluted volumes loosens the analytical ties that bind probability to certain well-characterised analytical regular forms such as the normal curve. In this simulation of folded and multiplied probability distributions, the lines between objective and subjective, or aleatory and epistemic probability, begin to shift not towards some total computer simulation of reality but towards a refolding of probability through world and experience. The subjective and the objective undergo an ontological transformation in which calculation lies neither simply on the side of the knowing subject nor inheres in things in the world. These practices perhaps make those boundaries radically convoluted.

Fig. 4.3 shows two plots. The histogram on the left shows the occurrence of 10,000 computer-generated random numbers between 0 and 1, and as expected, or hoped, they are more or less uniformly distributed between 0 and 1. No single number is much more likely than another. This is a simulation of the simplest probability distribution of all, the *uniform* probability distribution in which all events are equally likely. The uniform distribution could be assigned to a random variable. The plot on the right derives from the same set of 10,000 random numbers, but shows a different probability distribution in which events mapped to numbers close to 0 are much more likely than events close to 1. What has happened here? The reshaping of the flow of numbers depends on a very simple multiplication of the simulated uniform distribution by itself:

> A real function of a random variable is another random variable. Random variables with a wide variety of distributions can be obtained by transforming a standard uniform random variable $U \approx UNIF(0, 1)$ (Suess and Trumbo 2010: 32).

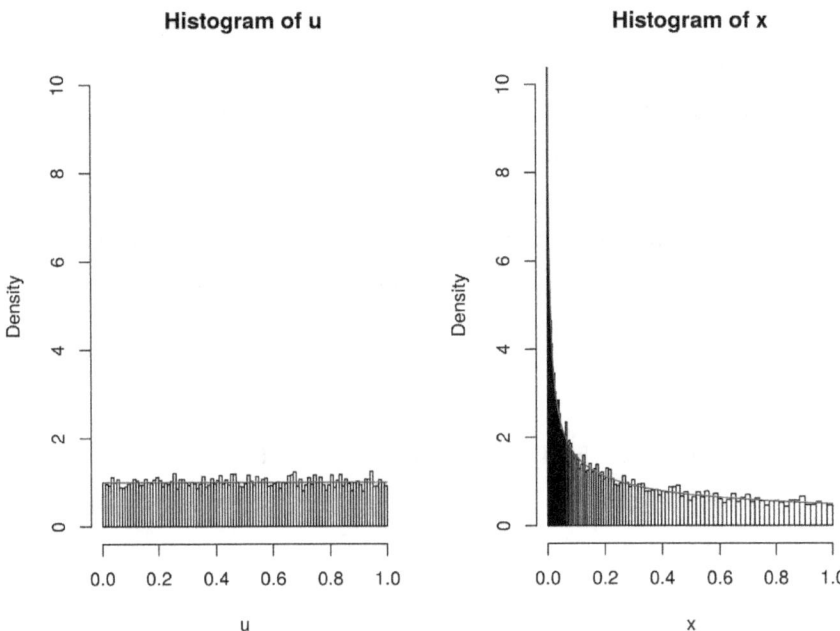

FIG. 4.3 Simulated distributions

It happens that multiplying the uniform variable by itself (U^2) produces an instance of another random variable, now characterised by the *Beta* distribution, shown on the right of Fig. 4.3. While generated by the same set of random numbers, this is now a different random variable. It would be possible to produce that curve of a beta distribution analytically, by plotting points generated by the *Beta* probability density function:

$$f(x; a, \beta) = \text{constant} \cdot x^{a-1} (1-x)^{\beta-1} \text{ where } a = 0.5 \text{ and } \beta = 1 \text{ in equation}$$

But in the case of the plots shown on the right of Fig. 4.3, the random variable has been generated from a flow of random numbers. So, from a flow of random numbers, generated by the computer (using a *pseudo-random* number-generator algorithm), more random variables result, but with different shapes or probability densities. As Robert and Casella write, 'the point is that a supply of random variables can be used to generate different distributions' (2010: 44). Indeed, this is the principle of all Monte Carlo simulations, methods that 'rely on the possibility of producing (with a computer) a supposedly endless flow of random variables for well-known or new distributions' (Ibid: 42). The example shown here is really elementary in terms of the distribution and dimensionality of the random variables involved, yet it illustrates a general practice underpinning the MCMC technique: the reshaping of the 'supposedly endless flow of random variables' to produce known or new distributions that map increasingly convoluted volumes and more intricately distributed events.

THE PATH PRECEDES THE TOPOGRAPHY

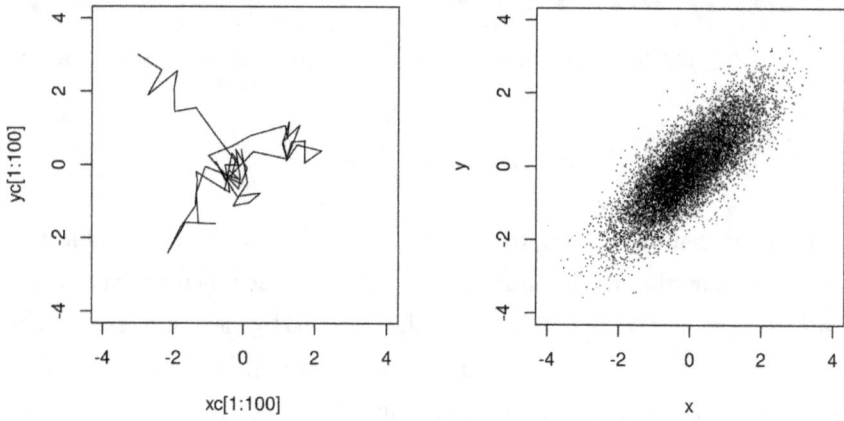

FIG. 4.4 Metropolis-Hastings algorithm-generated normal distribution

In Fig. 4.4, the density of a volume generated by many random numbers (shown on the right as a cloud of points) contrasts with the meandering itinerary of the line on the left. The former plots the now familiar bvariate normal distribution while the latter shows the path taken by the MCMC algorithm as it *generates* this volume. The path replaces the global analytical solution, the a priori analysis or indeed any simply numerical calculation that estimates properties of the volume or surface. Rather, and this difference matters quite a lot, the path constructs the volume as it maps it. The plot on the left precedes the plot on the right, which is effectively a simulated probability distribution derived from the path. Note too that the path shows only a small selection of the many moves made by the algorithm (approximately 100 of the 40,000 steps).

What form of rule regulates the itinerary of this path? 'Consider the Markov chain defined by $X^{t+1} = \sigma X^t + \epsilon(t)$ where $\epsilon(t)$?$(0, 1)$', write Robert and Casella (2010: 169). The Markov chain – the first MC in MCMC – knows nothing of the normal distribution, yet simulates it by using a flow of random numbers to construct random variables, and then using another stream of random numbers to nudge that random variable into a particular shape. The idea of using a 'random walk' to explore the folds of a volume dates back to the work of physicists Nicholas Metropolis and Stanislaw Ulam in the late 1940s modelling particles in nuclear reactions (Metropolis 1949).[4] Purely randomly sampled points are just as likely to lie in low probability regions (valleys and plains) as in the high probability peaks. Metropolis proposed a move which becomes the modus operandi of subsequent MCMC work (and hence justifies the high citation count): 'we place the N particles in any configuration [...] then we move each of the particles in succession' (Ibid: 1088). As well as generating a sample of random numbers that represent particles in a system, they submit each simulated particle to a test. Physically, the image here is that they displace each particle by a small random amount sideways. Having moved the particle/variable, they calculate the resulting slight change in the overall system state, and then decide whether that particular move puts the system in a more or less probable state. If that state is more likely, there is some probability that the move is allowed; otherwise the particle goes back to where it was. Having carried out this process of small moves for all the particles, they can calculate the overall system state or property. The process of randomly displacing the particles by a small amount, and always moving to the more probable states, effectively maps the possibly bumpy terrain of the joint probability density. In many minute moves, the simulation begins to steer the randomly generated values points towards the peaks that represent interesting high-valued features on the surface.

In contemporary MCMC, the folds and contours mapped by the Markov chains are no longer particles in physical systems but random variables with irregular probability distributions. But the connection between iteration and itinerary holds firm. By generating many itineraries, a topography begins to take shape and appear. The computationally intensive character of MCMC arises from the iteration needed to construct many random walks across an uneven surface in order to ensure that all of its interesting features have been visited. As we saw in Fig. 4.4, the surface appears by virtue of the Markov chain paths that traverse it.

CONCLUSION

What in the redistribution of events and beliefs in the world, the random variables as distributive individuals, or the paths that precede the terrain they traverse helps us make sense of what was happening: each night in the Obama election team; each time players are matched in Microsoft's Xbox Live player-matching system; in the epidemiological models of public health authorities forecasting influenza prevalence (Birrell, Ketsetzis, Gay, et al. 2011); or for that matter, in the topic models that have recently attracted the interest of humanities and social science researchers sifting through large numbers of documents (Mohr and Bogdanov 2013)? I have been suggesting that a redistribution of number is occurring in all these settings, and is perhaps generalised across them. In this redistribution, probabilities no longer simply normalise individuals and groups in partitioned spaces and ranked orders (Foucault 1977) as they might have in nineteenth-/twentieth-century statistical treatments of populations. What might be surfacing in somewhat opaque and densely convoluted forms such as MCMC is a post-demographic rendering of a world in which individuals become something like joint distributions. It is likely that these joint distributions, and their effects on the chances of donating or voting, were the target of the Obama data analytics team's night-modelling efforts.

This is not to say that a world is clearly and distinctly expressed in these techniques. Against the common tendency to see probability as split between two main interpretations, the aleatory and the epistemic, the frequencies-of-events versus the degrees-of-belief, we see their convoluted embrace in techniques such as MCMC. In this setting, neither the objectivist (frequentists) nor subjectivist (Bayesian) interpretations of probability work well. For the objectivist interpretations of probability, MCMC presents the difficulty that all parts of the statistical model potentially become random variables or probability distributions, including the parameters of the statistical model itself. For the subjective interpretations, while MCMC means that all parameters can become random variables, these variables only become available for belief via the long chains of numbers that arise in the computations, gradually converging towards the central tendencies or significant features we see in the contour plots. From the post-demographic perspective, both interpretations miss the redistribution of probability as randomly generated but topographically smooth surfaces whose many dimensions support complicated conjunctions of events.

What we might instead see in MCMC and similar techniques is a redistribution of chance, a refiguration of the chance tamed during the last few centuries in the development of concepts of probability and then the techniques of statistics with their reliance on controlled randomness. In these techniques, randomness is again redistributed in the world. This happens materially in the sense that computational machinery generates long converging series of random numbers in order to map the curved topography of the joint probability distributions. But it also happens more generally as a staging of events. Many of Gilles Deleuze's articulations of a baroque sensibility take the form of curves. He describes, for instance, the world as 'the infinite curve that touches at an infinity of points an infinity of curves, the curve with a unique variable, the convergent series of all series' (Deleuze 1993: 24). In Deleuze's account, curves act as causes: 'the presence of a curved element acts as a cause' (1993: 17). This claim begins to make more sense as we see the curved surfaces of joint probability distributions acting as the operational or control points in so many practical settings (asthma studies, multiplayer game coordination, epidemiological modelling, spam filtering, and so on). The particles, maps, images and populations figure in a baroque sensibility as curves that fold between outside and inside, creating partitions, relative interiorities and exteriorities.

Where are we in the folded volumes that result from this distributive treatment of numbers? Sensations of change, movement, texture, and increasingly of something happening are attributable to distributive numbers. These machineries stage new convergences between numbers coming from the world, numbers coming from belief or subjects, and numbers that lie somewhere between the world and knowing subject. I suggested above that we might need to reconceptualise individuals less as the product of biopolitical normalisation and more as a mode of including the world. To the extent that we monadically include the world in such stagings, to the extent that we become the most simple, individual distributive numbers, $1/\infty$ numbers that can only be integrated in simulated surfaces and volumes, then events or what happens are assigned according to the distributive numbers and their curves. What would it mean to be aware of those curves, to have a sense of the joint probability distributions that subtly shape the public health initiatives, the phone calls, or advertisements we receive from a marketing drive, or the price of a product? If normalisation and its statistical techniques sought to strategically manage human multiplicities, to what end do the redistributive numbers we have been discussing tend? The task here, it seems to me, is to identify in the joint probability distributions what is put together, and how assigning numbers to events changes in the light of this joining or concatenating of curves on folded surfaces. There is a kind of generativity here, since the demographic categories and rankings shift and blur on a more differentiated yet integrated or connective surface.

NOTES

1 This chapter will not trace the complicated historical emergence of probability and its development in various statistical approaches to knowing, deciding, classifying, normalising, governing, breeding, predicting, and modelling. Historians of statistics have documented this in great detail and tracked how statistics is implicated in power-knowledge in various settings (Stigler (1986); Hacking (1990); Daston (1994); Porter (1996)).

2 A rapid convergence on MCMC follows from the 1990s onwards. Gibbs samplers appear in desktop computer software such as the widely used WinBUGS ('Windows Bayes Using Gibbs Sampler'), written by statisticians at Cambridge University in the early 1990s (Lunn, Thomas, Best, et al. 2000), and MCMC quickly moves into the different disciplines and applications found today.

3 In making sense of the change described by Robert and Casella, scientific histories of the technique are useful. The brief version of the history of MCMC might run as follows: physicists working on nuclear weapons at Los Alamos in the 1940s (Metropolis 1949)

first devised ways of working with high-dimensional spaces in statistical mechanical approaches to physical processes such as crystallisation and nuclear fission and fusion. Their approach to statistical mechanics was later generalised by statisticians (Hastings 1970). It was taken up by ecologists working on spatial interactions in plant communities during the 1970s (Besag 1974), revamped by computer scientists working on blurred image reconstruction (Geman and Geman 1984), and then subsequently seized on again by statisticians in the early 1990s (Gelfand and Smith 1990). In the 1990s, it became clear that the algorithm could make Bayesian inference – a general style of statistical reasoning that differs substantially from mainstream statistics in its treatment of probability (Mcgrayne 2011) – practically usable in many situations. A vast, still continuing, expansion of Bayesian statistics ensued, nearly all of which relied on MCMC in some form or other (Thompson Reuters Web of Knowledge shows 6 publications on MCMC in 1990, but over 1000 *each year* for the last five years in areas ranging from agricultural economics to zoology, from wind-power capacity prediction to modelling the decline of lesser sand eels in the North Sea; similarly, NCBI Pubmed lists close to 4000 MCMC-related publications since 1990 in biomedical and life sciences, ranging from classification of newborn babies' EEGs to within-farm transmission of foot and mouth disease; searches on 'Bayesian' yield many more results).

4 It is hardly surprising that scientists working at the epicentre of the 'closed world' (Edwards 1996) of post-WWII nuclear weapons research should develop such a technique. In 1953, Metropolis, the Rosenbluths, and the Tellers were calculating 'the properties of any substance which may be considered as composing of interacting individual molecules' (Metropolis, Rosenbluth, Rosenbluth, et al. 1953: 1087) (for instance, the flux of neutrons in a hydrogen-bomb detonation). In their short but still widely cited paper, they describe how they used computer simulation to deal with the number of possible interactions in a substance, and to thereby come up with a statistical description of the properties of the substance. Their model system consists of a square containing only a few hundred particles. These particles are at various distances from each other and exert forces (electric, magnetic, and so on) on each other dependent on the distance. In order to estimate the probability that the substance will be in any particular state (fissioning, vibrating, crystallising, cooling down, etc.) they needed to integrate over the many-dimensional space comprising all the distance and forces between the particles (this space is a typical multivariate joint distribution). As they write, 'it is evidently impossible to carry out a several hundred dimensional integral by the usual numerical methods, so we resort to the Monte Carlo method' (Ibid: 1088), a method that Nicholas Metropolis and Stanislaw Ulam had already described in an earlier paper (Metropolis 1949). Here the problem is that the turbulent randomness of events in a square containing a few hundred particles thwarts calculations of the physical properties of the substance. They substitute for that non-integrable turbulent randomness a controlled flow of random variables generated by a computer. While still somewhat random (i.e. pseudo-random), these Monte Carlo variables taken together approximate to the integral of the many-dimensional space.

BIBLIOGRAPHY

Amoore, L., 'Lines of Sight: On the Visualization of Unknown Futures', *Citizenship Studies*, 13.1 (2009), 17–30 <http://search.ebscohost.com/login.aspx?direct=true\&db=a9h\&AN=36353240\&site=ehost-live> [accessed 19 May 2010]

Andrieu, C., N. De Freitas, A. Doucet, et al., 'An Introduction to MCMC for Machine Learning', *Machine Learning*, 50.1 (2003), 5–43

Besag, J., 'Spatial Interaction and the Statistical Analysis of Lattice Systems', *Journal of the Royal Statistical Society: Series B (Methodological)* (1974), 192–236

Birrell, P. J., G. Ketsetzis, N. J. Gay, et al., 'Bayesian Modeling to Unmask and Predict Influenza a/H1N1pdm Dynamics in London', *Proceedings of the National Academy of Sciences*, 108.45 (2011), 18238–18243 <http://www.pnas.org/content/108/45/18238.abstract> [accessed 14 November 2011]

Daston, L., 'How Probabilities came to be Objective and Subjective', *Historia Mathematica*, 21.3 (1994), 330–344

Deleuze, G., *The Fold: Leibniz and the Baroque* (London: Athlone Press, 1993)

Dempster, A. P., N. M. Laird, and D. B. Rubin, 'Maximum Likelihood from Incomplete Data via the EM Algorithm', *Journal of the Royal Statistical Society: Series B (Methodological)*, 39.1 (1977), 1–38

Edwards, P. N., *The Closed World: Computers and the Politics of Discourse in Cold War* (Inside Technology Series) (Cambridge, MA, and London: MIT Press, 1996)

Efron, B., 'The Efficiency of Logistic Regression Compared to Normal Discriminant Analysis', *Journal of the American Statistical Association*, 70.352 (1975), 892–898 <http://www.jstor.org.ezproxy.lancs.ac.uk/stable/2285453> [accessed 24 January 2015]

Foucault, M., *Discipline and Punish: The Birth of the Prison* (New York: Vintage, 1977)

Gelfand, A. E., and A. F. M. Smith, 'Sampling-based Approaches to Calculating Marginal Densities', *Journal of the American Statistical Association*, 85.410 (1990), 398–409 <http://www.jstor.org.ezproxy.lancs.ac.uk/stable/2289776> [accessed 14 January 2011]

Gelman, A., J. B. Carlin, H. S. Stern, et al., *Bayesian Data Analysis, Second Edition* (Boca Raton, FL: Chapman and Hall/CRC, 2003)

Geman, S., and D. Geman, 'Stochastic Relaxation, Gibbs Distributions, and the Bayesian Restoration of Images', *Pattern Analysis and Machine Intelligence, IEEE Transactions*, 6 (1984), 721–741

Gill, J., *Introduction to the Virtual Issue: Bayesian Methods in Political Science*, *Political Analysis*, 2 (2011) <http://www.oxfordjournals.org/our_journals/polana/virtualissue2.html> [accessed 9 January 2013]

Hacking, I., *The Emergence of Probability* (Cambridge and New York: Cambridge University Press, 1975)

——— *The Taming of Chance* (Cambridge: Cambridge University Press, 1990)

Hastings, W., 'Monte Carlo Sampling Methods using Markov Chains and their Applications', *Biometrika*, 57.1 (1970), 97–109

Issenberg, S., 'The Definitive Story of how President Obama Mined Voter Data to Win a Second Term', *MIT Technology Review* (2012) <http://www.technologyreview.com/featuredstory/509026/how-obamas-team-used-big-data-to-rally-voters/> [accessed 9 January 2013]

Knorr-Cetina, K., and U. Bruegger, '"Traders"' Engagement with Markets: A Postsocial Relationship', *Theory, Culture & Society*, 19.5.6 (2002), 161–185

Lunn, D., A. Thomas, N. Best, et al., 'WinBUGS – a Bayesian Modelling Framework: Concepts, Structure, and Extensibility', *Statistics and Computing*, 10.4 (2000), 325–337

Mcgrayne, S. B., *The Theory that Would not Die: How Bayes' Rule Cracked the Enigma Code, Hunted down Russian Submarines, and Emerged Triumphant from Two Centuries of Controversy* (New Haven, CT: Yale University Press, 2011)

Metropolis, N., 'The Monte Carlo Method', *Journal of the American Statistical Association*, 44 (1949), 335–341

Metropolis, N., A.W. Rosenbluth, M. N. Rosenbluth, et al., 'Equation of State Calculations by Fast Computing Machines', *The Journal of Chemical Physics*, 21 (1087) (1953) <http://link.aip.org/link/\%3FJCPSA6/21/1087/1> [accessed 10 October 2012]

Mohr, J. W., and P. Bogdanov, 'Introduction – Topic Models: What they Are and why they Matter', *Poetics*, 41.6 (2013), 545–569 <http://www.sciencedirect.com/science/article/pii/S0304422X13000685> [accessed 16 December 2013]

Porter, T. M., *Trust in Numbers: The Pursuit of Objectivity in Science and Public Life* (Princeton, NJ: Princeton University Press, 1996)

Robert, C., and G. Casella, 'A History of Markov Chain Monte Carlo-subjective Recollections from Incomplete Data', *arXiv:0808.2902* (2008) <http://arxiv.org/abs/0808.2902> [accessed 1 January 2011]

Robert, C. P., and G. Casella, *Introducing Monte Carlo Methods with r* (New York: Springer, 2010)

Scherer, M., 'How Obama's Data Crunchers Helped him Win', *CNN.com* (2012) <http://www.cnn.com/2012/11/07/tech/web/obama-campaign-tech-team/index.html> [accessed 20 November 2012]

Simpson, A., V. Y. F. Tan, J. Winn, et al., 'Beyond Atopy: Multiple Patterns of Sensitization in Relation to Asthma in a Birth Cohort Study', *American Journal of Respiratory and Critical Care Medicine*, 181.11 (2010), 1200–1206 <http://www.ncbi.nlm.nih.gov/pubmed/20167852> [accessed 16 May 2011]

Stigler, S. M., *The History of Statistics: The Measurement of Uncertainty before 1900* (Cambridge, MA: Harvard University Press, 1986)

Suess, E. A., and B. E. Trumbo, *Introduction to Probability Simulation and Gibbs Sampling with r. 1st edn.* (New York: Springer, 2010)

Wasserman, L., *All of Statistics: A Concise Course in Statistical Inference* (New York: Springer, 2003)

5

A BAROQUE SENSIBILITY FOR BIG DATA VISUALISATIONS

Evelyn Ruppert

SENSORY SOCIOLOGY AND THE EMPIRICAL BAROQUE

THE SENSIBILITIES AND VARIETIES OF EXPRESSION GATHERED UNDER WHAT John Law describes as resources of the baroque do not suggest a method but an orientation to thinking and research that departs from dominant modes of knowing in the social sciences and humanities. This includes concerns with excess, non-coherence, the senses, Otherness, affect, embodiment, movement, and heterogeneity as explored in cultural, postcolonial, feminist, and science and technology studies (STS). As he notes, these concerns resonate with intellectual and political currents that implicitly or explicitly draw from Gilles Deleuze. Coleman and Ringrose's (2013) edited collection, for example, point to recent Deleuzian inspired empirical research in the social sciences that is concerned with methods as messy, mobile, creative, open-ended, sensory, affective, and performative.

These concerns also resonate with another area of research that attends to the developing field of sensory studies in the social sciences and humanities (Puwar and Sharma 2011). For example, sensory studies have been taken up to conceive of a 'sensory ethnography', which takes as its starting point 'the multisensoriality of experience, perception, knowing and practice' and how this is integral both to the lives of the researched and how ethnographers practise their craft (Pink 2009: 1). While 'sensory experience and perception have "always" been central to the ethnographic encounter' (Ibid: 10), a sensory ethnography involves the explicit inclusion of new forms of sensory experience in the practices of doing ethnography. A key point coming out of Pink's approach, which focuses on perception, memory, embodiment, and place, is the dual attunement to the sensory of both the researched and the researcher.

There are many more examples of research that takes up the sensory as summarised by Puwar, Sharma, and Pink. What I set out to do here is to understand the sensory as not confined to the senses but to a broader repertoire of ways to apprehend and know worlds. I elaborate this repertoire under the description of a 'sensory sociology' with a specific attention to digital mediums.[1] This is not to exclude applicability to other mediums but to attend to one that presents specific challenges to methodological sensibilities in sociology. The repertoire is necessarily selective and partial. It is not intended to be a comprehensive survey and it is largely focused on recent writings; indeed, many of the concepts and understandings such as the performativity of methods that I elaborate below can be attributed to many different authors. Instead it is a synthesis of work in the social sciences and humanities that experiments with alternative modes of knowing and what this collection refers to as the resources of the baroque.

The second part of the chapter then exemplifies these sensibilities through an engagement with an empirical object, visualisations of 'excessive' digital data, or Big Data. I do this through a discussion of three approaches to visualisation: Anna Munster's (2013) work on network experience as perception rather than the perceptible; Adrian Mackenzie's (2010) concern with network theorising that de-animates relations and elides the flow of experience; and Lev Manovich's (2011) comparison between information visualisation and direct visualisation.

PART 1: A SENSORY SOCIOLOGY

That digitisation is having an impact on how social, political, cultural, and economic worlds are constituted, researched, and known is well documented.

Within the social sciences one evaluation of the impact is that it is challenging the expertise of sociologists in both the generation and analysis of social data and social life (Savage and Burrows 2007). Another assessment is that digitisation offers an opportunity to rethink the sociological craft and is leading to a revitalised concern with what 'the empirical is and how it matters' in the discipline (Adkins and Lury 2009: 4). For Adkins and Lury, digitisation is destabilising sociology and closing a gap between the practices of sociologists and those of social worlds. The challenge then is to invent sociological methods in ways that can adapt, repurpose, and engage with such digital mediums and the data that they generate (Adkins and Lury 2009; Back 2012). For one, they argue that digital mediums involve continuous feedback loops that change the relations that make up research, and call for

> a sociology 'not of social fact but of the sensate empirical'[...] not at ideal conditions but 'real existing stuff, real existing social processes', that can 'deal with uncertainty, chaos, complexity and multiplicity' [...] 'multiple, contingent and in process rather than fixed and a priori' [...] 'requires the discipline to confront a newly co-ordinated reality, one that is open, processual, non-linear and constantly on the move' (Adkins and Lury 2009: 18).

All of the qualities that Lury and Adkins cite here, from uncertainty and chaos to a reality that is constantly on the move, call for sensibilities that are quite different from the crafted and strategic methodological approaches typical of the sociological craft. For one, digital mediums reconfigure the relations between researchers and the researched by offering new opportunities for engagement through innovative forms and modes of presenting and conducting sociology in 'live' mediums (e.g. social media platforms). Through a variety of examples, Adkins and Lury raise questions about how sociology might be reconfigured to do this and how we might then reimagine data not as simply a conversation and dialogue with publics 'out there' but engaged in different ways and in relation to the very methods deployed.

This conception of relations to publics and mediums is of course not entirely new. The Mass Observation project is one well-cited example.[2] It involved studying the ordinary lives of ordinary people in the UK to counteract the stereotypes that held sway in the British media in the early part of the twentieth century. It could be considered a form of crowdsourcing since a key medium was photographs produced by volunteers documenting intimate aspects of their lives, from their lounges and closets to their gardens. What digital mediums have done is mobilised and made possible the multiplication of forms of engagement that are more recursive, multisensory (image, text, sound, and so on), interactive, live, and happening.[3]

Digital mediums have also folded the everyday lives of publics into research methods. On the one hand, social media platforms are mediums of digital sociality and the doing of social relations. The data they generate in the cultural sphere on platforms such as Facebook, Spotify, and Flickr are also part of everyday popular cultural forms that are actively both produced and consumed via myriad acts of 'playbour' (Beer and Burrows 2013). Such data is lively as it is recursively taken up and reappropriated as a part of contemporary popular culture. At the same time social researchers and others develop methods for analysing and interpreting the data these platforms generate to make sense of, interpret, and know digitally mediated lives (Ruppert, Law, and Savage 2013). Thus digital mediums both open up the possibilities for creative, interactive, and collaborative research engagements with publics and at the same time can render them unknowing research subjects. Their engagement is thus variably configured by the method relations of which they are not separate from but are a part.[4] Digital mediums are thus implicated in both the performance and knowledge of contemporary sociality, and changing who subjects are, how they are known, or apprehended, and their forms of engagement.

The relation between the researcher and researched is but one aspect that digital mediums open up. More generally, the concerns that Lury and Adkins raise call for reimagining methods with a different set of sensibilities that are not part of the standard repertoire. Conceptually, I capture these sensibilities, which necessarily overlap and play off each other, under the description of a sensory sociology: medium specific, live, performative, and inventive.

Medium: Specific

Different mediums are different ways of 'telling about society', as Becker (2007) has expressed it. From statistical graphs, historical narratives, and novels to films, maps, and theoretical discourses, there are myriad ways of telling about society that are not only the province of social science researchers. While visual mediums such as photography are modes of knowing that have a long history in academic disciplines, publics also do photography and produce visualisations as part of their everyday lives and now are also generators, observers, and analysts of their digital lives. Building on Becker's argument, Back then asks what is sociological about the images, recordings, and traces generated by digital mediums. If 'one of the first principles of social science is that nothing speaks for itself' (Back 2012: 33), then critical and ethical questions must be asked about the methods deployed to speak for things. But, as he asserts, then we must attend to how mediums – the digital, visual, sonic, textual, and so on – are specific and different ways of sensing worlds and not simply add-ons to research methods or to which we can apply already existing methods. Instead, methods need to be (re)imagined in relation to their mediums.

Such a sensibility alerts us to mediums as 'just openings'; we need to go beyond them because 'data pictures do not give up their meaning in a single glance […] the pictures require more work before they give up their full meaning' (Becker 2007: 169). How photos are taken to how they are interpreted involve specific framings; the task then is to make the invisible chain of translations involved in generating the photo visible and part of the analysis (Guggenheim 2013). Attending to the medium thus calls for going 'behind' the arrangements of the photo, the digital image, or the sound recording and attending to the different human, material, and technical organisation of mediums and how these participate in and configure concepts and modes of knowing (Ruppert, Law, and Savage 2013).

So, for instance, changes in the relations between researched and researcher are not simply a matter of differently positioned or engaged people but also their relations to what is assembled in a medium. This includes particular forms of expertise, theories, and conceptions of the social to different materialities, tools, and technologies that get folded into the methodological apparatuses organised and taken up by the researcher. Modes of knowing are saturated with all that compose the medium and which make it distinctive.[5] For instance, digital mediums such as social media platforms are made up of specific forms of expression such as keyword selections, hashtags, or hyperlinks that are 'born online' (Rogers 2013) and generative of distinct modes of sociality (Marres and Weltevrede 2013). The same forms of expression can be repurposed to become both the object of and actively inform social research through 'native' methods that follow the medium (Rogers 2013). Rather than importing techniques and concepts used to research other mediums, medium-specific sensibilities involve attending to the unique cultures of mediums and all that compose them. A sensory sociology is thus attuned to medium specificities as not simply add-ons but as constitutive and inside modes of sociality – how the social is done – and also social research – how knowing is done. At the same time, the attention to medium specificities is not a call for separate subfields or to suggest what Guggenheim (2013) criticises as a 'media-determinism'. Instead, it is to recognise specific forms of expression that may or may not correspond to other mediums but yet share other qualities of a sensory sociology elaborated below.

Live: Qualities

A sensory sociology understands 'sociology in-the-making' and focuses on the process of sociological research rather than its products (Lury 2012). It is attuned to what Back has called 'live' rather than 'dead' sociology (Back 2012). The latter is objectifying, comfortable, disengaged, and parochial. Instead, live sociology draws attention to many of the qualities of the social that are not captured by existing social science methods which are dominated by narrative/words and number/statistics, and which deal poorly with qualities. In characterising live sociology Back summarises Law and Urry's call for the social sciences to renew the sensibilities of its methodological inheritance, which are 'under pressure from an alternative, complex and performative sense of social inquiry' (2004: 403). Twenty-first century methods are, for example, not well positioned to address the

- *fleeting*: is here today and gone tomorrow, but only to reappear the day after tomorrow,
- *distributed*: that which is to be found here and there but not between or which slips and slides between one place and another,
- *multiple*: that which takes different shapes in different places,
- *complex*: of the non-causal, the chaotic,
- *sensory*: that which is subject to vision, sound, taste, smell,
- *emotional*: of time-space compressed outbursts of anger, pain, rage, pleasure, desire, or the spiritual, and
- *kinaesthetic*: of pleasures and pains that follow movement and displacement of people, objects, information, and ideas.

The different ways of sensing the social call for reimagining social research not in a way that is against narrative or number but to 'extend the range, texture and quality of what passes as academic representational practice and writing' (Back 2012: 28). For example, an equality of the senses and 'attentiveness to the multiple registers of life' (Ibid: 29) includes approaches such as 'sonic geographies' (Kanngieser 2012) that open up the affective and ethical political force of voice and those with a sensitivity to the multisensory ambiences, sensibilities, and work of the senses of everyday urban life (Rhys-Taylor 2010). Or the ways that Puwar (2011) has explicitly demarcated the sensory as a field within postcolonial studies to engage with questions of difference, alterity, migration, and belonging through the media of musical composition, poetry, and film.

There are numerous other possible approaches and meanings that Back and Puwar (2004: 403) document in their 'manifesto for live methods', which consists of eleven provocations for how sociology can be done. Building on the understanding of live methods and the changing nature of the empirical, their collection of articles covers 'real-time' and 'live' modes of research (Marres), speculative designs that actively seek out empirical objects and events that are 'idiotic' (Michael), an 'amphibious sociology' that lives in at least two media (Lury), new forms of curating public performances and collaborations (Puwar and Sharma), attentiveness to the doing of social life (Back), and how the 'make believe' might aid the sociological imagination (Motamedi Fraser). These are just some of the qualities of what live methods mean for paying attention to the social world through a range of sense-making. But as the contributions also establish, this involves 'placing critical evaluation and ethical judgement at the centre of research craft' and 'debat[ing] the forms of work we are doing, the kinds of academics we are producing, and the institutional and life worlds we occupy as well as make' (Back and Puwar 2004: 15). These issues are confronted in the final two qualities of a sensory sociology.

Performative: Effects

The entanglement of methods, mediums, researched, and researcher is captured in the understanding that methods have social lives. Interwoven in the foregoing is an implicit argument that reimagining methods in relation to different mediums and sensibilities does not simply involve representing worlds differently but also enacting them in new ways. Methods do not stand apart as representations of social worlds; they also perform those social worlds and enact them. This is different from an epistemological argument that practices construct representations of realities which depend on holding the world (acted upon, and constructed) separate from practices such as methods and their representations – or as perspectives on a stable, accessible 'real' (Law and Urry 2004). Instead enactment is based on an ontological claim that both representations and the phenomena they describe come into being through methods. Theory, method, and social worlds are thus entangled and methods are social theories in practice, whether or not this is made explicit or remains implicit.

A sensory sociology thus not only involves going behind the medium to interrogate its specificities, but to also understand how it is inside and part of enacting modes of being and knowing. This includes the performative effects of the medium when it is part of a method apparatus. One approach to this is to think of methods as having double social lives, shaped by and shaping of the social worlds of which they are a part (Law, Ruppert, and Savage 2011). For the former we can ask, 'what are the specific sensibilities demanded and afforded by a medium when we fold it into our methods'? For the latter, 'what then are the performative effects of our methods so composed'? This calls for rethinking theoretical assumptions and attuning to a number of qualities and their performative effects that are specific to a medium. The following are some questions about how the qualities and affordances of digital mediums can come to shape the performative effects of methods and the social worlds they enact:[6]

- *Transactional actors*: by making sense of doings – of movements, actions, transactions, interactions, choices, and statements – how do methods enact worlds as the outcome of not only what people say but also do?
- *Heterogeneous relations*: by attending to the associations, links, switches, connections, exchanges, flows, and networks between not only people but also things, how do methods enact worlds as mixes of relations?
- *Visualisation of patterns*: by making sense not in words or numbers but through images, graphics, and designs that reduce 'excessive' information into visual forms, how do methods enact worlds as patterned arrangements?
- *Continuous time*: by following the ongoing, real-time, dynamic, and continuous digital traces of the activities and movements of people and things, how do methods enact worlds as processual rather than static entities?
- *Granular being*: by focusing on particularistic identifiers of people such as their microscopic details, unique profiles, and specifications, how do methods enact them as monads and particulars?
- *Mobile and mobilising*: by engaging people actively in digital mediums that circulate between numerous sites, how do methods enact worlds in participatory yet configured, designed, and perhaps dominating ways?
- *Non-coherent accounts*: by taking up digital mediums along with other analysts (governments, businesses, publics) and for different purposes, how do social science methods enact worlds that are implicated in the normative purposes of others and multiply and compete with their accounts?

There are many examples of how digital mediums provoke these questions and constitute specific modes of sense-making. For example, Gabrys (2012) explores environmental sensing as a complex ecology of networked devices and citizens actively engaged in sensing and knowing pollution, flora, fauna, and sustain-ability. As she further articulates, rather than approaching 'the senses' as given, she considers how 'sensing-as-practice' is differently articulated in relation to specific entanglements of technologies, data, and humans.[7] Sense making is thus an entanglement between people, devices, and data that perform environ-ments in complex ways. Such ecologies draw attention to modes of knowing as 'happenings' that are full of contingencies, adjustments, and oriented to the open-endedness of social worlds (Lury and Wakeford 2012).

Inventive: Answerable

Methods understood as performative and happening introduce a fourth sen-sibility: the inventiveness of sociology as a craft. If methods are performative, then we can think of them as creative and inventive, but in ways that may not be intended or knowable in advance. The openness of the social world and of methods means that there is indeterminacy about how either plays out and which cannot be anticipated or pre-determined. Through their liveliness, worlds and methods are inventive in ways that are beyond the determinations and expectations of the researcher.

Like the other qualities of a sensory sociology, to think of methods as inventive is not new and does not simply apply to contemporary methods that mobilise digital mediums. Methods more generally are means by which the social world is not only investigated, but may also be engaged. However, such inventiveness is often not attended to or acknowledged. That is, researchers are often not attentive to the unexpected and instead explain these as anomalies, or ignore them because they don't fit the methodological paradigm, expectations, or original problem (Lury and Wakeford 2012). Lury and Wakeford thus sug-gest that 'the inventiveness of methods is to be found in the relation between two moments: to a specific problem, and the capacity of what emerges in the use of that method to change the problem' (2012: 7). Regarding the latter, they argue that this calls for answerablility to what is provoked and emerges when a method is activated:

> Inventiveness is a matter of use, of collaboration, of situatedness, and does
> not imply the ineffectiveness of methods, only that their inventiveness –
> their capacity to address a problem and change that problem as it performs
> itself – cannot be secured in advance (Lury and Wakeford 2012: 7).

Answerability to inventiveness means to excavate the versions of social worlds initially implied or explicit in methods but then brought to life by them and made to happen including that which cannot be anticipated. The performativity and inventiveness of methods means they are not innocent but political: 'They help make realities. But the question is: which realities? Which do we want to help make more real, and which less real?' (Law and Urry 2004: 404).

There are multiple possible moments of answerability. In addition to how a problem is formulated and what this then provokes, there is accountability to the sensibilities that methods attend to and make more real. By attending to 'that which has conventionally escaped or troubled social science – the virtual, the affective, the ephemeral', methods can possibly 'expand the actual, invent and/or strengthen particular worlds' (Coleman and Ringrose 2013: 8). There is also answerability to the ethical relations to the researched that methods enact. Rather than the 'intrusive empiricism' of confessional and voyeuristic methods such as interviews (Back 2012), answerability can be built into methods. For example, Puwar (2011) has created a call-and-response methodology that engages artists and creative practitioners in music, poetry, and film as active collaborators in the research process and publics not simply as audiences but as dialogic participants. Feminist methodologies have attended to these folded relations between researcher and the researched in the process of sense-making as an ethics of research (Coleman and Ringrose 2013: 12). Barad (2007) names this agential realism: at issue is not representations of a separate real but the real consequences, interventions, creative possibilities, and responsibilities of intra-acting within worlds.

Taken together, the four sensibilities – medium specific, live, performative and inventive – are attuned to what this collection has set out as baroque modes of knowing. As modes of knowing, the sensibilities are far from prescriptive or programmatic, as the examples I have referenced attest to. Much of what I have called a sensory sociology is more suggestive than specific, and that is one of the reasons I work with all of the variations of 'sense': from sensory, sensibility, to sense-making, and the myriad meanings associated with these words: to perceive, feel, experience, detect, understand, comprehend, grasp, test, or expound the meaning of worlds.[8]

In the next part of this chapter I will engage with what I have described as a sensory sociology to think through some examples of dominant and alternative visualisations of Big Data generated by social media platforms. I first start by outlining how visualisation has become a key method through which sense is made out of excessive data. I then turn to examples of work that treat visualisations as openings to the challenge of the empirical that I set out at the beginning of this chapter: the articulation of sensibilities that depart from dominant modes of knowing in the social sciences and humanities.

PART 2: ENCOUNTERS WITH DATA EXCESS

> St. Pierre describes how she also began to ruminate on the status of 'data', and how certain kinds of data 'were uncodable, excessive, out-of-control, out-of-category'. Paying attention to such 'transgressive data', St. Pierre argues, is an ethical project, in that it is concerned with responsibility, with 'theorising our own lives, examining the frames with which we read the world, and moving toward an ongoing validity of response' (Coleman and Ringrose 2013: 12, citing St. Pierre 1997: 179, 186).

> When we imagine a network these days, it is hard to stave off the flood of visualisations – tangled threads, fractal webs, uneven distributions of inter-connected circles and lines – that populate our contemporary connectionist imaginary (Munster 2013: 1).

The 'data deluge' is one common term used to describe the volumes of accumulating digital data on the internet and in database archives. Increasingly referred to as Big Data, both the volume and digital format of data has led to visualisation emerging as a key method of social analysis. While numbers and text have long dominated the social sciences, digital visualisation has become a means of reducing 'excessive' data to forms that are stabilised and represented in patterns that can be 'more easily' interpreted. That visualisation is increasingly being taken up as a tool of social enquiry is also a matter of concern, especially in relation to how they are 'guiding' attention in particular ways (Madsen 2013). But the problem of and solutions for analysing and making sense of large volumes of data is not only a challenge of Big Data. Ethnographers, for example, struggle with the flood of data that field sites present and problematise the necessity of drawing boundaries around what is to be included and enacted (Candea 2013; Law and Singleton 2013). What they suggest is that attending to excess is not simply a technical matter of magnitude and its processing but about the choices made to reduce, bound, sort, organise, categorise, represent, and interpret data. Yet these explicit ordering and rationalising techniques also encounter what Saint Pierre calls the 'uncodable, excessive, out-of-control, out-of-category' and that which is 'transgressive', all that is in excess or beyond the frames of enacted worlds. This includes the 'ordinary affects' of the everyday that exceed and evade meaning and representation and that which can only be sensed, as it cannot be grasped by structures of signification.[9]

Encounters with Big Data as excess – of what is included in sense-making and what is absent, out of control, and beyond – can be interpreted through a sensory sociology. I explore this by contrasting two modes of visualising excessive data that enact social relations, which really are two different empirical strategies. One is a popular mode called the network diagram, which reduces and controls excess to make it perceptible and interpretable. It has become a dominant mode of knowing and showing how 'excessive' information can be reduced to a form that can be meaningfully, if partially, rendered for interpretation (Ruppert, Law, and Savage 2013). Another conveys the uncodable, which is beyond signification and involves a mode of knowing that provokes and calls for the sensibilities of a sensory sociology. This comparison is inspired by Anna Munster's (2013) work on network experience as perception rather than the perceptible, Adrian Mackenzie's (2010) conception of the embodied and sensory experience of networking and 'wirelessness' and Lev Manovich's (2011) differentiation between information visualisation and direct visualisation. Their work provides a number of openings for doing a sensory sociology through visualisation.

As the quote from Munster at the beginning of this part of the chapter notes, network diagrams are a particular visual form that uses nodes, lines, and simple geometrical shapes to represent relations between data objects and is used to render data visualisations on almost every aspect of life, from social networks to financial transactions. Gephi is one popular open source platform for generating such network diagrams out of social media, from billions of tweets to hundreds or thousands of Facebook friends: 'It helps data analysts to intuitively reveal patterns and trends, highlight outliers and tells [sic] stories with their data'.[10] Entering the words 'Gephi' and 'Twitter' in a search engine will immediately return thousands of images of network designs generated by individuals, organisations, and researchers.

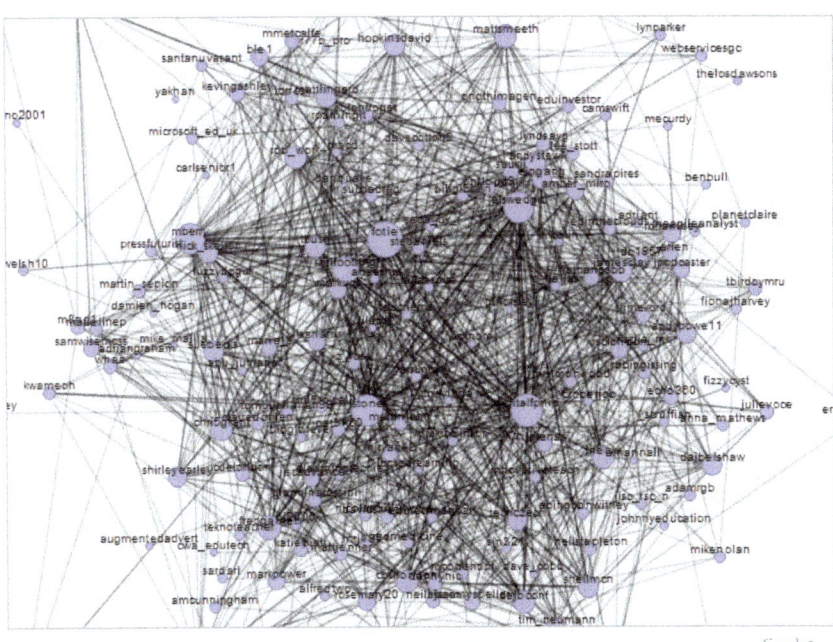

FIG. 5.1 Network diagram by Martin Hawksey (2011)[11]

While these are not of the scale of some large quantitative network analyses (e.g. Watts (2007)), the form is similar. As Manovich (2011) describes, they typically do two things: use 'graphical primitives' (points, lines, curves) that reduce the specificities of each data object to only about 1% of its characteristics.[12] In this way they follow the dominant science paradigm that involves the calculation of totals and averages and their representation in histograms, scatter plots, and line graphs. The second thing they do is use spatial variables such as relative positions to reveal particular patterns and relations. Spatial variables are privileged over other properties while less important qualities are represented in tones, shading, and colours. While there are some practices that veer from this, the majority are based on this configuration. Manovich suggests that this is due to the privileging of everyday ways of seeing spatial properties as well as the affordances of available graphic technologies.[13] In this regard, they constitute particular 'web-visions' or valuations of what is attention-worthy in data, such as provoking sensitivity to invariants and anomalies that are within and internal to the framing of the diagram (Madsen 2013).

While Manovich critiques the reduction and privileging of spatial dimensions, he doesn't attend to the kind of experience and sense of the social that network diagrams enact, promote, and provoke. This is something that Anna Munster (2013) takes up when she argues that the network diagram blinds the viewer to qualities such as unevenness and asymmetry and constitutes a particular kind of network experience. Its pervasiveness, sameness, and repetition are generative of a visual and conceptual slide into what she names network anaesthesia: 'a numbing of our perception that turns us away from their unevenness and from the varying qualities of their relationality' (Munster 2013: 3). Instead, she argues for ways of sensing the patchiness of the network, its particularities, and complexities, such as the closing and opening of relations and their changes and durations over time. That is, she seeks to undo the frozen quality of the network diagram, its coherence, tidiness, and 'repetitive mode of managing quantity' (Ibid: 5) that is anaesthetised and numbing and a normalising dispositif that does not maintain processuality but codifies relations into recognisable patterns.

To accomplish this she proposes a shift from the perceptible to perception, by drawing on pragmatist philosopher William James' work on experience where perception involves the making of worlds where sensing itself is done 'as we go' or a kind of happening. In contrast, the perceptible is the outcome of perception-action, where 'to recognise is to see something already seen: a pattern seen in data is an example of the perceptible' (Ibid: 5). It involves generalising experience by making something recognisable through recurring patterns that humans can comprehend and experience. What is perceptible often comes to stand for what is perceived.

A second move she makes is to avoid reducing perception to human experience but to understand network experience as happening through the 'heterogeneous togetherness' of humans and nonhumans. This does not involve understanding how humans experience technology, as typically done in studies of human-technology interaction. Rather, she inverts the relation to focus on how *networks experience,* or what she calls the aesthesia of networks. Network experience is not given but involves recursive relations between humans and nonhumans that are actively forming and which tend toward repetition and difference. She takes up James' concept of concatenation – the 'determinately varied hanging together' – to express network experience as the radically novel and individuated moment that has no prior convention for understanding it:

> The point is not to map, model, and systematize the network or experience but to account for, to sense and to encounter novel network aesthesias.... But *networking* – processes, proto-formations, and imperceptible human/ machine currents that conjoin social, info-technical, and aesthetic elements in novel ways – is what generates an aesthesia of networks (Munster 2013: 8–9; emphasis in original).

While the novel is imperceptible it is a becoming perceptible, an emergence that signals the presence of something else, a radical empiricism that is inventive, and creative, and 'proffers new sensibilities, and so the possibility that other ways of sensing, relating, and indeed living might thereby emerge' and of 'generating novel networking sensibilities' (Ibid: 10). For Munster, the 'felt force' of networking comes out of expressing the heterogeneous, inventive, and novel relationality, and collective experience that makes up visualisations that are not ontologically given nor prior to dynamic experience.

Mackenzie also critiques network-oriented theorising and argues that since the 1980s it has turned 'every scale, order, and variety of phenomena' into a network form (2010: 9). Like Munster, he takes up William James' conception of experience but attends more to the specific material and infrastructural elements of networks and their mediations of sense-making. Experience is understood as immersive entanglements with and often fleetingly felt sensations of the flow of wireless networks, things, gadgets, and infrastructures that escape codification, symbolisation, or quantification in network diagrams. He names this experience 'wirelessness', which he argues captures James' conception of 'the processes of moving, making, changing, altering, and connecting of feelings, things, events, images, textures, ideas, and places' (2010: 13) and a 'feeling of incompletion or openness' (Ibid: 14). For Mackenzie, then, a radical empiricism needs to 'engage with experiences ranging from the infrastructural to the ephemera of mediatised perception and feeling' (Ibid: 17).

Mackenzie also attends not to networks but networking as processual where experience involves what James called 'transitions'. It is the sense of continuous or discontinuous transitions that allow experience to flow, and holding onto this flow from one experience to another is what makes empiricism radical (2010: 18). As Munster also argues, this means attending to tendencies, trajectories, emergence, and inventiveness. To an extent this is what Manovich does when he identifies challenges to the visualisation paradigm that has dominated the last 300 years of practice. With the advances in computing in the twenty-first century, new forms of visualisation, especially in the humanities, are fundamentally changing and foregrounding animation, interactivity, and more complex visualisations. Specifically he calls these emerging forms 'direct visualisation', where data objects such as an image are not quantified, reduced, and translated into points and graphic signs but maintained to varying extents in their original complexity, such as visualisations of whole texts or complete corpuses of photos.[14] They also can be dynamic, animated, and interactive rather than frozen in time and include sound and textures. Direct visualisation maintains complexity and excess where revealing patterns is still central, but vision can be mixed with sound, tones, interactions, and movements and thus generative of multisensorial and affective experiences of data.

There are many experiments with visualisations that in varying ways and degrees go beyond the calculative and reductionist approach of the network diagram to explore network experience in the ways Munster, Mackenzie, and Manovich suggest. I state this as 'varying ways and degrees' to capture how they involve a play between the perceptible and perception, are simultaneously recognisable and novel, but at the same time make the boundary between the two experientially present. This is what Mexican artist Agnes Chavez does in her visualisations of the same kind of social networking data used in the social sciences to generate network diagrams. Her visualisations enact not the network but networking, and call on empirical sensibilities that are radically different. The choice of an artwork to explore this could be criticised since art has stronger claims to the sensibilities I have outlined.[15] But it is because Chavez takes up the same digital data that is very popular in social science analyses and network visualisations that I think the example is compelling for exploring how alternative visualisations could be enacted.

She describes her (x)trees project as an exploration of data visualisation and video-mapping technologies to create immersive contemplative spaces around the theme of trees. One version (Fig. 5.2), integrates the data mining of social networks and text messaging to generate branches of messages containing designated keywords (trees, nature, rights) on a wall in 'real time' as they happen online.[16] When exhibited at the Albuquerque Museum in 2012–13, people could text or tweet live in front of the installation and see their messages as they floated up and disappeared. The trees also incorporated quotes about nature collected from the internet and the articles of the Universal Declaration of Rights of Mother Earth. Finally, the installation included interactive audio created by Alessandro Saccoia out of sounds collected from nature, crowds, and a repeating Prana breath to instil an awareness of breath. The (x)trees were designed as an experience and catalyst for contemplative states of being for people to sense their global and local relationship to others, and to contemplate the value of trees and the rights of nature.

There are of course many explorations of art as a mode of knowing. In drawing on this example I am not arguing that social scientists should become visual artists or that art introduces the subjective and makes up for its erasure in objective

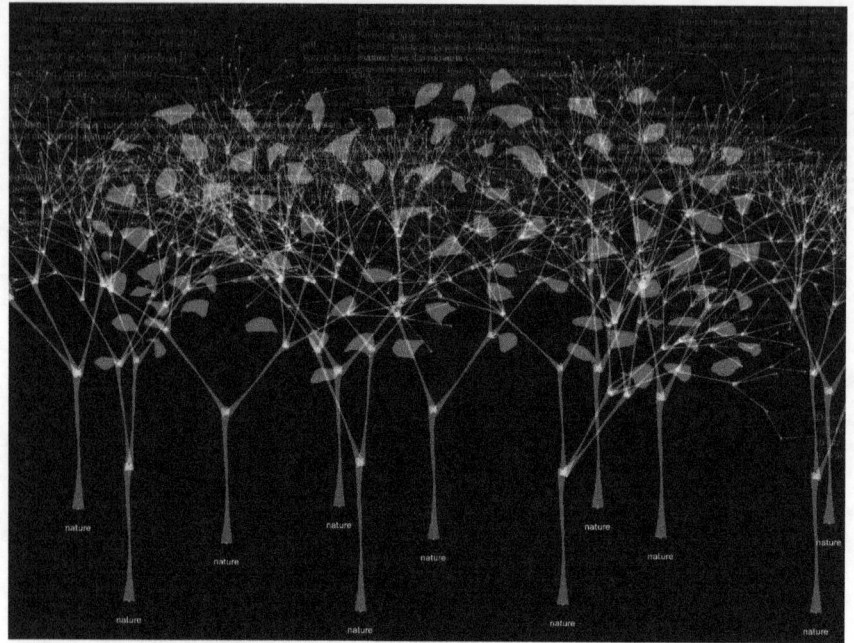

FIG. 5.2 (x)trees by Agnes Chavez and Alessandro Saccoia (2012)[17]

network diagrams.[18] My point is to draw attention to the sensibilities that this other form of data visualisation and mode of knowing enact and open up. It is a mode of knowing that has interesting crossovers with data-driven approaches in the social sciences, but how it is 'driven' by data involves different sensibilities. For while there are many examples of data visualisations in the social sciences that innovatively experiment with the possibilities of digital mediums, they are limited in their engagement with the sensibilities I have outlined above.[19] Most importantly, they do not capture the immersive and embodied encounter of (x) trees. For example, they typically retain the network diagram as a container and mode of knowing even though they may modify it by making it more dynamic or interactive.

Instead, I want to think about how (x)trees *does* a network experience. The researched – who I will now call a subject – stands outside and observes but can also become part of and see herself as a subject together with others and things in the making of a network experience; she doesn't simply interact with a given dataset but performs and is part of the experience through her networking with various technological devices. She is folded into and experiences a kind of communion with people, trees, and technologies. As Law writes in his introductory chapter, she is entangled and asked and required to submit and participate. Yet it is through familiar elements of trees, branches, colour, sounds, lines, screens, light, points, and text that data is rendered perceptible as a 'heterogeneous togetherness'. And while a repetition of what is already recognisable and thus also perceptible to others, difference is introduced – if ever so slightly – by the subject's presence and intervention that now becomes part of what the network experiences. But this I think is also Chavez's point. The subject is but one within a complex ecology, whose utterance is a fleeting moment compositionally part of the network and simultaneously collective and novel. The relation is dynamic, temporal, and dependent on the networking experience between the interface as framed by the artist and the flow of words of distant subjects. Temporality trumps spatial relations (as diagrammed in connections between text) in the dynamic formation and flow of fleeting but sometimes repeating text.

While reducing social media data through keyword selection, the (x)trees also maintain the whole data object (tweets, quotes, messages) as streaming text. The scale and quantity of this content are not enumerated – there is no possibility of knowing how much – and it is instead experienced as qualities. Quantity thus becomes a sensory quality to be immersed in and feel but also to see oneself reflexively and individually as part of its very generation and experience. While 'small data' such as thick and detailed ethnographic accounts are often put forward as an answer to what is subjectively 'missing' from the reductionist and thin analyses of Big Data, (x)trees performs quantity as a subjective and sensory experience. In this way it also complicates the conventional boundaries between quantitative and qualitative methods and accounts.

Nature and its qualities are both a matter of concern and of experience. Living, breathing, moving, and flowing are heard and seen, and the subject is inside of these. While the subject also reads text, it is with the same qualities of the sound and image. That is, text flows and moves quickly, like sounds, and some of it repeats such as quotes; some is never to be seen again, and some flows by without the possibility of being apprehended. Excess is not contained but flows, is part of a process rather than a product, and disappears as part of a lifecycle like its matter of concern. The entirety is thus not graspable or analysable, but that is one of its qualities: to perceive the collective as a sensation of 'the presence of something else' (Munster), of ephemera, surpluses, and overflows (Mackenzie), and of not-knowing that can be made 'experientially real'.[20]

It is hard not to imagine that the artist intentionally sought to create an experience that enacts an ecological sensibility.[21] And for this reason the mediums she chooses – visual, sonic, textual – are not external but internal and consequential to the very ecological phenomenon she seeks to enact. What I think Chavez has achieved is a merging of mediums, subjects, and objects, and that these together constitute the network experience. She prepares a stage that is configured yet happening as it compositionally changes such that each performance is new. Through such a merging the force of networks is felt and experienced as momentary, dispersed, multiple, and multiplying, elusive, chaotic, normative and affectual, and alive, and in motion. Yet, at the same time, much is reasonably and recognisably conveyed through words and repetitions.

There is more that can be said here. I could make explicit how the four sensibilities of a sensory sociology are actualised by the (x)trees. Some of this I have already done above and could extend to the enactment of live, lively, and existing social processes, of attuning to complexity, heterogeneity, and the performativity of the (x)trees. Its juxtaposition against the network diagram certainly has done some of this work. Instead I will reflect on the quality of inventiveness and answerability and offer some comments on the sensibilities they make more real.

In the simplest terms, the network diagram closes what (x)trees opens up. Through reduction, classification, and stabilisation, it settles on a version of networking that makes unproblematic its own terms of closure and its performative effects. These are terms that render the object – relations – calculable and actionable. In these ways they reproduce dominant modes of analysing 'quantitative' data in the social sciences. The view is informed but not informing of all that has come to compose it, and it is productive of passive viewers whose data traces may be part of the data network but which they cannot see.

(x)trees provokes, activates, and enacts something else, a different way of sensing, relating, and knowing that is open and changeable not by one subject but by an unseen yet sensed collective of humans and non-humans. In this way (x)trees opens up and activates the emergence of what Munster calls the becoming perceptible while resisting its taming and containing and what Mackenzie describes as the peripheral and overflowing. What is knowable escapes, yet at the same time is felt and apprehended as relations between humans and non-humans that are enacted but irreducible to the figure of the network. Rather than reduction, the subject perceives the irreducibility of knowing and its matter of concern – nature. Yet the encounter with such uncertainty and unknowing enacts something. That something includes experiencing the possibility of other ways of sensing and relating to worlds that open up experience to the multisensorial, contemplation, and the ineffable, and how we are entangled in our matters of concern.

The concerns about nature and ecology and our place within them that (x)trees enacts are often appealed to in declarations and political narratives. Such appeals beckon through words and rhetoric the activation of reason and responsibility to protect nature, and sometimes also mobilise and play on affect to achieve the same purposes. Knowledge politics are thus advanced as a deliberative competition between argument, persuasion, and normative affirmations that subjects receive and evaluate. I think (x)trees performs politics instead as an encounter that is a multiple, complex, and perpetual composition made up of the self in relation to other people, things, ideas, technologies, and nature. The real it does, opens up, and makes more real is one that compels the active, contemplative, and engaged subject. It is a real that is not simplified, classified, and organised but the 'felt force' of a collective that beckons a sensibility of the subject as a bit player but also composer of the real. In this way it ends with a question rather than answers: what will you contribute, and what will you create?

ACKNOWLEDGEMENTS

I am thankful for the feedback on earlier versions of this chapter from John Law, Adrian Mackenzie, and Rebecca Coleman.

NOTES

1 I am grateful for the insights, ideas, and contributions towards thinking about a sensory sociology in the writings of colleagues in the Department of Sociology, Goldsmiths, both past and present. In particular, Noortje Marres and Nina Wakeford conceived of and prepared the general outlines of a Masters course called 'Sensory Sociology: Imagining Digital Social Research' that I taught with Rebecca Coleman in 2013 and through which I developed my understanding.

2 Founded in 1937 by anthropologist Tom Harrisson, the poet and journalist Charles Madge, and the surrealist painter and filmmaker Humphrey Jennings.

3 #Citizencurators, for example, is a history project that recorded the experience of Londoners during the Olympic fortnight in 2012. Created for the Museum of London, it involved the 'real-time' collecting of tweets, objects, and images compiled by citizens to 'tell the story of everyday life in the capital' <http://citizencurators.com/about> [accessed 16 July 2014].

4 This is captured by the concept 'agencement', the French version of assemblage as elaborated by Deleuze, which focuses attention on how agency and action are configured by and contingent upon the sociotechnical arrangements that make them up (Ruppert 2009).

5 Compare for example the mundane and distributed devices such as statistical procedures, skilled interviewers, and clipboards of surveys, focus groups, or interviews to the digital platforms, algorithms, APIs, software designers, and so on, of digital mediums.

6 These are selected and re-cast from nine propositions about how we might rethink the theoretical assumptions of social science methods to take into account the specificities of digital devices and data (Ruppert, Law, and Savage 2013).

7 See project description at <www.citizensense.net/sensors/sensing-practices-seminar-series>.

8 'Sense, v.'. OED Online. <www.oed.com.catalogue.ulrls.lon.ac.uk/view/Entry/17595 5?rskey=XKORSF&result=2> [accessed 01 March 2014].

9 I have taken the understanding of ordinary affects from Coleman and Ringrose's (2013) discussion of Kathleen Stewart's (2007) book by the same title. On beyond representation, see van de Port in this collection, and his engagement with Žižek and Eagleton on the Real to think about that which is always beyond representation and what structures of signification cannot grasp.

10 'Gephi: makes graphs handy' <https://gephi.org/about/> [accessed 10 Jan 2015].

11 This work is licensed under a Creative Commons Attribution 3.0 Unported License. CC-BY mhawksey <http://mashe.hawksey.info/2011/10/live-twitter-data-from-fote-fote11/>.

12 Manovich adopts the term 'information visualisation' rather than data visualisation. I agree with the former, since visualisations are the outcome of particular procedures and operations on data; data is not visualised, but it is information – the outcome of these procedures – that is made perceptible and 'seen'.

13 Colour, for example, became more prominent with the adoption of computers for design which allowed for millions of unique colours. Despite this, colour is not a significant quality of network visualisations because their focus is on discovering spatial variables, which are not known a priori.

14 Manovich provides a number of examples from the humanities that he notes involve different degrees of reduction in data objects.

15 Adrian Mackenzie raised this in his review of an earlier version of this chapter. While I take his point, there is a convergence of interest in visualisations as a method of analysing digital data, from that of data-driven art to that of data-driven science. It is this convergence that I think calls for investigating how visualisations are comparatively being done in the arts and social sciences.

16 The (x)trees are presented in different versions and cities. One version was first on display at the Albuquerque Museum of Art and History from September 2012 to January 2013, and more recently, on 26 September 2014, another version was displayed on the streets of Taos, New Mexico: <http://www.agneschavez.com/xtreeproject/projections>. The installation is best experienced by watching the video clips.

17 See <https://agneschavez.see.me/>. Permission to reproduce this image courtesy of the artist: (x)trees v.2. Data Visualization Projection: Agnes Chavez and Alessandro Saccoia, 2012 [accessed 14 March 2015].

18 This is a point Guggenheim (2013) makes about claims that visual mediums such as photographs are more subjective than objective and thus compensate for what is not rendered by other mediums such as text.

19 This includes interactive visualisations; some specific and innovative examples include controversy and issue mapping; see the work of Marres (2013) and Venturini (2010).

20 I take this from van de Port's discussion in this collection of the collective as a sensation, not a representation or of being representable.

21 The artist provides very little in the way of such an interpretation and I have been unable to find any produced by others. Minimal text and explanation are provided, perhaps reasserting the emphasis on experiencing data.

BIBLIOGRAPHY

Adkins, L., and C. Lury, 'Introduction to Special Issue "What Is the Empirical"', *European Journal of Social Theory*, 12 (2009), 5–20

Back, L., 'Live Sociology: Social Research and Its Futures', *The Sociological Review*, 60 (2012), 18–39

Barad, K., *Meeting the Universe Halfway: Quantum Physics and the Entanglement of Matter and Meaning* (Durham, NC, and London: Duke University Press, 2007)

Becker, H., *Telling About Society* (Chicago: University of Chicago Press, 2007)

Beer, D., and R. Burrows, 'Popular Culture, Digital Archives and the New Social Life of Data', *Theory, Culture & Society*, 30.4 (2013), 47–71

Candea, M., 'The Fieldsite as Device', *Journal of Cultural Economy*, 6.3 (2013), 241–258

Coleman, R., and J. Ringrose, eds., *Deleuze and Research Methodologies* (Edinburgh: Edinburgh University Press, 2013)

Gabrys, J., 'Sensing an Experimental Forest: Processing Environments and Distributing Relations', *Computational Culture*, (2012)

Guggenheim, M., 'What Was Visual Sociology?', in *CSISPOnline* (Goldsmiths: 2013)

Kanngieser, A., 'A Sonic Geography of Voice: Towards an Affective Politics', *Progress in Human Geography*, 36.3 (2012), 336–353

Law, J., E. Ruppert, and M. Savage, 'The Double Social Life of Methods', in *CRESC Working Paper Series*, Paper No. 95, 2011

Law, J., and V. Singleton, 'Devices as Rituals: Notes on Enacting Resistance', *Journal of Cultural Economy*, 6.3 (2013), 259–277

Law, J., and J. Urry, 'Enacting the Social', *Economy and Society*, 33.3 (2004), 390–410

Lury, C., 'Going Live: Towards an Amphibious Sociology', *The Sociological Review*, 60.S1 (2012), 184–197

Lury, C., and N. Wakeford, eds., *Inventive Methods: The Happening of the Social* (London: Routledge, 2012)

Mackenzie, A., *Wirelessness: Radical Empiricism in Network Cultures* (Boston: MIT Press, 2010)

Madsen, A. K., '*Web-Visions: Repurposing Digital Traces to Organize Social Attention*', PhD Thesis, Copenhagen Business School, 2013

Manovich, L., 'What Is Visualisation?', *Visual Studies*, 26.1 (2011), 36–49

Marres, N., and E. Weltevrede, 'Scraping the Social? Issues in Live Social Research', *Journal of Cultural Economy*, 6.3 (2013), 313–335

Munster, A., *An Aesthesia of Networks: Conjunctive Experience in Art and Technology* (Boston: MIT Press, 2013)

Oxford English Dictionary [online], (Oxford: Oxford University Press, 2013) <www.oed.com.catalogue.ulrls.lon.ac.uk/view/Entry/175955?rskey=XKORSF&result =2> [accessed 01 March 2014]

Pink, S., *Doing Sensory Ethnography* (London: Sage, 2009)

Puwar, N., 'Noise of the Past: Spatial Interruptions of War, Nation, and Memory', *Senses and Society*, 6.3 (2011), 325–345

Puwar, N., and S. Sharma, 'Introduction: War Cries', *Senses and Society*, 6.3 (2011), 261–266

Rhys-Taylor, A., '*Coming to Our Senses: A Multi-Sensory Ethnography of Class and Multiculture in East London*', PhD Thesis, Goldsmiths University, 2010

Rogers, R., *Digital Methods* (Boston: MIT Press, 2013)

Ruppert, E., 'Becoming Peoples: "Counting Heads in Northern Wilds"', *Journal of Cultural Economy*, 2.1.2 (2009), 11–31

Ruppert, E., J. Law, and M. Savage, 'Reassembling Social Science Methods: The Challenge of Digital Devices', *Theory, Culture & Society, Special Issue on the Social Life of Methods*, 30.4 (2013), 22–46

St. Pierre, E. A. (1997). 'Methodology in the Fold and the Eruption of Transgressive Data', *International Journal of Qualitative Studies in Education*, 10 (2), 175–189

Savage, M., and Roger Burrows, 'The Coming Crisis of Empirical Sociology', *Sociology*, 41.5 (2007), 885–899

Stewart, K., *Ordinary Affects* (Durham, NC, and London: Duke University Press, 2007)

Venturini, T., 'Building on Faults: How to Represent Controversies with Digital Methods', *Public Understanding of Science*, iFirst (2010), 1–17

Watts, D. J., 'A Twenty-First Century Science', *Nature*, 445 (2007), 489

PART TWO

EXPERIMENTING WITH THE BAROQUE

6

BAROQUE AS TENSION: INTRODUCING TURMOIL AND TURBULENCE IN THE ACADEMIC TEXT

Mattijs van de Port

WHY DO I NEED THE BAROQUE TO MAKE SENSE OF MY ANTHROPOLOGICAL research findings, or rather, what can the baroque bring out in these materials? What I take the baroque to be – an aesthetic impulse, rather than a clearly deline-ated, historically situated style; an intuition about the failure of representation, rather than an alternative representational mode; a sensibility, rather than an art – will be elaborated below. Here, at the beginning of this essay, I would like to point out that this baroque that I have been introducing in my thinking and writing over the last years came into being in response to very particular ethno-graphic materials. I had therefore best start this essay by briefly introducing you to my work so that you may get an idea as to what 'materials' I am talking about.

My research has taken me to tumultuous places: the war-ridden Yugoslavia of the early nineties with its all-out destruction and disintegrating life worlds (Van de Port 1998); the Dutch underworld, with its unpredictable and incalculable violence (Ibid: 2000); and, for the last decade, Salvador da Bahia, where spirit-possession cults and ecstatic religiosities blossom as never before in the context of a global metropolis (Ibid: 2011). One of the things that struck me most about these worlds was the vast gap between life-as-it-presented-itself-to-my-interlocutors and the way they represented this life to themselves and others. I found myself in places where, as David MacDougall (2006) would phrase it, *being* and *meaning* were frequently at odds with each other, where there was an almost palpable absence of reliable narrative frames that might provide guidelines as to how to interpret events, how to act, what direction to choose.

In my continuing attempts to theorise this gap between life and its cultural representations, some fieldwork scenes have become emblematic. For Yugoslavia, I keep returning to that old woman in the blackened ruins of her shelled home in the East Slavonian town of Vukovar. Given her old age, and knowing what atrocities were committed in this region in World War II, the war of the early 1990s must have been the second devastating event this woman had been forced to live through. Standing amidst the rubble, she lamented the loss of an indoor plant. With tears running down her cheeks, she described how big and lustrous it had been. 'Such enormous leaves it had', she added, waving with her arms to indicate the size. The way she said it evoked an image of her watering that plant every day, from one year to the next, watching it grow and become fuller, and the growth of that plant strengthening her faith in the new Titoist era, an era that had promised that wars were a thing of the past, and had allowed her to build a home with indoor plants that can grow to maturity. Yet amid the ruins she was forced to see that she had framed her life in a particular image of what life is like, and that the world in which she lived did not comply with that image.[1]

For the Dutch underworld, I immediately think of the certainty with which drug traffickers would talk of 'the laws' of the underworld. 'We all *know* that if you mess up in such and such a way, you get the bullet', they would tell police investigators. But they knew full well that there are no such 'laws' in their business. You may get the bullet for 'messing up', but you may also get away with it. Or get the bullet for reasons beyond your calculations. The self-assured tone with which these drug dealers spoke of the rules that governed their lives was not an expression of confidence – far from it. It was more of a mantra which served to screen off the fears and paranoia that the absence of law generates (Van de Port 2001).

For Bahia, I often recall the shock of José, a young shop assistant, with whom I had seen the Hollywood movie *A Beautiful Mind* in a local movie theatre. This

BAROQUE AS TENSION

movie casts the delusions of the mathematician and Nobel Prize winner John Nash as schizophrenia, forcing José to reconsider the nature of all the spirits he himself had seen during his life. José lives in a world where the reality of spirits interfering in human affairs is pretty much taken for granted. He had been telling me countless stories of spirits visiting him at night, giving him messages, taking him places. Yet now he had been confronted with a powerful reframing of these experiences. 'Am I really mad?' was the first thing he asked me when we left the movie theatre.

These recollections keep reminding me just how much anthropology had taught me to approach my interlocutors as people who are secure in the knowing of their life worlds, and how little my training had prepared me for the frailty of that knowing vis-à-vis life-disrupting events. I found – and keep finding – myself insufficiently prepared for the extent of people's not-knowing; their doubts; the fluidity and incoherence of their views; for the amount of guessing and ad-hoc opinionating that goes into the construction of meaningful worlds; for the way people may find themselves lost between irreconcilable paradigms.

My struggle as an anthropologist and writer is therefore increasingly this: how can I move my readers closer to this sense of being lost? How can I instil in them the appropriate mood from which to observe and interpret the world-making[2] of Yugoslavs, drug traffickers, and Bahians? One would think that this should not be that much of a problem. After all, the fact that life is always in excess of our knowing is as defining a feature of our own being as it marks the lives of the people we study. As academics, we too are caught up in attempts to dream up a coherent, well-signposted world, firmly embedded in our representations of it, just as we are also plagued by the fact that real life keeps interrupting such daydreaming. We keep instructing ourselves, however, not to dwell on the shaky grounds on which our representations rest. We write about what we know, not about what we don't know. And we thus seek to temper that uncomfortable suspicion that 'the world itself lies largely beyond our linguistic and intellectual grasp' (Jackson 2012: 29). Subjecting the world to our orderly aesthetic of straight lines, clear categories, coherent narratives, transparent methods, neat schemes, and learnt vocabularies, we provide our readers with a sense of being in control. The people we study may be lost. We are not.

167

In anthropology, the 'writing culture' debates of the 1980s questioned many of the stylistic conventions of academic world-making (see Marcus and Fisher 1986; Clifford 1988; Crapanzano 2004; Geertz 1989).[3] A much discussed – but unfortunately much less practised – 'literary turn' sought to face the inadequacies of academic modes of representation, and opened up a space for the fuzziness, ambiguity, and indeterminacy that pervades life-as-it-is-lived, allowing a poetic register to play its part in ethnographic writing. However, it only takes one little step out of the confines of the 'writing culture' debate to see how its propositions have been marginalised in the social sciences and humanities, which are strongly committed to the idea that the university is a fact-producing industry. The critical reflections that were put forward in these debates have been reduced to an option ('ah, I see, you are into "writing culture"! How interesting!'), rather than an epistemological turning point.

Allow me to present you some other emblematic images in order to underscore my point that it is very hard to escape the moulds into which academia casts its representations of the world-out-there. Picture me, struggling to evoke those dark and mud-smeared tragedies of war-ridden Yugoslavia in a vacuum-cleaned conference room, full of spotless white Formica tables. Me, trying to bring the all-pervading fear that ties the lives of drug dealers to my audience's conscience, while in the background the projector produces a reassuring humming sound. Me, trying to summon up the mind-boggling dimensions of a Candomblé spirit-possession ceremony with a chair waving a note saying '5 minutes', adding that 'at 11 a.m. sharp there is coffee and tea'. Don't get me wrong; I am all in favour of strict chairs at conferences. What I am trying to hint at is that there is something utterly unbending in the formats that academia offers us to report on our research findings; something utterly impossible in the ways we seek to transport other worlds into academic settings and representational practices. Therefore, when I read John Law's admirable attempt to invent a 'sociology of mess' two decades later, his arguments sound as fresh and as urgent as if the 'writing culture' debate had not taken place at all:

> parts of the world are caught in our ethnographies, our histories and sta-
> tistics, but other parts are not, or if they are, they are distorted into clarity

[…] if much of the world is vague, diffuse or unspecific, slippery, emotional, ephemeral, elusive or indistinct, changes like a kaleidoscope, or doesn't have much of a pattern at all, then where does this leave social science? How might we catch some of the realities we are currently missing? (Law 2004: 2)

Which brings me to the baroque. Part of the problem I have sketched is about aesthetics, about issues of style, indeed, about the lack of recognition that our academic reports are as much subject to stylistic conventions as novels, poems, paintings, and buildings and not merely 'neutral reporting'. To adopt a term from Birgit Meyer (2010: 751), academic reports are 'sensational forms' (i.e. 'authorized structures of repetition that tune the senses and allow for particular experiences to occur'). As many have pointed out, the particular stylistic conventions that rule in academia are heavily marked by earlier attempts to mimic the natural sciences (see Lepenies 1986). Sociologist Alvin Gouldner (1974) wrote about Classicism as one of the deep structures of the social sciences, whereas Clifford Geertz subsumed the stylistic imperatives of academia under the label 'literalism'. Geertz succinctly articulated the tacit understandings underlying this style, when he wrote

[t]he strange idea that reality has an idiom in which it prefers to be described, that its very nature demands we talk about it without a fuss – a spade is a spade, a rose is a rose – on pain of illusion, trumpery, and self-bewitchment, leads on to the strange idea that, if literalism is lost, so is fact (1988: 140).

Hindered by this invisible straightjacket of academic sensational forms, a number of social scientists, philosophers, and cultural analysts have explored the baroque to find possible alternatives for academic practices of representation.[4] Clearly, scholars have moved in very different directions in their explorations of this aesthetic, so much so that in her detailed exposition as to how 'the baroque' has figured in debates in art history and philosophy, Helen Hills sighs that 'the term readily lends itself to extension such that it becomes meaningless' (2007: 67). One of the constants in these explorations, however, is that these scholars found themselves seduced by the expressive forms the baroque has on offer, and the promise of epistemological innovations they contain. The baroque's preference for excess, fragmentation, instability, metamorphosis, labyrinthical complexity, polycentrism, irregularity, distortion, disharmony, and boundlessness (to mention but a few of the formal traits that have been gathered under the label baroque) suggests possibilities for an alternative organisation of textual representations, one which arguably suffers less from the academic imperative to 'distort reality into clarity', and which might make this sense of finding oneself gone astray amidst tumult and turmoil present in our texts.

With this prospect in mind, I have recently joined the search for a baroque alternative to the sensational forms of academia (Van de Port 2011; 2012; 2013a; 2013b; 2013c).[5] The most immediate incentive for this move was the rich baroque legacy I encountered in the Bahian capital Salvador, where I have conducted fieldwork since 2001. In Salvador, the baroque is being pointed out to you almost everywhere: in the colonial churches and palaces; in monuments, artworks, fountains, and museums; in the pomp of religious processions and the ecstatic mood of religious celebrations; in the aesthetic preference for over-the-top exuberance, glitz, and theatrical excess displayed in the acts and attitudes of the Bahian popular classes (which ethnologist Pierre Verger famously described as Bahia's 'street-baroque'); or in the curly, flowery rhetoric with which Bahian academics and public officials tend to address their audiences. Bahians explicitly instructed me to take notice of their baroque ethos, using the term to characterise their ways of being: 'we are very *barroco*', is what they would say over and over again.

The second incentive to adopt the term was the reading of a most inspiring book by the Dutch art historian Frank Reijnders, *Metamorfose van de Barok* (1992).[6] In this study, Reijnders discusses the baroque as the anti-art par excellence. The spirit of the baroque – which he finds to be operative in various moments in the history of the arts, not just in the historical period labelled 'the baroque'[7] – disrupts an understanding of the arts as the articulators of all that is perfect, good, true, essential, and pure in the world. Hence the title of Reijnders' work: far from being a unified style, Reijnders' baroque is in a process of constant metamorphosis, continuously trying to break into harmonious dream-worlds, whether they be of a classicist, romantic, fin-de-siècle, or modernist signature.[8] In Reijnders' vision, the baroque is a creative intuition that appropriates artistic vocabularies and techniques, but uses these as a crowbar with which to break open worlds of perfection, so as to bring out the lack in all artistic representations of life and being.

Following Reijnders' take on multiple 'baroques', I will take my encounters with the Bahian baroque (and with the other 'baroques' I encountered in the body of literature on the style, as well as during my travels in Middle- and Southern Europe) as the empirical starting point for an exploration of what this disruptive aesthetic can do to bring the tumult and turmoil of the world into a scholarly text. In other words, my conceptualisation of the baroque in this text is 'intersubjective': the concept helps me to mark the differences between the way my Bahian interlocutors assemble their world, and the way a Dutch academic tends to go about this.

Juxtaposing academic and baroque ways of world-making brings up a number of interesting issues for consideration. The first issue I faced was how to avoid the 'domestication' of the baroque's capacity to produce turbulence and tumult, and the accompanying sense of 'being lost'. Take the image below (Fig. 6.1), which shows a so-called 'miracle room' in a sanctuary in Candeias, a small town in the Bahian interior. The room is full of ex-votos and gifts that were left there by the devotees of Nossa Senhora das Candeias. To subject this site to a formal academic analysis – picking apart the constituent elements of this jumble, classifying them, and explaining their meaning – runs the danger of dulling the shrieking, unsettling, and confusing assault on 'straight thinking' that this site so powerfully calls into being. In other words, to subject the baroque to the orderly aesthetics of academia threatens to render its disruptive powers harmless, which would make this whole project of exploring baroque alternatives to our modes of representation redundant. John Law's suggestion to shift the focus from discussing what a baroque aesthetics *is* to a focus on what a baroque register *does* – how this aesthetic 'enters into *experience*' (Law, this volume) – might help us out of this problem.

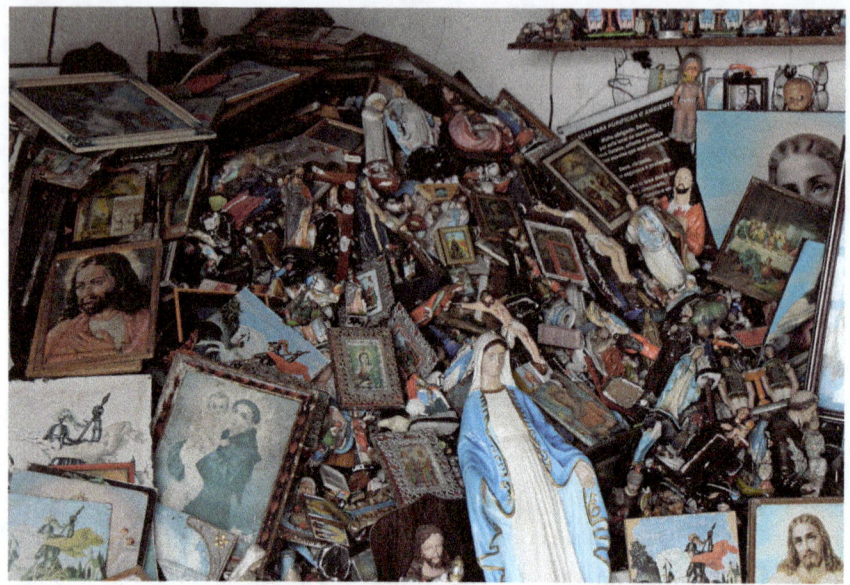

FIG. 6.1 Miracle Room in Candeias, Bahia[9]

Which brings me to a second issue I had to ponder. For me, to think of the baroque is to conjure up images in my mind, rather than texts. Say 'baroque' and I see the endlessly folded garments of the statues of the saints in the Museu da Arte Sacra in Salvador, the ornate decorations of Bahian church interiors, the *trompe l'oeil* ceilings, the complicated play of the gaze in baroque paintings, or the jumble of Bahian 'miracle rooms'. I am aware that there is a 'textual' baroque, a corpus of literature that might be explored for its tropes, rhetorical strategies, and undisguised 'mannerisms'. Yet I must admit that for me (and I venture the opinion that I am not the only one), the lure of the baroque lies in its visual appeal to the senses, its *folie du voir* (Buci-Glucksman 1992). I found myself challenged to think through how the experiences evoked by baroque visuals might be brought into my texts; in other words, what kind of 'cross-pollinations' are possible between textual and visual mediums?

A last issue I needed to address in my explorations of the baroque is the fact that Bahian baroque occurs in a thoroughly religious society. Its work of disruption is driven by metaphysical concerns (and the politics therein implied). As I will elaborate below, it sought (and seeks) to articulate humans' relation to the

Divine, or to be more precise, it sought (and seeks) to bring the lack in human-made worlds of meaning to consciousness, to thus produce a yearning for the transcendent, omnipotent power of the Divine – the *luz divina* (divine light) that is capable of replenishing the world and making it whole. I will argue that it is exactly this capacity to bring a transcendent realm beyond representation to consciousness that makes an exploration of the Bahian baroque useful for the epistemological innovations that I am after. I am of course aware that the religious motivations underlying baroque expressivities are hardly a selling point in academia, an institute that takes pride in being heir to the Enlightenment. To make a baroque intervention appealing – and I am, indeed, thinking quite strategically here – it is necessary to explore the similarities and differences between the 'God' of the baroque and more secularist contemplations of the 'wholly other'. I will do this by making two hitherto unrelated scholarly discussions speak to each other. The discussions I am referring to are, on the one hand, those of art historians and cultural analysts like Reijnders, who took the baroque to be an ever-metamorphosing spirit of disruption, an aesthetic impulse that seeks to heighten a sensibility for the limits of all representational practices (Reijnders 1991; Calabrese 1992; Ndalianis 2004). On the other hand, I refer to the discussions of a number of philosophers and social scientists of the Lacanian notion of the Real (Žižek 1989; Stavrakakis 1999; Eagleton 2009), the dimension of being that confronts us with the lack in our representational capacities, and tears our reality definitions out of joint.

In what follows, I will elaborate on these issues in reverse order, starting with a discussion of the baroque as a religious 'aesthetics of persuasion'.

THE BAHIAN BAROQUE AS A RELIGIOUS 'AESTHETICS OF PERSUASION'[10]

The montage-like statuettes that you see in Fig. 6.2, examples of a popular art form from nineteenth-century Bahia, are my favourite illustration of the spirit that pervades the baroque that I encountered in Brazil. They are called *O Menino Jesus no Monte*, the Child Jesus on the Mountain. They are sometimes

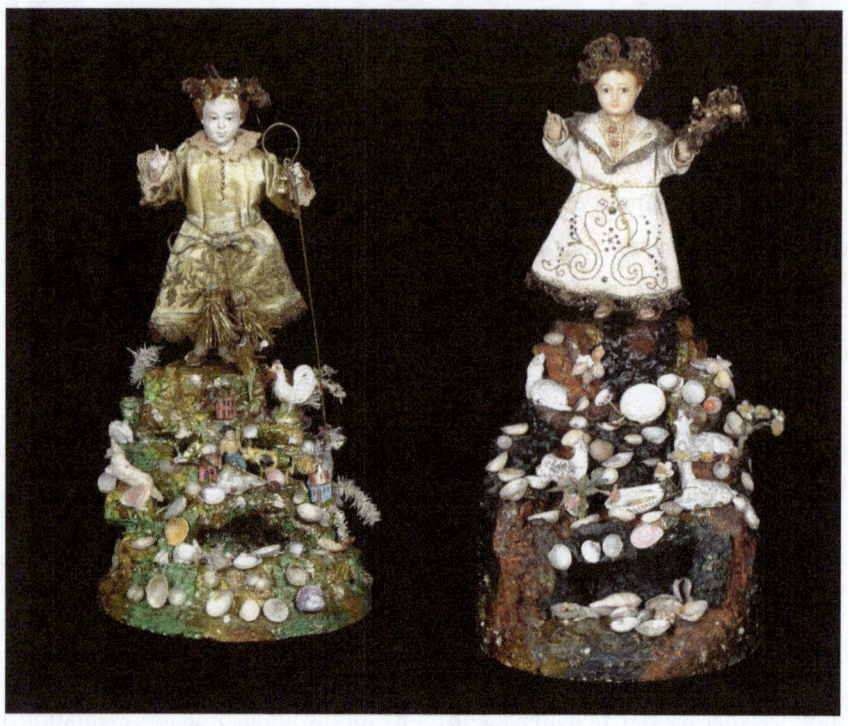

FIG. 6.2 Lapinhas[11]

also referred to as *lapinhas*, 'little caves', as many of them exhibit a dark void in the middle of the mountain, suggestive of a cave. What little information I found on these *lapinhas* reveals that they were made in convents in the Bahian Recôncavo area. The nuns from the town of Santo Amaro de Purificação were particularly famed for their artistic skills, and produced these lapinhas in great numbers (Marques and Araújo 2006; Silva 2007).

In their basic structure, the lapinhas are all alike. What you see is the child Jesus who, in king-like posture and outfit, reigns over a world that is represented as a messy pile of fragments: rooster, seashell, rabbit, house, little man, flower, duck. Glued to the mountain in random fashion, these individual elements are mere emblems: their meaning does not exceed the depth of a pictogram. Nothing in these lapinhas invites you to ponder the deeper significance of those roosters, flowers, or ducks, nor their mutual relations. Quite to the contrary: they invite you to ponder the *absence* of pattern, harmony, and synthesis, and entice you to contemplate the lack of 'wholeness' to the world that they so strikingly express.[12] In some of the lapinhas that are on exhibit in a small museum in the centre of the Bahian capital Salvador,[13] the piling up of fragments goes even further than the two examples presented above. The result is a veritable jumble of figurative elements. Watching these lapinhas, one can almost see those poor nuns, tucked away in their convent, fully absorbed in their frenzied attempt to recreate the world from which they had been banned by gluing ever more emblems to the mountain. Soldier. Church. Carriage. Horse. Negro-with-guitar. Bridge. Bottle. Peacock. More seashells. Mermaid. More flowers. And yet, all that the resulting encrustation of the mountain does is to dramatise the utter failure to grasp the world in its entirety by piling up its separate elements. Indeed, the thick crust of emblems first and foremost highlights that dark, empty cave in the middle of the mountain: a void that underscores the hollowness of this universe, its lack of inner meaning and substance.

The one element that brings harmony to these statuettes is the figure of the Menino Jesus. The divine child on top of the mountain, stretching out his little hand in a gesture of blessing, allows the fragments to cohere (and to be perceived as 'the world') just as it is this divine presence that is able to negate the emptiness of the cave below. And yet, for as much as the posturing of the kingly child speaks of a triumphant faith that brings order to an incoherent world, these lapinhas are tinged with a certain melancholy. For everything about them – most strikingly the disproportional size of the child Jesus in relation to the world below and its uninvolved and strangely directionless smile – works to suggest that this divine presence may be at work *in* the world of men, but is certainly not *of* this world.

This interpretation of the lapinhas takes its main cues from the work of Walter Benjamin on the baroque and a number of scholars who followed his line of argument.[14] They have argued that the highlighting of the incompleteness of human-made worlds of meaning – and the notion of the Divine as an *absent truth* that might replenish this lacking world – spoke to the experiences of people who were living the turbulent religious–political developments of the sixteenth and seventeenth centuries. Being the art of the Counter-Reformation, as well as the art of the 'conquest, seizure and subjugation' of the pagan peoples of the New World (del Valle 2002), the baroque sought to impose a revitalised

Roman Catholicism on a world ridden with religious conflict and schisms, where the taken-for-grantedness of a divine omnipresence was under siege. It was an aesthetic that expressed the disintegration of the sacred canopy *and* sought to counter it; it registered God's receding from the world of men *and* sought to stop this from happening; it was informed by people's despair over the fact that the presence of metaphysical truth in the world of men could no longer be taken for granted *as well as* by their hope that truth might reside elsewhere. 'Desperate faith' is how Bainard Cowan (1981: 119) labelled these two opposite dimensions of the religious mood that pervades the baroque. The tragic awareness of the imperfection of human-made worlds fuelled the yearning for a transcendent, divine agent who might mend the rents and fissures. A verse from songwriter Leonard Cohen beautifully captures this duplicity in baroque aesthetics: 'there's a crack, a crack in everything, that's how the light gets in' (in Fabian 1998: 34).

Two baroque churches in Bahia may serve as an example to spotlight how these 'cracks' were played out aesthetically in a religious setting, not only to bring that all-powerful yet absent God to presence, but indeed to provoke an encounter with that absent God in ecstatic experiences.

The Igreja de São Francisco in the Bahian capital Salvador is part of a Franciscan convent, and was built between 1708 and 1723 (Talento and Hollanda 2008).[15] Somewhat hidden at the far end of the Terreiro de Jesus, the central square of the historical Pelourinho district, it comes across as 'yet another baroque church' (Terreiro de Jesus alone counts four huge baroque churches, the city many more). To enter the church's interior, one has to pass through a narrow and rather uninviting corridor which entirely fails to prepare the visitor for what is coming (or indeed, adds to the shock effect); stepping into the church, one finds oneself in the midst of what is best described as a 'golden storm', an overwhelming, whirling jumble of gilded ornaments, which produces a veritable 'blast' to one's sensory apparatus.

The most noticeable aspect of the interior of the Igreja de São Francisco is what some have called the *horror vacui* of the baroque, its 'fear of empty spaces' (Hansen 2006). Wherever you look, there are woodcarvings smothered in gold leaf, panels of *azulejos*, paintings of biblical scenes, or statues of saintly figures. The rectangular, hexagonal, rhombic, and star-shaped surfaces in between the complicated geometrical patterns of the vaults on the ceiling all contain paintings with more biblical scenes. The multicoloured marble floor is decorated with wild, curly vegetal motives. Every single object – chandeliers, candle stands, balustrades, balconies, altars, columns, doors, holy-water fonts – seems to have spurred on the decorative zeal of the builders and become a pretext for more ornamentation. The interior is like a lapinha turned inside out: the jumble is no longer to be found on an object you can hold at a distance so as to contemplate it: you are now inside it.

Trying to take in the excessive decorations, the eye soon gets lost in what seems to be an unstoppable movement of curling, curving, and spiralling, producing an acute sense of dizziness. Adding to this dizziness is the fact that the designer's indulgence in ornamentation leads to the blurring of all clear lines. All sharp divisions and forms are covered by a thick crust of decorative elements, leaving them amorphous, like an old shipwreck on the bottom of the ocean, covered by shells and corals.

Clearly, this space does not want you to maintain your distance so as 'to get the picture straight'. Its aesthetic tactic is to overwhelm you, to engulf you,

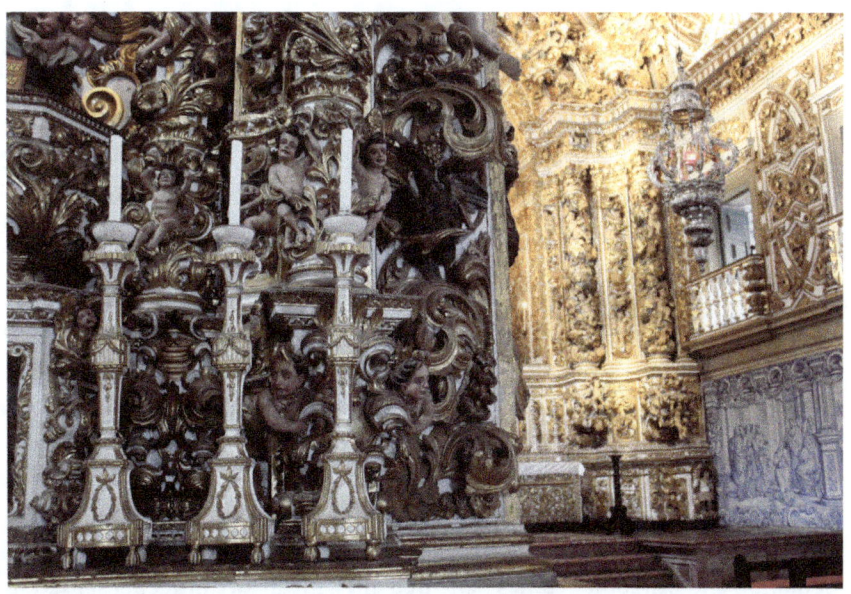

FIG. 6.3 Igreja de São Francisco, Salvador da Bahia[16]

to break down the control that 'observation' allows. The sensation it seeks is to push you off track, to provoke a sensation of falling, of being lost, of losing one's grip.

This sensation continues at a semantic level. Transformations and metamorphoses are everywhere. Decorative curls become plants, which in turn become human figures. When giving them a second, more attentive look, acanthus leaves reveal the features of a lion's head. Human limbs, not connected to any body, hold out chandeliers: reduced to mere decorative elements, they prohibit the idea that the category 'human' would somehow be a privileged category in the order of things. Everything could well be something else. Are these angels really angels? Many offer their nakedness to the congregation as ever so many flashers. Some seem pregnant. Some have remarkably erect nipples. Some look at us as if they were a prostitute soliciting at a street corner. Most of them boast silly smiles and other rather idiotic facial expressions, so stupid that you can't help thinking that the slaves who did the woodcarving must have had a good laugh mocking the facial expressions of their Portuguese masters (a point that is also stressed by the black tour guides who take tourists into the church and help them to 'read' the interior).

And yet, for all the dizziness that the interior of the Igreja de São Francisco provokes, a description of my impressions would not be complete without mentioning its experiential antidote. For as much as this place seeks to induce in its visitors a sensation of losing their grip, no one actually falls when entering the church, or loses control. And intriguingly, it might well be again the design of the interior that brings about this sensation. For in the storm of whirling ornamentation, the statues of the saints remain calm and serene, resting points for the eye in spite of their flowing robes. More importantly, the overall structure of the interior has a theatrical set-up – the corridor of the nave, flanked by dark wooden pews, and the arched aisles all draw attention to the altar, thus bringing into focus the huge statue of Saint Francis embracing Jesus on the cross.

It is in this simultaneity of 'losing one's grip' and 'being led towards the Saviour' that this church interior is at its most effective: the sensation of disorientation and instability comes hand in hand with an awe inducing sensation that a transcendent power, capable of keeping it all together, is present in this space. Dizziness is produced to derail the subject, only then to grab this falling subject and lead him up to salvation.

The *trompe l'oeil* ceilings found in many of the Bahian baroque churches (Fig. 6.4) and elsewhere (Fig. 6.5) offer a second intriguing example of the baroque capacity to unsettle sense perceptions so as to provoke a head-spinning encounter with the blissful, transcendent realm of the Divine.

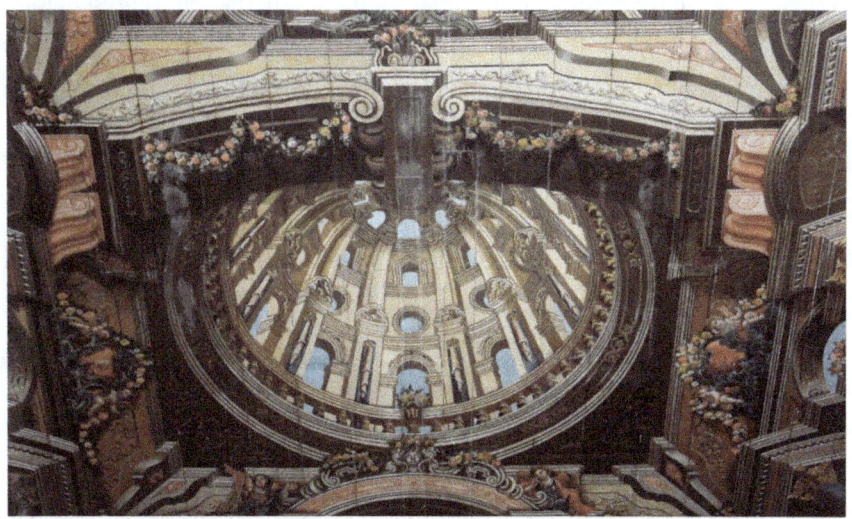

FIG. 6.4 Igreja da Matriz, Santo Amaro da Purificação, Bahia[17]

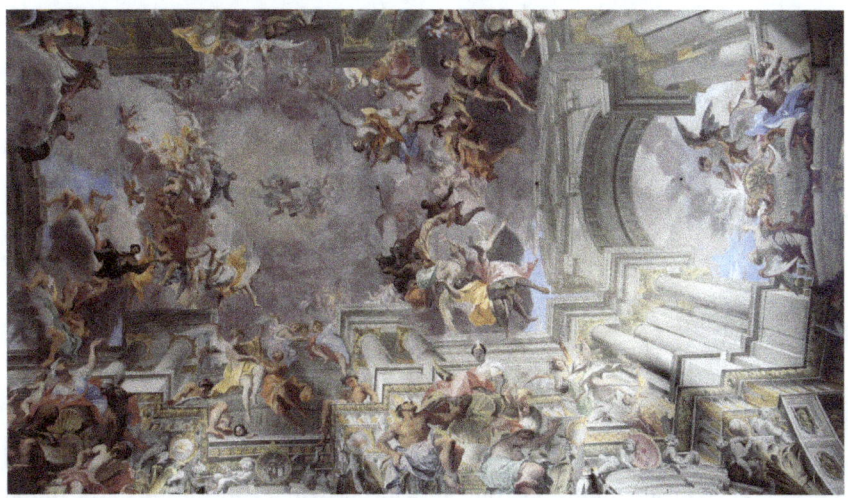

FIG. 6.5 Gesú, Rome[18]

Evidently, these ceilings negate the closure of an architectural space and suggest that the believers who have gathered for worship under this roof gain access to an infinite 'beyond'. They are, quite literally, a material expression of the thought that it is through the 'cracks' that the light gets in.

Yet the power of these ceilings does not rest in their being the illustration of a 'thought'; it rests in their capacity to make that thought experientially real. When I look up to these ceilings, I am of course aware that this representation of the heavens is a painting, an illusion, a 'trick' that is played on the eye (as the term *trompe l'oeil* suggests). Such knowing, however, does not prohibit a powerful, dizzying sensation of having access to – and partaking in – the infinite heights that are depicted. In other words, when I visit these churches and look up, I cannot fully dismiss the trick as being 'merely a trick'. Even though I am fully aware that my senses are being 'played' by the architectural space and the painted ceilings, part of my experience escapes this knowing. The knowing that the encounter with the 'transcendent' is 'in fact' a bodily sensation does not undo the mystery either. Film scholar Vivian Sobchak's insightful observations of her relation to the image on a film screen easily translate to the *trompe l'oeil* ceiling: 'As the image becomes translated into a bodily response, body and image no longer function as discrete units, but as surfaces in contact, engaged in a constant activity of reciprocal realignment and inflection' (Sobchak 2011). Watching the image is thus the 'commingling of flesh and consciousness, the human and technological sensorium, so that meaning and where it is made does not have a concrete origin in either bodies or representation but emerges from both' (Ibid.). This 'meaning without concrete origin' – which has been called 'the sublime' in discourses on the arts, and the 'numinous' or the 'ineffable' in religious studies – opens a window onto a mysterious 'beyond', a larger, overarching reality plane that, while fully real, remains ungraspable for the intellect: an absent truth.

The instances of a religiously inspired baroque that I have discussed are fine examples of what Birgit Meyer calls 'an aesthetic of persuasion' (Meyer 2010). Clearly, the Catholic Church sought to inscribe the subject's experiential encounters with an 'infinite beyond' into its particular conception of the moral and political order, to thus endow that order with a touch of the sacred. Ecstatic experiences of the ineffable were to be invoked via images, the *Gesamtkunstwerk* of religious architecture, music, and pompous ritual and at the same time to be controlled through catechism and theological explanation. The ecstatic experiences of the great mystics of the baroque were brought to the community of believers in poetry, essays, tracts, and autobiographical reports: the mystical experience of an encounter with the Divine was to contribute to a 'science of the soul'. In other words, the experiential *je ne sais quoi* evoked in baroque art and architecture was attributed, *post hoc*, with a concrete origin: it was an experience of the Divine.

The attempts by religious institutions to 'colonise' the experiences of the ineffable they produced in their arts are what the baroque anthropology I seek to design would want to undo. But then again, my idea is not to reject the authority of the religious 'coloniser' of the ineffable in order to replace it with the authority of academia. Instead I would suggest toppling the Menino Jesus from the mountain, but then to leave its place vacant.

THE-REST-OF-WHAT-IS

The term I ended up working with to conceptualise this vacancy, this 'beyond' to all representation, is 'the-rest-of-what-is' (van de Port 2011), a catchphrase which summarises the writings of philosophers and cultural analysts such as Yannis Stavrakakis (1999), the early Slavoj Žižek (1989; 1997; 1999), Alain Badiou (2002), and Terry Eagleton (2009) on the Lacanian concept of 'the Real'.

The Lacanian 'Real' refers to the existential human condition that the symbolic orders that promise us to make sense of ourselves and the world fail to capture the experience of ourselves and the world in its entirety. The Real is thus not to be confused with 'reality'. On the contrary, these authors keep stressing that the Real is the *other* of reality, the dimension of being which makes us aware just how much our reality is dependent on our representations of it. In *The Sublime Object of Ideology* (1989), Slavoj Žižek describes the Real as

the starting point, the basis, the foundation of the process of symbolization [...] which in a sense *precedes* the symbolic order and is subsequently structured by it when it gets caught in its network: this is the
great Lacanian motif of symbolization as a process which mortifies, drains
off, empties, carves the fullness of the Real of the living body. But the
Real is at the same time the product, remainder, leftover, scraps of this
process of symbolization and is as such produced by the symbolization
itself (1989: 169).

Intriguing contradictions abound in this Lacanian notion of the Real. First of all,
the Lacanian Real must be conceptualised as a radical negativity in that it resists
all symbolisation, representation, and narration. 'Cancelling out the Real, the
symbolic creates "reality", reality as that which is named by language and can
thus be thought and talked about', writes Yannis Stavrakakis (2002: 526). 'The
Real is what remains outside this field of representation, what remains impossible to symbolize' (Ibid.). Any claim to be able to articulate the Real is false,
for an articulation of the Real would imply that this 'beyond-of-our-knowing'
now finds itself *within* the horizons of the known – and is thus no longer what
it was. The-rest-of-what-is must therefore be conceptualised as forever strange.
It is the elusive, mysterious, ungraspable, inarticulable, inexplicable, baffling
dimension of being. In his remarkable study *Trouble with Strangers: A Study of
Ethics* (2009), Eagleton puts it like this:

[The Lacanian Real is] a version of Kant's unknowable thing-in-itself [...]
we can grasp this alien phenomenon only by constructing it backwards,
so to speak, from its effect – from how it acts as a drag on our discourse,
as astronomers can sometimes identify a celestial body only because of its
warping effect on the space around it (Eagleton 2009: 149).

And yet, for all of its ungraspable characteristics, the Real derives its solid-
sounding name from its unchanging and stone-like nature: it is, as Žižek puts
it, 'the rock upon which every attempt at symbolization stumbles', and 'the hard
core which remains the same in all possible worlds' (1989: 169).

The other major contradictions that are to be faced when pondering the notion of the Real concern the way people experience and evaluate its presence in their lives. As I have just suggested, the Real reveals our structures of signification to be lacking: it is the excess, the surplus, the 'beyond' of our realities; the inevitable by-product of the process whereby form is carved out of the formlessness that Michael Jackson – following William James – has called the 'plenum of existence' (1988: 3). The Real is experienced as a constant threat to the stability of cultural definitions of what is possible, normal, credible, or true. Unrelentingly, the forces of the Real besiege the fortresses of meaning in which we have taken refuge. It is therefore not surprising that people shy away from confrontations with anything or anyone who raises an awareness of the Real and erect taboos and prohibitions to prevent this from happening.

And yet it is exactly because of its location beyond representation that the Real is also positively evaluated as fullness, totality, healing, and wholeness. As the-rest-of-what-is, it is the promise of having access to the infinite that the baroque *trompe l'oeil* ceiling holds out to the congregation of believers. Traumatic encounters with the Real may be experienced as blissful *plenitude*, or the 'All' that mystics have described as 'the oceanic feeling'. 'Nothing is lacking in the Real', says Žižek. 'The lack is introduced only by the symbolization' (1989: 170).

The focus of these writers on the 'failing' of the symbolic order does not mean that they find lack and incompleteness always and everywhere. On the contrary: it is exactly because of the awareness of the lack in symbolic modes of worldmaking that these thinkers have come up with such wonderful and insightful descriptions of the pivotal role of fantasy in covering up the rents, fissures, and black holes in the structure of meaning (see Žižek 1997; Stavrakakis 1999; Veenis 2012; Thoden van Velzen and van Wetering 1988). As Stavrakakis argued, fantasy is not the opposite of reality (as colloquial wisdom has it), but supports reality: it emerges exactly in the place where the lack of reality definitions becomes evident (1999: 46). Indeed, reality can only acquire a certain coherence and become desirable as an object of identification by resorting to fantasy.

This line of thought offers some striking correspondences with the (religiously inspired) baroque insistence on the incompleteness of man-made worlds of meaning and the evocation of a potentially redemptive 'beyond' to these worlds. Žižek's observation that 'nothing is lacking in the Real', that 'the lack is only introduced by the symbolization' (1989: 170), is fully compatible with a baroque discourse on the plenitude of the Divine, which presents the lack – via such forms as the *trompe l'oeil* or mystical ecstasy – as the beyond. Lacanian understandings of the Real are even more reminiscent of negative theologies, which insist that God is unfathomable and maintain that the Divine can only be understood in terms of what it is not; or radical theologies such as developed by Karl Barth, who sought to differentiate the human affair called 'religion' from the absent truth that is God: 'For Man, God is always on yonder side, always new, far, strange, sovereign, never within reach, never in his possession: saying God means saying *miracle*' (Barth 2008: 95). In these theologies, the difference between 'God' and the-rest-of-what-is seems to be reduced to a mere choice of terms.

The differences between religiously inspired baroque and Lacanian articulations of the human condition are as striking. In Lacanian thought, the baroque construct of a divine being called 'God', capable of imposing its all-encompassing meanings and morals onto the world, can only be understood as a desirable fantasy object, the imaginary solution to the lack that pervades the worlds of meaning and morals in which human beings dwell. To replace the Menino Jesus on top of the mountain with the Lacanian Real is to replace it with an empty signifier. It is indeed, to leave its place vacant.

BAROQUE WAYS OF KNOWING

I opened this essay with the observation that the stylistic conventions of academia are not very appropriate to instil in readers that sense of 'being lost' which I deem crucial to understand the world-making that goes on in turbulent places such as the former Yugoslavia, the Dutch underworld, and Bahia. I suggested that the baroque is a rich repository of sensational forms with which to reveal that sentiment, and I found in Lacanian musings over the notion of the Real an apt academic equivalent. The suggestion now presents itself that we might simply 'go Lacanian', instead of 'going baroque'. Undoubtedly, such a move would produce a whole set of resistances (Lacanian thought is controversial, to say the least), but at least one would be working with ideas and arguments put forward by intellectuals in a thoroughly academic style. In other words, with Lacan our ideas would be challenged, but our ways of knowing would not be messed up.

The problem, however, is that replacing the baroque with its Lacanian avatar is exactly the kind of 'domestication' of baroque expressivities that I would like to avoid. No mistake about it, I have been much inspired by Lacanian scholars, in that they have enabled me to intellectually grasp the lack that lies at the heart of all representational forms and see the overlap in the existential plight of people in places as far apart as Vukovar, Amsterdam, and Bahia. They have helped me to think about the fact that the world does not comply with our narrations of it and to chart the implications of this observation for the anthropological study of world-making. Yet the way these scholars address me as a reader is very much within the modes in which we academics 'go about knowing': their vocabulary is experience-distant with contrived intellectual formulations and abstractions; they require me to think hard and deep; and they force me to stay attuned to the development of their argument, to follow them along, sentence by sentence, paragraph by paragraph, chapter by chapter. They thus take me further and further from the ethnographic situation that I want to report on and ever more into academia. In addition, there is the intellectual satisfaction that is offered in this kind of writing: working hard to grasp the complicated arguments, the reader is continuously provided with a sense of mastery that is well caught in the very verb 'to grasp', which my dictionary of the English language translates as 'to seize and hold firmly'. It is for such reasons that these scholars only get me halfway to where I want to go: in allowing me to stay in the academic universe, and allowing me to experience this sense of mastery, they separate me – and my readers – from that old woman in her ruined home, from those paranoid drug dealers, and from the fears that a Hollywood movie caused in the mood and mindset of a young Bahian shop assistant.[19]

The baroque – or rather, the baroque that is being designed here: one from which an omnipotent and beneficiary God has been evicted – does not offer the satisfaction of a sense of mastery or being in control. It seeks to make the lack that is at the heart of all world-making 'experienceable', not graspable. It is ecstatic, in that its movements are centrifugal, transporting its subjects out of familiar intellectual terrain, away from those rooms with white Formica tables and humming projectors. It seeks to shock, to confuse, and to derail by alerting its subjects to the-rest-of-what-is, and unlike the Lacanian thinkers, it does not seek to make up for the tensions it produces. It does not shy away from the discomfort it gives rise to – a sense of non-accomplishment, unfulfillment and impotence – but seeks to add such affects to its palette. This, then, is why I am seduced by the baroque: it holds out the promise that its rich repository of expressive forms might bring me (and my readers) experientially closer to what it is like to be lost in the rest-of-what-is.

One may ask, of course, whether these propositions still fall within accepted ideas as to what academics are supposed to do. After all, one might argue that experience-centred modes of knowing, and emotional and affect-full apprehensions of life, pertain to the realm of poetry, literature, music, and the arts. I do think, however, that a separation between academics who cater for the 'thinking', and artists who cater for the 'experiencing' reproduces a false dichotomy of the disembodied knowledge practices of the academic versus the experience-full knowledge practices of the artist. As argued above, reading an academic text is an experience-full activity, producing all kinds of sensations, albeit sensations *of a certain kind*. It is exactly because the academic writer seeks to limit the range of sensations that are admissible in his or her text that we can think of 'academism' as a style, an ensemble of aesthetic conventions that casts the world in a particular light and produces particular reality effects.[20]

Just how much academics are performing 'emotion-work' became clear to me when I came back from war-ridden Yugoslavia. The emotional overtones in the demands of my audiences to undo the 'bloody mess' of the world I had studied were hard to miss. The intense news coverage of massacres and atrocities in 'a place where we used to go on holiday' (as the often repeated phrase had it)[21] had unsettled them. They wanted to be released from the tensions caused by shocking televised images. They sought to be *soothed* by my texts, comforted by the thought that it all appeared very chaotic and unfathomable, but that an expert might actually show that underneath the bloody mess 'it all made sense'.

My resistance to delivering that comforting experience of release and relaxation, my stubborn refusal to clean up the mess, my attempts to send my readers into the mud, and the opposition this approach encountered (not least by a rather positivistic alter ego in my head) made me aware of how much we are under pressure to instil a particular kind of emotion in our reader's minds and bodies: the tranquillity and peace of mind that pertains to a world brought to order, the contentment that follows the illusionary sensation of being in control again. In response to hesitancy about bringing in emotion, I would say that maybe that is what we've been doing all along. The question is not whether we would want to open up our academic texts to emotions, but whether we want to expand the range of emotions that we deem admissible.

As I have made clear by now, a broadening of the experiential world that is an academic text is exactly what the baroque attention to the-rest-of-what-is might accomplish: to infuse our intellectual conquests of the rest-of-what-is with our not-knowing, our bafflement, our missing-out-on-things – and the feelings of discomfort, despair, and excitement this infusion may give rise to: to make our readers aware of the emotional undercurrents that accompany the eternal struggle to make a-story-to-live-by out of a world that is 'vague, diffuse or unspecific, slippery, emotional, ephemeral, elusive or indistinct, changes like a kaleidoscope, or doesn't have much of a pattern at all' (Law 2004: 2).

'How then to realise this?' one might ask. Introducing literary modes of writing which allow for more poetic registers of articulation are one way to go. In contrast with academic instructions to the author – to define, to fix, to delineate, to make explicit, to explain, to give 'the complete picture', to conclude – literary modes of writing wilfully produce 'gaps' and open ends to engage and activate the reader's imagination, inviting the reader to bring the narrative to life with his or her own idiosyncratic associations. As Wolfgang Iser puts it, in his masterful analysis of 'the reading process',

> no author worth his salt will ever attempt to set the *whole* picture before his
> reader's eyes. If he does he will very quickly lose his reader, for it is only by
> activating the reader's imagination that the author can hope to involve him
> and so realise the intentions of his text (1972: 287).

I am aware that inviting the reader to search for experiential or emotional overlap between his or her moments of derailment and being lost, and those of the people he or she is reading about, may strike the academic as odd and unwanted. For indeed, this implies the transfer of emotions that pertain to the reader's situation to the ethnographic setting: for instance, the life drama of that old woman in bomb-shelled Vukovar becomes experientially linked with, say, the drama of the loss of a dear friend due to illness, or even something as banal as losing him because of his move to another city. Such transfers of emotion may seem preposterous, or even disrespectful of the greater plight of others. But then again, in the reading process, these transfers of emotions of the reader to the characters and events that figure in the text are an inescapable given. Identification with a story implies this kind of emotional trafficking. It is not as if this is an 'option'. Rather, it is given with the act of reading. Moreover, as Wolfgang Iser explains, the inescapable fact that the reader brings in his or her own emotions does not mean that the encounter with the other does not take place.

The manner in which the reader experiences the text will reflect his own disposition, and in this respect the literary text acts as a kind of mirror; but at the same time, the reality which this process helps to create is one that will be *different* from his own (since, normally, we tend to be bored by texts that present us with things we already know perfectly well ourselves). Thus we have the apparently paradoxical situation in which the reader is forced to reveal aspects of himself in order to experience a reality which is different from his own. The impact this reality makes on him will depend largely on the extent to which he himself actively provides the unwritten part of the text, and yet in supplying all the missing links, he must think in terms of experiences different from his own; indeed, it is only by leaving behind the familiar world of his own experience that the reader can truly participate in the adventure the literary text offers him (Iser 1972: 287).

Readers are emotional and sentient interpreters of our words and always already implied in the making of our texts. In that sense, the moves I propose are towards a recognition of the role of the reader's imagination, and an exploration as to how that imagination can be played differently. They are *not* the clearing of a new path.

The other road to a realisation of a baroque anthropology, that is more welcoming to the idea that there is a 'rest-of-what-is', is a reconsideration of the role that visuals might play in our reports. As stated, the baroque immediately conjures up images in one's mind. Visual anthropology, a subdivision of the discipline where the form of knowing that is 'looking' has been intensively discussed, has recently introduced some very inspiring ideas as to what images might do in academia. David MacDougall, for instance, systematically compared writing/reading and filming/watching as knowledge practices, and explains how images are always in excess of what the producer of the image wants from it: 'Shots are filled with both relevant and (to me) extraneous matter at every level [...] they drift constantly toward the actual complexity and indeterminacy of the experienced world' (2006: 41). Whereas the containment of this 'extraneous matter' is the never-ending problem of the filmmaker, it is also the great potential of film as a medium, for it is exactly in this surplus that one may catch 'glimpses of being more unexpected and powerful than anything we could create':

> in films the complexity of people and objects implicitly resists the theories and explanations in which the film enlists them, sometimes suggesting other explanations, or no explanations at all. In this sense, then, film is always a discourse of risk and indeterminacy. This puts it at odds with most academic writing, which, despite its caution and qualifications, is a discourse that advances always towards conclusions (MacDougall 2006: 6).

The digital age greatly facilitates the use of images in texts, and with online publishing all kinds of hybrids between texts, images, moving images, and sounds become imaginable. The exploration of these opportunities is only the beginning. By and large, images appear in texts as illustrations of an argument already made. The illustrations in this article are a case in point. And yet even here, the sovereignty of these images is not restricted by my narrative. For example, take the photograph of the miracle room in Candeias (Fig. 6.1). I introduced this image in my text to illustrate the baroque receptivity for mess. The upper right corner of the photograph, however, reveals an (earlier?) attempt by the caretaker of this site to neatly arrange the ex-votos on shelves. This detail does not undo my reading of the image, but signals other possible readings.

A more radical example of the way images may introduce the-rest-of-what-is into our reports is the photograph below. It shows the statue of a bleeding Christ in yet another Salvadorian baroque church, São Domingo de Gusmão. I might use this image of a human corpse thrown in front of an elegant Rococo altar, frozen in its convoluted rigor mortis, and with wide open eyes, to 'serve' an argument about the baroque insistence that the mystery of being escapes our intellectual grasp. Yet as it 'hits us in the stomach', as it jeers at such attempts to control it by typing a caption under it saying 'Fig. 6.6, Christ figure, Igreja de São Domingos de Gusmão', this image also catapults us out of the universe of this text. It is no longer an illustration of arguments made about the Real, it is a frightening encounter with it.

Instead of shying away from artistic resources in our reports on reality, I plead for crossovers into the realm of the (visual) arts. Why not grant the image a larger role than that of *illustrating* our arguments? Why not profit from the stubborn resistance of images to be fully subjected to our intellectual grasp? And given the fact that we are not artists ourselves, why not cooperate with artists and their capacity to provoke experiences of the sublime? I have long thought that to make such moves towards a new role of images needs to be justified. But I am more and more convinced that what needs to be justified is the decision to keep the power of images at a distance.

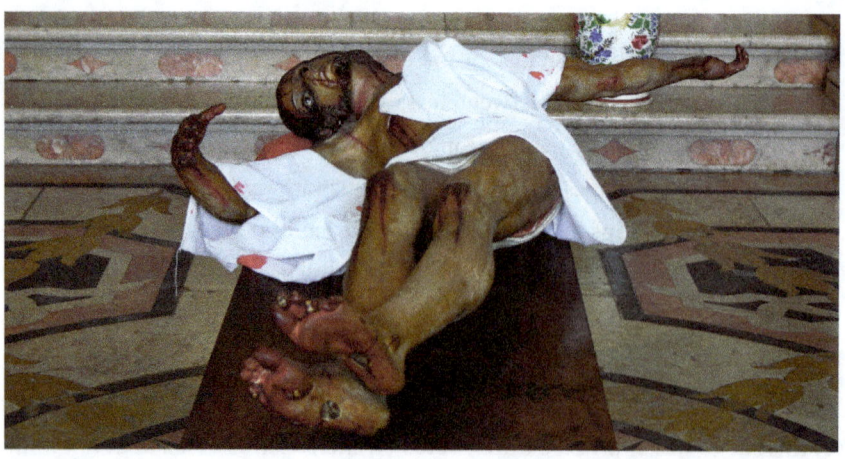

FIG. 6.6 Igreja de São Domingos de Gusmão, Bahia[22]

INSTEAD OF CONCLUSIONS: APERTURES

In this chapter, I have sought ways of making the gap between life and its representations present in anthropological reports, and so to counter the stylistic conventions that dominate academia and disrupt their comforting effects on readers. In the baroque I found a rich repository of sensational forms to express the intuition that all representations are ultimately lacking, as they cannot host 'the plenum of existence' (Jackson 1988: 3). Or rather, the baroque seeks to make that tension present, by hinting at the beyond of each and every representation, a field that I called the-rest-of-what-is.

I take this tension to be given with the condition of being human, the symbolising animal whose dependence on cultural representations is 'so great as to be decisive for his creatural viability' (Geertz 1973: 99). To phrase it with the grandiloquence and bombast that befits the baroque: as cultural beings we are all required to store our life and being in narratives which fail to deliver on their totalising promises. Moreover, I would argue that it is this common human experience that provides the meeting ground for anthropologists, the people they report on, and the readers of anthropological reports. We have all been derailed at some point, torn off the track we thought we were on, heading towards the future of our imaginations. And to a differing extent, we have all encountered the upheaval and despair – or the excitement and bliss – that may invade our consciousness at such moments. It is this commonality that might bring our readers experientially close to that old woman in Vukovar, to the 'desperate faith' with which those drug-traffickers clung to the thought that the underworld is subjected to strict laws, to the confusion of José that the spirits he interacts with are possibly a sign of schizophrenia.[23]

The other possibility for introducing turmoil and turbulence in academic modes of report lies in a further exploration of our 'modes of address', the way in which we engage our readers to partake in the stories we have to tell. Acknowledging that the act of reading is not only an intellectual activity but also an embodied and experiential one opens up avenues for interpolating our readers as affective and sensuous beings. The baroque teaches us that there are ways to make the encounter with the rest-of-what-is happen in the act of reading. Instilling in the reader 'a sense of being lost' might bring about a deeper identification of the reader with the subjects portrayed in the ethnography, and a greater commitment to find ways to relieve their plight.

For those of you who detect in this last 'vista' yet another fantasy to screen off the lack that lies at the heart of the anthropological project – yet another fantasy of comfort – I can only say 'yes indeed'. I find relief and comfort in the thought that the world does not comply with anyone's narration of it, and might therefore be a more welcoming place than we make it to be.

ACKNOWLEDGEMENTS

I would like to thank my colleagues Birgit Meyer and Freek Colombijn for their comments on earlier drafts. The presentations and discussions during the workshop 'The Baroque as Empirical Sensibility' (11–13 June 2011 at the Manchester Museum in the University of Manchester), organised by John Law and Evelyn Ruppert, were crucial in helping me to articulate the position put forward in this essay.

NOTES

1 For a full account, see Van de Port (1998) and (2013c).

2 I use the term 'world-making' for people's ongoing attempts to carve meaningful worlds out of the plenum of existence. I take anthropology to be the study of these attempts.

3 In an interesting special issue of *Etnofoor* (2011, XXI: 2), a number of authors – Michael Jackson, Kirin Narayan, Paul Stoller, and Barbara Tedlock among them – revisit the writing culture debate.

4 Next to the works that are referred to throughout the text, my readings on Brazilian baroque include Averini (1997); Ávila (2001); Bastide (1945); Freire (2006); Grammont (2008); Hansen (2006); Montes (1998); and Underwood (2002). For the use of the baroque in imagining the social I have acquainted myself with the work of Deleuze (2006); Benjamin (1977); Buci-Glucksman (1992); Calabrese (1992); Ndalianis (2004); and Wolin (1994).

5 As stated, the baroque served to articulate the tensions between life and its representations, which my earlier work in Serbia and the Netherlands had already brought to the fore. The main concepts I had used in this earlier work were the 'Dionysian', the 'wild', the 'primitive', and, more specifically for Serbia, the 'Balkan'.

6 I thank my colleague Jojada Verrips for bringing this book to my attention.

7 This point is also made by Calabrese (1992), who speaks of the baroque as an artistic 'impulse'.

8 Elsewhere, I have discussed the baroque dimensions of camp (van de Port 2012) and punk (van de Port 2013a).

9 Photograph by Mattijs van de Port.

10 For a full discussion, see Van de Port (2012), pp. 159–181.

11 Photograph by Sergio Benuti. Copyright courtesy of the Acervo Fundação Instituto Feminino da Bahia.

12 The *presepios* (cribs) that are set up in homes in the Bahian interior around Christmas time share the characteristics of the lapinhas. Next to images of the Holy Family they contain all kinds of items that aesthetically appealed to the women who assemble them – including empty shampoo bottles, canned sardines, and potted plants, producing a proliferating, messy mountain that sometimes takes up half the space of their living room. This particular 'messy' aesthetic is also a striking characteristic in the 'miracle rooms' of Bahian pilgrimage sites, as the photograph from the Bahian town of Candeias illustrates (Fig. 6.1).

13 The collection of 'Meninos no Monte' can be found in the Museu Henriqueta Catharino, which pertains to the Instituto Feminino da Bahia, once an old boarding school for rich girls in the centre of Salvador, now with a wonderful collection of popular religious art.

14 Benjamin (1977); see Owen (1980); Cowan (1981); Wolin (1994).

15 For a full account of this particular church interior, see Van de Port (2013b).

16 Photograph by Mattijs van de Port.

17 Photograph by Mattijs van de Port.

18 Photograph by Mattijs van de Port.

19 For a full discussion of this theme, see Mattijs van de Port, 'Reading Bruno Latour in Bahia. Or: How to Approach the Great, Blooming Buzzing Confusion without Going Mad' (2015).

20 One only needs to read Roland Barthes' *The Pleasure of the Text* (1975), a wonderful treatise on 'reading', to be reminded that reading is as much an experiential activity as an intellectual one (or else recall the phenomenologist's understanding of the embodied ground of all mindful activity).

21 There was always a striking tone of *indignation* in the way people would say this, a sense of having been *betrayed*.

22 Photograph by Mattijs van de Port.

23 Highlighting this commonality is by no means an invitation to forget about the specificity of individual cases, to ignore that there are different ways in which worlds may fall apart (that there are different intensities of collapse – slaps and blows). I urge ethnographers to always zoom in on the particular and culture-specific modes of dealing with moments of derailment.

BIBLIOGRAPHY

Araújo, E., *O teatro dos vícios. Transgressão e transigência na sociedade urbana colonial* (Rio de Janeiro: José Olympio, 2008)

Averini, R., 'Tropicalidade do Barroco', in A. Ávila, ed., *Barroco. Teoria e análise* (São Paulo: Perspectiva, 1997), pp. 23–31

Ávila, A., 'The Baroque Culture of Brazil', in E. J. Sullivan, ed., *Brazil: Body & Soul* (New York: Guggenheim Museum, 2001), pp. 114–128

Badiou, A., *Saint Paul: The Foundation of Universalism* (Stanford, CT: Stanford University Press, 2009)

Barthes, R., *The Pleasure of the Text* (New York: Farrar, Strauss and Giroux, 1975)

Bastide, R., *Imagens do Nordeste místico em branco e prêto* (Rio de Janeiro: O Cruzeiro, 1945)

Benjamin, W., *The Origin of German Tragic Drama* (London: NLB, 1977)

Buci-Glucksman, C., *La folie du voir. De l'esthétique baroque* (Paris: Galilée, 1992)

Calabrese, O., *Neo-Baroque: A Sign of the Times* (Princeton, NJ: Princeton University Press, 1992)

Chiampi, I., *Barroco e modernidade. Ensaios sobre Literatura Latino-Americana* (São Paulo: Editora Perspectiva, 1998)

Clifford, J., *The Predicament of Culture: Twentieth-Century Ethnography, Literature and Art* (Cambridge, MA: Harvard University Press, 1988)

Cowan, B., 'Walter Benjamin's Theory of Allegory', *New German Critique*, 22 (1981), 109–122

Crapanzano, V., *Imaginative Horizons: An Essay in Literary-Philosophical Anthropology* (Chicago: Chicago University Press, 2004)

Deleuze, G., *The Fold: Leibniz and the Baroque* (New York: Continuum, 2006)

Freire, L. A. R., *A talha neoclássica na Bahia* (Rio de Janeiro: Versal, 2006)

Geertz, C., *The Interpretation of Cultures* (New York: Basic Books, 1973)

——— *Works and Lives: The Anthropologist as Author* (Stanford, CA: Stanford University Press, 1986)

Gouldner, A., 'Romantiek en classicisme. Dieptestructuren in de sociale wetenschappen', *De Gids*, 136 (1974), 3–29

Grammont, G. de, *Aleijadinho e o aeroplano. O paraíso barroco e a construção do herói colonial* (Rio de Janeiro: Civilização Brasileira, 2008)

Hansen, J. A., 'Barroco, Neobarroco e outras ruínas', *Floema Especial*, 2 (2006), 15–84

Hills, H., 'The Baroque: Beads in a Rosary or Folds in Time', *Fabrications: The Journal of the Society of Architectural Historians, Australia and New Zealand*, 17 (2007), 48–71

Iser, W., 'The Reading Process: A Phenomenological Approach', *New Literary History*, 3 (1972), 279–299

Jackson, M., *Paths Toward a Clearing: Radical Empiricism and Ethnographic Inquiry* (Bloomington: Indiana University Press, 1988)

────── In Sierra Leone (Durham, NC: Duke University Press, 2004)

────── Between One and One Another (Berkeley: University of California Press, 2012)

Law, J., After Method: Mess in Social Science Research (London: Routledge, 2004)

Lepenies, W., 'Über den Krieg der Wissenschaften und der Literatur. Der Status der Soziologie seit der Aufklärung', Merkur, 40 (1986), 482–494

Marcus, G. E., and M. M. J. Fisher, Anthropology as Cultural Critique: An Experimental Moment in the Human Sciences (Chicago: University of Chicago Press, 1986)

Meyer, B., 'Aesthetics of Persuasion: Global Christianity and Pentecostalism's Sensational Forms', South Atlantic Quarterly, 109 (2010), 741–763

Montes, M. L., 'As figuras do sagrado: entre o público e o privado', in L. M. Schwarcz, ed., História da vida privada no Brasil 4 (São Paulo: Companhia das Letras, 1998), pp. 63–171

Ndalianis, A., Neo-Baroque Aesthetics and Contemporary Entertainment (Cambridge, MA: MIT Press, 2004)

Owens, C., 'The Allegorical Impulse: Toward a Theory of Postmodernism', October, 12 (1980), 67–86

Port, M. van de, Gypsies, Wars and Other Instances of the Wild: Civilization and its Discontents in a Serbian Town (Amsterdam: Amsterdam University Press, 1998)

────── '"It Takes a Serb to Know a Serb". Uncovering the Roots of "Obstinate Otherness" in Serbia', Critique of Anthropology, 19 (1999), 7–30

────── Geliquideerd: criminele afrekeningen in Nederland (Amsterdam: Meulenhoff, 2001)

────── 'Circling around the Really Real: Possession Ceremonies and the Search for Authenticity in Bahian Candomblé', Ethos, 33 (2005), 147–179

────── Ecstatic Encounters: Bahian Candomblé and the Quest for the Really Real (Amsterdam: Amsterdam University Press, 2011)

────── 'Genuinely Made Up: Camp, Baroque and the Production of the Really Real'. Journal of the Royal Anthropological Institute, N.S., 18 (2012), 864–883

────── 'The Natural is a Sham: the Baroque and its Contemporary Avatars', Forum, 16 (2013a), 1–10

────── 'Golden Storm: The Ecstasy of the Igreja de São Francisco, Salvador da Bahia, Brazil', in O. Verkaaik, ed., Religious Architecture: Anthropological Perspectives (Amsterdam University Press/ University of Chicago Press, 2013b), pp. 63–83

────── 'On the Necessity of Daydreaming', in F. Enns, and A. Mosher, eds., Just Peace. Ecumenical, Intercultural, and Interdisciplinary Perspectives (Eugene, OR: Pickwick Publications, 2013c)

────── 'Reading Bruno Latour in Bahia: Or: How to Approach the Rest-of-what-is Without Going Mad', in M. Jackson, and A. Piette, eds., What is Existential Anthropology? (Oxford: Berghahn, 2015)

Reijnders, F., Metamorfose van de Barok (Amsterdam: Uitgeverij 1001, 1991)

Sobchack, V., 'What My Fingers Knew: The Cinesthetic Subject, or Vision in the Flesh', (2011) <http://www.sensesofcinema.com/2000/5/fingers/> [accessed 17

December 2015]

Stavrakakis, Y., *Lacan and the Political* (London: Routledge, 1999)

Talento, B., and H. Hollanda, *Basílicas & capelinhas. Um estudo sobre a história, arquitetura e arte de 42 igrejas de Salvador* (Salvador: Bureau, 2008)

Underwood, D. K., 'Toward a Phenomenology of Brazil's Baroque Modernism', in E. J. Sullivan, ed., *Brazil: Body & Soul.* (New York: Guggenheim Museum, 2002), pp. 504–524

Valle, I. del, 'Jesuit Baroque', *Journal of Spanish Cultural Studies*, 3 (2002), 141–163

Wolin, R., *Walter Benjamin: An Aesthetic of Redemption* (Berkeley: University of California Press, 1994)

Žižek, S., *The Sublime Object of Ideology* (London: Verso, 1989)

——— *The Plague of Fantasies* (London: Verso, 1997)

——— *The Ticklish Subject: the Absent Centre of Political Ontology* (London: Verso, 1999)

7

INNOVATION WITH WORDS AND VISUALS: A BAROQUE SENSIBILITY

Helen Verran and Brit Ross Winthereik

INTRODUCTION

INNOVATING TO EFFECT THE DISCIPLINE OF DEDUCTIVE PROOF IN ANCIENT Greek mathematics by mixing words and visuals; to accomplish the compromises needed in the conduct of an elected monarchy in sixteenth-century Denmark; to lubricate the workings of a public-private partnership (PPP) in contemporary Denmark; and to inspire a baroque style of empirical analysis in the contemporary academic discipline of science and technology studies. These are the sites of innovation that figure in our paper (albeit some more fleetingly than others). We connect them by embroidering each with that 'now you see it, now you don't' thread of innovation in mixing words and visuals.

Flick through our text and the visuals will stand out – an odd mixture of PowerPoint images and photographs of a tapestry. The words of course will take more time to get your head around. When you have done so (dear reader), we ask you to undertake an exercise of the imagination. Imagine our text, this particular mixture of words and visuals, as a performance: two speakers with spoken words and screened visuals. By undertaking that exercise of imagination you will correct an imbalance which we, writing on different sides of the world, are unable to attend to. In our performance of this text, our imagined embodied storytelling, we hope our initial, almost unreasonable, juxtaposition of the life of two Danish cities modernising in different centuries creates a tension strong enough to contain the further tensions we create in mixing visuals and words. The tensions are crucial in making our argument for expanding our modern repertoire for 'doing diagrams'. Our juxtapositions put the four worlds we listed in the beginning in tension, accepting that they are detached and different in myriad unknowable ways while effecting an attachment, a working sameness within that wonder-filled difference.

JUXTAPOSITION: GROWTH CENTRES IN DENMARK

In the sixteenth century Helsingør was a centre of innovation. But here we set the life of that city of long ago against the contemporary life of Hanstholm, a twenty-first-century centre of innovation on the other side of Denmark. We juxtapose these temporally and spatially distinct places for no other reason than developments in these places both harvest opportunities offered by the sea. Or more precisely, we juxtapose the collective practices involved in their being places, by connecting them with this (rather slight) thread. This unlikely juxtaposition might be seen as expressing a baroque sensibility, but whether or not it does it is the first move in the comedy that is our paper.[1]

Helsingør commands the strait that is the entrance to the Baltic Sea. As a sixteenth-century centre of economic development, it grew out of the extraction of dues from ships that wished to pass through the strait. Hanstholm, in contrast, faces the North Sea and while it is already Denmark's largest fishery harbour, it is hoped that this town will become a future engineering city through the extraction of energy from the waves that pound its shores. Both development events might be construed as cutting-edge events concerned with innovation and growth, and taking place on different geographical edges. Recognising these edges is to recognise stories of entrepreneurship as stories of working relations between people, technology, and nature.

Narrating and exhibiting devices garnered from the life of these two different places on the edge of the sea, we first draw attention to a diagram of innovation and its roles in instituting innovation. This diagram emerged into our field of vision through fieldwork in a Danish wave-energy research and development collective where participants are hoping to move towards commercialisation and promote Danish know-how on marine renewable energy technology in Denmark and abroad. We take the diagram of the stages of innovation as a device designed to allow participants to sift through the complexity of wave-energy development and effect partnership among developers and potential private and public sector investors.

The second diagram we display is historical and emerged in archival work we undertook as a way of analysing the innovation diagram with a baroque sensibility. Looking for inspiration as to how a baroque sensibility might be expressed, we turned to Helsingør as exemplary of a Danish baroque time and place. Here we encountered a baldachin, a tapestry throne canopy woven in a tapestry workshop established in Kronborg Castle in 1585. As the town expanded into a centre of commerce, drawing on its strategic location between the North Sea and the Baltic, and capitalism emerged as an economic order, the Danish aristocracy was radically reorganised through successive upheavals. These were associated with the institutionalisation of Protestantism and the establishment of an elected monarchy. We take the baldachin as a device designed to intervene in that emergent polity.

Through juxtapositions, we offer stories in the form of non-explanation. We frame and reframe in order to generate something new from within the field of study, rather than reflect on 'what is' from a meta position (Law 2004). We work within the 'folds' (see introduction to this volume by Law), pushing and pulling at the interfaces we feel ourselves enmeshed in.

The work diagrams do in collectives is the focus of our attention in this chapter, and we acknowledge that our understandings of what diagrams are differ from the technical understandings adopted by our colleagues in wave-energy capture innovation, our engineering and financial PPP co-participants. Our reframing through focussing on diagrams draws on a recent novel account of diagrams offered in the history of mathematics. Instead of taking diagrams as involved only in epistemic practices linking the mess of the actual and the ideal of the future, this account of diagrams focuses on their unique contribution in rhetoric. This account allows us to recognise the work diagrams do in collective way-finding, in working in the present.

Diagrams as we present them here are graphics, images, or visuals that fill two-dimensional physical spaces – e.g. screened images of the stages of techno-logical innovation, or the graphic images that cover the surfaces of a tapestry. The visuals we are interested in are those performing in a graphic register that is in tension with linguistic registers. We refer to these figurations that are designed to work with text as diagrams, and open up a space for imagining their capacities as agential devices. Our concern is with how diagrams and their associated texts intervene in the organisation and governance of institutions like the wave-energy partnership. In showing the workings of such diagrams they emerge as objects of governance and organisation that embed working imaginaries exercised in the present. In contrast to baroque diagrams like the baldachin, the diagram-matic devices of technoscience that we met in the wave-energy capture PPP are designed to enforce non-equivocation and non-contradiction, the standard rhetoric of Western scientific thought and argument. Devices enacting such norms make it difficult to manage ambiguities and ambivalences that might generatively make it possible to go on together doing difference.

MEETING A WORKING DIAGRAM

When we began our involvement with wave-energy commercialisation we were working on the edge in several senses of the word. In an attempt to get an edge in environmental energy generation, Denmark's government has invested money, on and off, in local initiatives in Northern Jutland over a thirty-year period. However, since a change of government in 2001, state funding in renewable energy has taken on a particular form. Any application should now involve private as well as public partners. Whether an innovation project is fundable depends on its ability to successfully enrol various stakeholders in the project. The imaginary at work in this vision of funding is that cutting-edge projects will necessarily involve developers, financial partners, research institutions, local government, and so on.

Before 2001, government funding in renewable energy in Denmark focused on supporting the renewable energy developer communities and expert engineers in whatever organisational form they chose to present themselves. It is different today. If you go to the geographical edge where the North Sea waves energetically batter the Danish coast, you will find the Danish Wave Energy Center (DanWEC). Located in the town of Hanstholm, DanWEC has, as one of its main missions, the institution of a PPP around marine renewable energy in Denmark.[2] One full-time employee attends to this along with a number of helping hands from several different public and private institutions. As part of research in the context of the project 'Marine Renewable Energy as Alien', we have witnessed some of the sociotechnical means by which the partnership hopes to turn wave-energy devices into cutting-edge infrastructure.[3]

Work to stabilise and move forward the partnership is ongoing, as is fieldwork.[4] The partnership has taken upon itself a number of tasks, one of these being to map all the ongoing stakeholders and technology projects geographically and in terms of progress (which means how far they are from commercialisation).

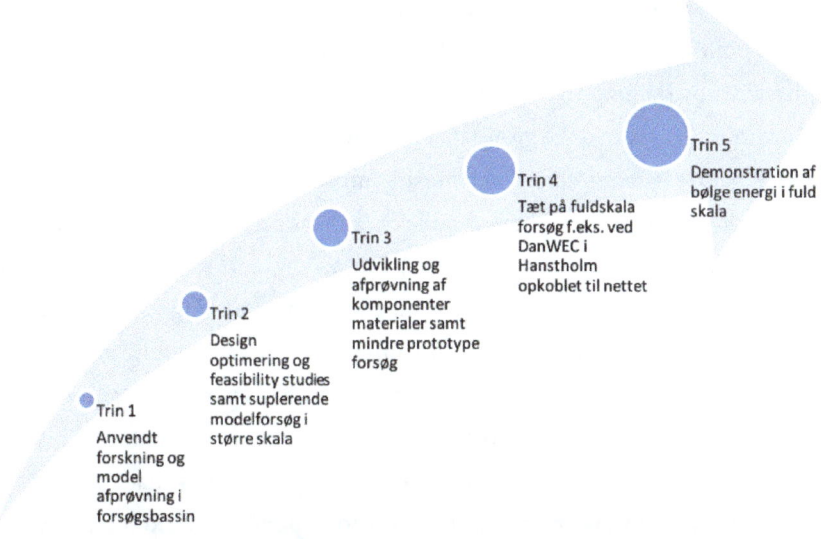

FIG. 7.1 Diagram of Innovation, reproduced from the draft report presented at the strategy meeting[5]

On the basis of web searches and interviews, core members of what is known as 'The Partnership' constructed a list of core actors in Danish wave-energy development. The initiative was guided by a worry that the developers did not collaborate enough to benefit from each other's insights. Another main task the partnership set itself was to draft a national strategy for wave energy and hand it over to the organisation that represents the interests of Danish energy companies and to the Ministry for Climate and Energy. A varied group of people make up 'The Partnership': wave device developers, local politicians from north-western Denmark, energy company representatives, suppliers of technology and materials, and scientists. Members of the partnership have a number of rather different concerns and participate in the partnership for various reasons. Nevertheless, the coordinating actors repeatedly highlight two concerns: 1) to create visibility around wave-energy innovation among politicians and ordinary people as this, it is hoped, will generate increased funding, and 2) to collaborate around particular technical issues that they all seem to share (secure seabed anchoring is an issue that is often mentioned at meetings in the partnership as being of shared concern). What they may each gain from demonstrating the vitality of the wave-energy technologies and community differs, but participants are adamant that individual inventors must collaborate to gain political visibility. Collaboration is facilitated by wave-energy scientists (physicists by training) from a Danish University located in the same region as Hanstholm. This is also the group that introduced the innovation-cum-funding model that was presented at a partnership meeting in 2011.

I sit at the horseshoe-shaped table in a meeting at the Montra Hotel in Hanstholm. The room has soft carpets, and a view, and an ambition, it feels, to perform its visitors as 'elegant'. The meeting I am attending today is one in a series of meetings instituting a new organisation, a private–public partnership around wave-energy development in Denmark. Its forty participants range from inventors of wave-energy technology to environmental consultants, politicians, and engineers. There are familiar faces and newcomers, a few that I'd expected to see are absent; this is a busy crowd. Of the forty participants, four are women. The purpose of the meeting that was stated in the invitation and repeated by the chair is to discuss the first draft for a national wave-energy strategy. The meeting is the last in a series of meetings held by a smaller working group and the draft report has been circulated. A consultant who has been chairing the working group walks us through the sections of the report. Everybody listens attentively and no comments are made until a model depicting five steps and purporting to describe the 'stages' of wave-energy innovation is presented.

When the diagram (reproduced as Fig. 7.1 above) appeared on the screen, several of the people in the audience requested explanation. As the consultancy personnel identified and narrated its five steps, a vision of orderly progression emerged as actual locations of the physical work of testing wave-energy technologies: from the test basin, to the fjord, and to the open sea. The final step (5) referred to nowhere in particular and everywhere in general – commercialisation. Upon enquiry we learnt that this diagram was introduced into the national strategy by the consultant in collaboration with university partners. The diagram distinguished three reality 'factors', or control variables, relevant to the process of wave-energy innovation. The factors were variables influencing translation of kinetic energy to electrical energy; variables relating to environmental robustness; and social factors. These factors were held to 'add up to' criteria salient to assessing the viability of this type of environmental energy infrastructure. The diagram seemed to propose that these various classes of 'factors' enter the innovation process in this specific order.

The discussion heats up as the accuracy and truthfulness of the diagram is discussed. Overall, the participants do not disagree over whether the form of the diagram is an apt representation of innovation. The problem seems to be that it locates specific technological prototypes differently on the arrow of progress. Several of the developers disagree with how their devices are ranked in the vision of progress envisioned in the diagram. The diagram seems to be fomenting dissension. I raise my hand to ask if there might be a way of representing the many differences at play. Are there other ways apart from one arrow pointing towards one future? The answer is swift: 'No, that would not be wise. We need to demonstrate that we stand united as an industry'.

We will come back to this moment below, for, albeit belatedly, we wish to respond to this swift and definitive answer.

Back in the meeting, as the walk-through of the report continued, a different diagram appeared on the screen. It outlined a number of funding schemes that had been identified by the working group. By means of colours these schemes were linked to the stages of the innovation diagram and hence to specific wave-energy prototypes. This diagram introduces a specificity into the reading of technological innovation in wave energy that is likely to have significant consequences for many of the entrepreneurs gathered in the room. If members of the partnership follow the strict logic created in putting these two representations of reality together, then some entrepreneurs will find their future possibilities severely constrained.

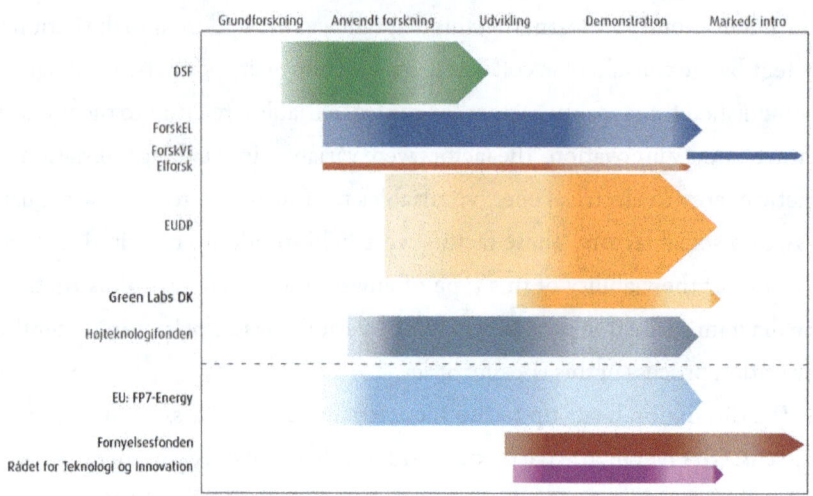

FIG. 7.2 A diagram depicting funding sources for the various stages of the innovation process proposed in Fig. 7.1[6]

Some months later I again sit at a horseshoe-shaped table. Once more the innovation diagram is shown on the screen, but this time it figures as part of a presentation by one of the partnership's developers. The entrepreneur uses the diagram to argue why 'his' prototype is located at step three and not at step two, which was how it was classified during the previous meeting.

The innovation-cum-funding diagram is at the same time both authoritative and contested. But the diagram's role as more or less a truthful representation is not the only issue contested on this occasion. The assumption that the diagram is only doing representation also becomes a point of contention. We take this as an important ethnographic finding, since the wave-energy partnership tends to exist and work around such diagrammatic representations. The university scientists introduced the innovation diagram with the intention of creating shared ground, an object for wave-energy developers to gather around. They envisaged it as a thing that would make possible simple (optimistic) representation of an emerging field to politicians and potential investors. As we noted earlier, at the same time as a spatially organised depiction of progress from a real past to an imagined future, the diagram also seemed to embed certain mechanisms for differentiation and even exclusion, so that not all devices would travel equally fast into the future.

Let us stay in the second meeting a little while longer. One of us was present amongst those representing various public institutions and along with private sector representatives who were helping to 'bring innovation to market'. The puzzle of our participation at that moment was about discerning exactly what these people were in fact gathering around: how did they make sense of the diagrammatic figurations presented to them?

The influence of the orthodox interpretation that pervaded the diagram's appearance in the room meant that while there was space for negotiation in the meeting, it could only proceed within the fixed logic of the five steps implied by the diagrammatic representation of stages. It was mutually and tacitly agreed that this is how innovation happens. Man-made devices ride into the future on arrows of progressive tinkering with heterogeneous things.

But then the next presenter steps forward. He is a developer who takes a rather different approach than the consensus to the problem of classifying wave-energy devices according to this vision of progress. A central part of his presentation is a newspaper clipping of a huge Atlantic Ocean wave smashing onto the coast of Portugal. A surfer is riding the wave and spectators are watching from the shore. The presenter asks the wave-energy capture consortium audience: aren't we all looking for the perfect wave? The main point of his presentation is that wave-energy models are different; alternative mechanical means of wave-energy harvesting each carry their own requirements. Specifically, different models need waves with different physical characteristics, different locations for model testing, and different funding schemes to bring the models to market. We paraphrase this timely (it seems to us) intervention by a member of the partnership as 'let us refuse the general account of progressive technological innovation the diagram proposes; each of us is an individual inventor'.

Key to our argument here is that this inventor steps forward with an alternative understanding of what it is that diagrams do. As this inventor explained in a subsequent interview, he was not opposing the logic of the innovation diagram (he is not refusing its role in representing passage of a domain of innovation from past to future) but seeking to add to it (interview Jan 2013). Of course he was, in actuality, adding further words. In these further words the argument goes in a different – and in some ways opposed – direction to the flow of words within the text associated with the graphic when it appeared initially. In adding further words to the graphic's milieu (or to put it another way, adding another distinct set of words to those already embedded within the graphic), this canny inventor seeks to enhance the diagram's institutional potency. He imagines the diagram could be capable of supporting entrepreneurs in thinking about the differences between their models while still accepting that they are all the same in capturing kinetic energy and translating it to electrical energy.

However, it is clear in this meeting that he is failing in this endeavour since nobody is picking up the invitation to respecify the innovation graphic. His presentation does not have any impact in this or the subsequent meetings, and is not referred to by others. Later, we are told that this may be a matter of trust. We are told that people in the sector do not trust this man because of previous business history. Nevertheless, regardless of his lack of success in infusing the diagram with a new sort of potential through further linguistic means, we see his attempt as pointing to the possibility of a generative tension around the diagram. More precisely we see the possibility of adding more and different texts to the graphics, and perhaps in consequence altering the spatial designs of the graphics.

This dissenting entrepreneur offers us the possibility of methodological pause, and has given us opportunity to announce the device that we are following here. The device we have 'locked onto' and which we will simply name as diagram, is a juncture: text-graphic/graphic-text as an ephemeral clot of material semiotic resources where words are embedded in graphics as much as graphics are buried in words. In the account we have just given of meeting the diagram of technological innovation in wave-energy capture during ethnographic fieldwork, we noted that it appeared along with a normative iconography which has the diagram as representing. And we told how subsequently a dissenting entrepreneur attempted unsuccessfully to introduce ambiguity and even internal contradictions into the diagram, by adding a further (contradictory) interpretation of what it depicted.

A NORMATIVE ICONOGRAPHY OF TECHNOLOGICAL INNOVATION

Following the diagram representing the stages of innovation and its accompanying text as it contributes to launching the national strategy for wave power in Denmark, a means by which the inventors seek funding opportunities offers a glimpse of how the complicatedness of innovation processes is managed in practice politically. It also offers insight into how the authors of the strategy see the management of innovation processes as a matter of controlling the relation between a model energy capture device and various natural environments.

Embedded in the diagram as a representation of technological innovation is the assumption that technological innovation in wave-energy capture begins with physics as fundamental knowledge: the translation of kinetic energy to electrical energy and the variables that influence the efficiency of that translation. Knowledge relating to environmental and social contextualisation of the techniques described by physics, the constitution of environmental robustness, and how social acceptability might be achieved, are identified by the diagram as additives; that knowledge becomes relevant at later stages in the life of the model asserted by the diagram. Negotiation and strategy reside outside the purview of the diagram – in the realm of subjects – and thus cannot be represented. Subjects, those who do the organising and the governing, do not belong to the 'core' that the diagram claims to represent (what it is that can be organised and governed) and to do so truthfully.

The diagram precisely represents actual specific organisational locations which are at different geographical places. Yet in simultaneously rendering innovation as a general event of an unspecifiable future that is progressed towards, the diagram also idealises the times and places of these affairs, and in a way that does not allow the questioning of these sites as obligatory passage points for innovation in wave energy. The diagram in its first appearance claims for itself a capacity to realistically map a stable system, although as we noted in reporting a revision subsequently offered by one of the members of the group, a revision which attempted to open up the arena the diagram represents, to render it instead as a complex and emergent system embedding ambiguity and contradiction, that claim to be a realistic map can be contested. Nevertheless, embedded in the diagram read through the normative iconography of technoscience, is a cartography of stable entities and stable relations.

Lurking within this orthodox iconography of diagrams, as Isabelle Stengers points out, is an epistemological map. It has a

'tree' shape, arising from a relatively simple but fundamental 'law' (or 'laws') to its application in increasingly complicated situations. The tree is a hierarchical representation: passing from the fundamental 'trunk' to the tiniest branch should ideally pose technically complicated questions but not fundamental ones. In practice it goes without saying that knowledge of the 'branches' includes a conception of the trunk, or at least a way to pass from the trunk to the branches...The finished operation, however, leaves few traces of this. To understand is to understand how the trunk generates the branches, and that is what is learnt and transmitted by specialists (Stengers 1997: 8).

Yet, as Stengers goes on to say, inevitably such a complicated rendering of the real comes at a cost in technoscientific discourse. Along with the reassuring singular technical story comes congress with another often unnoticed shadow domain – an ideal zone. Stengers alerts us to 'the gods and demons that populate physics' (1997: 9) constituting the ideal zone that accompanies such representations. We do not dispute the capacity of the diagram as representation, nor deny the importance of such representation in the workings of the wave-energy capture inventors' collective. But we also recognise that the inventor who reminded his fellow members of their differences was correct that representation is not all that this diagram does. We interpret the dissenting engineer as claiming that the diagram could and perhaps should offer possibilities for members of the partnership to each find their path within the general arena of innovation. Each might be supported in finding what their wave is if the design of the diagram were to be somewhat altered, or the words around it supplemented modifying the diagram to depict other things or different flows. In short, we suggest that he envisaged possibilities for diagrams to offer pilotage.

We will introduce the notion of pilotage shortly, but for the moment let us just observe that this diagram contributes to collective way-finding in the present, to going on together while recognising 'our' differences. In identifying this, a second insight emerges. Insisting, or assuming, that diagrams only represent gets in the way of their capacity to offer pilotage. What is it about the diagrams' work in representing that gets in the way of pilotage? Stengers' insights are helpful here.

What allows judgements to be made in the

> complicated real with [...] approximations that limit us [...] [are only] identified by reference to [the real's] demonic alter ego [...] a more or less implicit dualism that entails the rejection and enclosure within the domain of 'nonscientific' or 'simply subjective' of anything that cannot be reduced to the canon of the 'simple' model (Stengers 1997: 9).

The diagram of orthodox iconography, the diagram as representation (Stengers' 'simple model') is generative: it produces what comes to count as 'the real', but this constitution of reality happens on the basis of an unnoticed, implicit dualism. In our view this is a very costly dualism. An unnoticed expectation of diagrams understood in this way, as representations that come to function as the real, is that diagrams can reach into the ideal zone: diagrams embed reference to the ideal (this reference is essential to their functioning as reality), but dissemble over the question of how they represent the ideal zone, over whether the 'ideal' is the real. This is why we as participants in this PPP strive to re-narrate what realities are made in the collective and how. And this sometimes means reframing and transporting the discussion somewhere else.

While privately many participants in the wave-energy community might have reservations about the innovation diagram that we describe above and which features in meetings and reports, the diagram, with its embedded reference to an ideal zone 'of gods and demons', does particular work. Participants appreciate its social workings and for the most part do not feel that those workings are something to disapprove of or disagree over. However, some get upset about some of its doings. For example, some dislike the way it allocates their position in a hierarchy, or they feel uncomfortable about how the model seems to exclude some members of the partnership from funding opportunities without being transparent about this effect. Not all partners are equally at risk of such exclusion. Those at risk of not making it to the future of harnessing energy at the open sea are those inventors who have not been able to test their wave-energy devices at the geographical locations specified by the model in the order defined by the model.

A NOVEL ACCOUNT OF WHAT DIAGRAMS DO AND HOW THEY DO IT

In developing our argument about the work of 'other than representing' that diagrams do in collectives, we learn from a recent analysis of the diagrams of ancient Greek mathematics (Netz 1999) and an enthusiastic commentary on this text by Latour (2008). Reviel Netz's analysis proposes diagrams as offering pilotage, opening up possibilities for particular forms of collective way-finding in mathematical argument. In mathematical proof, of course, it is a way to be certain that matters and, as Netz (1999: 6) argues, this is what combining the graphics of the diagram with argument pursued with words was contrived to achieve in making mathematical arguments. Netz reveals the origins of the diagram as a formalism in the rather banal practices of Greeks orally performing arguments with words and visuals. As Latour points out, the move that Netz is making here is quite a standard move in science studies (Latour 2008: 442).

In fact, in a rather similar shift, one of us has previously revealed origins of the formalisms of enumeration and the capacities of numbers to interpellate their users, in routine, rather banal, practices involving words and gestures associated with particular forms of life (Verran 2001: 99–107).

Of course, in the collectives we are involved with here – a twenty-first-century PPP and the polity of a baroque elected monarchy – the 'absolute certainty' of the mathematician is not desirable, but, as our dissenting entrepreneur pointed out, support for collective way-finding, explicitly pursued in light of the profound differences with which the partnership is necessarily riven, is something that diagrams might be expected to offer.

Elaborating the unconventional understanding of diagrams that Netz offers us, we will go on to juxtapose the diagram of technological innovation with the baroque baldachin, comparing and contrasting their capacities in the dual functions of representation and pilotage. If we think of our paper as comedy, this is the second move in the three steps – contriving a device that can precipitate connection and attachment. We constitute a particular form of sameness between diagrams in taking them both simultaneously as devices of representation and of pilotage in collectives that are complex, emergent, open systems. This is a sameness by which we strategically hinge them together as a diptych. We propose that as organisational forms, neither the collective that is the twenty-first-century Danish PPP, nor the collective that was a sixteenth-century northern European polity governed as an elected monarchy, conform as stable closed systems. A baroque sensibility would be equally appropriate in navigating the complexity of the two administrations, attending to the internal differentiation in which all the elements are subject to emergent rules.

Through juxtaposing the diagram of technological innovation and the baldachin, we develop the suggestion that the innovation diagram is inadequate to the tasks it must perform. It promotes an organisational regime that proceeds by conforming to standards of non-contradiction and non-equivocation in its rhetoric. In contrast, the baldachin's design explicitly recognises complexity, openness, and emergence as pervading the working of the sixteenth- to seventeenth-century kingdom of Denmark and Norway within which it performs; the baldachin offers pilotage and representation in participating in an organisational regime that simultaneously abides by and evades these norms of rhetoric, with its blatant equivocation over contradiction. We propose, then, that the baldachin might serve as an object that inspires the cultivation of a baroque sensibility in developing PPPs in emerging industries like Danish wave-energy capture. In doing so it will promote a change in the way these PPPs understand their organisational forms and culture.

Recognising that the model of meaning-making that diagrams initiate was invented by ancient Greek mathematicians and appropriated by the politicians of the ancient Greek polity within which this mathematical meaning-making came to life, Netz insists that the graphics we call diagrams and texts that they are embedded within should not be separated if we are to understand how this model of meaning-making works (Netz 1999: 12). Diagrams and their associated texts work tightly together in simultaneously naming distinct sets of relations and relationally manipulating these distinct sets of relations. In this model of meaning-making, one set of relations is worked spatially, and the other set of relations is worked linguistically. While the grid of the diagram maintains an order as originally proposed (and spatially imagined), flows in the text accomplish shifts between the differentially (spatial versus linguistic) articulated sets of relations (Ibid: 19). In working these two distinct sets of relations, specified and worked in contrasting modes of thought (spatial and linguistic), meaning-making in geometry proceeds in a particular way, a way that generates deductive proof.

This is a model derived from oral performance, which works to make meaning in a performance of words uttered and lines traced. These processes are conducted strictly in tandem. Seen in this light of oral performance, the standard understandings of those who routinely encounter diagrams as seemingly embedded within written texts, as graphics embedded within flows of words, should be reconsidered. By contrast, oral performance diagrams and their texts should be taken as words embedded within the graphically rendered relations of diagrams (Netz 1999: 14). In the PPP meetings described above, the graphics framed the words, while in the written reports of course the words frame the graphics. But taking the PPP more vaguely, as a form of life, we can begin to accept that sometimes relations graphically plotted frame the relations plotted in flows of words, and, alternatively, sometimes the situation can be reversed. Diagrams – graphics and their texts – are highly labile in their forms of participation in collectives.

Going on from his insights into the invention of a particularly efficacious form of certainty-generating rhetoric by ancient Greek mathematicians, Netz proposes that Greek politicians appropriated this particular model of argument which the geometers had invented (Netz 1999: 276). One way to summarise the significance of the argument made by Netz on the basis of recognising the oral performance origins of meaning-making with diagrammatic devices, is to contrast the rhetorical strategies of speaking from the graphic and speaking to the figuration (Ibid: 293). In speaking from, words are imagined as embedded within the graphic, and performers (and listeners) must attend to relations con-tracted in the present. Speaking to the diagram is a form of presentation where the diagram presents a proposed 'found' past in an idealised future. Whereas speaking from the graphic offers possibilities of pilotage of the emergent rela-tions of an open and complex system emergent in the here and now, speaking to the diagram proposes it as a realistic map of a given set of relations as they pertain in a found, closed, stable system.

We find the work of Netz inspiring and suggestive, but still we wish to embel-lish it, to add a further layer of embroidery. As well as recognising the complexity of manipulating sets of relations expressed graphically (and thought about spa-tially) with those expressed in wordy texts (and thought through linguistically), in developing a contrast which offers possibilities for rhetorically distinguishing between 'speaking from' and 'speaking to' – allowing for shifts which can effect very significant moves in collective meaning-making – we want also to introduce a third, little-noticed, aspect of the workings of diagrams, the device we propose as capable of effecting useful connections between a twenty-first century PPP and a baroque elected monarchy. A third capacity that diagrams have concerns the rhetorical norms of non-contradiction and non-equivocation – norms originating in Aristotelianism.

Seeing herself in much the same way that Netz seems to, in 'displaying "our" modern commonplaces out of the place they are coming from', classics scholar Barbara Cassin points out in her contribution in the catalogue that accompanied the Making Things Public exhibition put together by Bruno Latour and Peter Weibel (2005) that

> [Aristotle] still does constitute a huge part of our [modern] conscious and less conscious background [to thought]. We are still Aristotelian, whether we know it or not [...] in our regulation of speech [...] we live under the regime of non-contradiction and of non-equivocation (Cassin 2005: 858).

In embroidering the fabric of Netz's argument we offer a qualification to Cassin's assertion. We claim that – alert to possibilities for differentially manipulating sets of relations specified in visuals and in words, and to possibilities for speaking to and from graphics – it is possible to cultivate possibilities for carefully contriving the means to simultaneously abide by and escape the commonplace Aristotelianism that ties up public life in non-contradiction and non-equivocation. Mixing visuals and words in doing diagrams and texts felicitates navigation of complexity. We point to the baroque as a source of inspiration in doing so. In particular in our next section we will demonstrate how a Danish baroque baldachin does just this.

A BALDACHIN AND ITS ICONOGRAPHY

Beginning our archival search for a text that might offer inspiration for attending to our disconcertment around the diagram of the innovation process, and its participation in that partnership, we were led to a lavish publication from the Metropolitan Museum of Art, New York, and Yale University Press: 'Tapestry in the Baroque: Threads of Splendor'. A large and heavy book with many full-colour images, it celebrates an exhibition mounted by the museum from 2007–08, funded by a consortium of public and private institutions. The museum wished to remind its patrons of the importance of tapestry as a traditional art form 'associated with the lifestyle of courts and churches ever since [Europe's] early Middle Ages [...][that] during the sixteenth and seventeenth centuries [...] continued to exercise its fascination for the grander and more visionary patrons'. Featured as part of the New York exhibition was a tapestry that had travelled from Stockholm, a throne baldachin 'of such quality that were it not for the survival of its contract, one would think it had been made in one of the major Flemish weaving centers' (Campbell 2007: 28–35).[7]

In this section we display the baldachin by offering an interpretive iconography of its images. Our iconographic reading contests that of the curator of the New York exhibition, who also authored the text that accompanies images of the baldachin in the book assembled in association with the exhibition. Perhaps echoing the dissenting inventor who unsuccessfully tried to introduce ambiguity into the diagram of technological innovation in wave-energy capture, and so bring to the fore the 'other than representation' capacities we discern as embedded within the baldachin, we find ambiguity and ambivalence in the arrangements of the icons on the tapestry which hung, glittering, over the Danish king and queen during banquets and other events of the court in the 1560s. We propose that the contradictions and equivocations we recognise in the design of the baldachin are not only an accurate representation of the workings of the baroque Danish polity, but that they also enable the graphic to offer pilotage.

Confiscated from Danish territory during 1657 by the forces of King Charles X of Sweden, the baldachin entered the art collection of the Swedish monarchy. Lent to the State Museum in 1887, it seems that its journey to New York in 2007 precipitated a determination that this item properly belongs to the Swedish State, not the Swedish monarchy. Currently the item is lent to the Danish state (while the Swedish state museum is renovated) to adorn the walls of Kronborg Castle in Helsingør, which is a prominent tourist site. These are the walls for which it, with nearly sixty further tapestries, was designed. It was woven in a tapestry workshop established in Kronborg Castle in the peaceful and prosperous times during which King Frederick II and his wife Sophie presided over the workings of Denmark's remarkable elected monarchy.

The baldachin culminates a series of twenty Old Testament tapestries, three of which depict Danish hunting scenes, and forty of which picture one hundred and eleven Danish monarchs, a series completed with a portrait of Frederick II and his heir Christian.

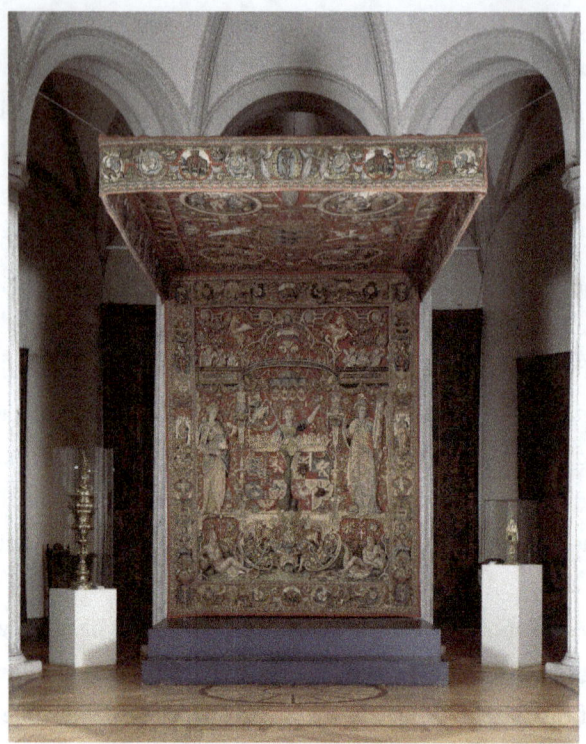

FIG. 7.3 A baldachin, or throne canopy, woven in a tapestry workshop established with Flemish craftsmen in Helsingør, Denmark, in the late sixteenth century[8]

Designed specifically for the proportions of the Great Hall [of Kronborg Castle], the tapestries covered all available wall space, even the sloping walls on either side of the twenty-three window bays. This was an inspirational moment of proto-Baroque theatre on the part of Frederick and his advisors: in a room encircled by more than a hundred previous rulers in tapestry, the centrepiece would be the actual ruler himself, living, breathing, and framed against a tapestry surround (Campbell 2007: 33).

While we applaud the enthusiasm of the curator – he is clearly enthralled by the tapestry – we think he has missed something here, and thus we contest his reading. For when we examine the image of the baldachin to discern what lies at its centre, what strikes us is that it is not actually the 'ruler himself, living, breathing and framed', but clearly the rulers themselves. While the monarchy lies near the centre it is not a single ruler nor is it a monarchy that lies at the centre. There are two armorials situated side by side but not directly engaged: Frederick, the King, and Sophie of Mecklenburg-Schwerin, a rich and learned woman who is, if we are to believe this baldachin, clearly a force to be reckoned with.

In continuing his iconography and contradicting his assertion that the monarchy lies at the baldachin's centre, the curator later notes that

> [i]n the centre, the allegorical figure of Justice, sword and scales in hand, is flanked by the coats of arms of Frederick II and of his wife Sophie of Mecklenburg-Schwerin. Knieper [the cartoon artist and master weaver] has wittily represented a canopy within this canopy, above Justice's head, its valence decorated with the device of an elephant repeated four times [two pairs facing each other], alluding to Frederick II's chivalric order of the elephant. To the left of the royal armorials stands Temperance; to the right, Fortitude (Campbell 2007: 39).

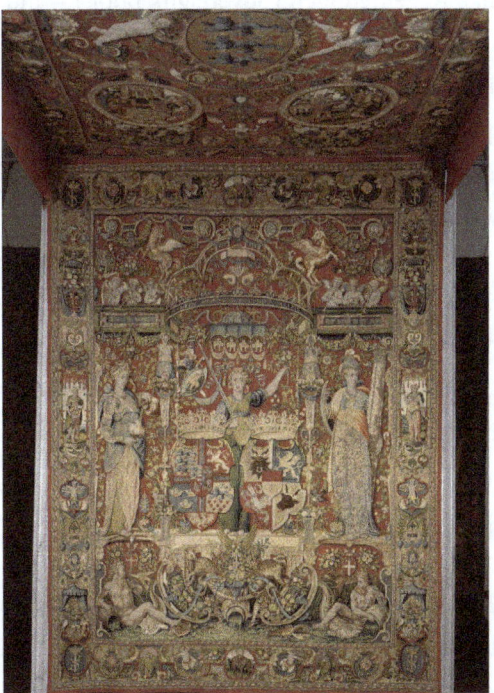

FIG. 7.4 Detail of the central panel of the baldachin[9]

The sumptuousness of the Helsingør-woven baldachin could rival that of any contemporary piece. The weaving contains so much gilt and silver-wrapped thread that it shimmers. The effect during candlelit court festivities and banquets would have been breathtaking. When the baldachin was in use with King Frederick and Queen Sophie seated beneath it, their subjects facing them would enjoy the full effect of the crowned armorials above their monarchs' heads.

We agree that it is the figure of Justice that lies at the centre of the baldachin, presumably claiming that justice lies at the centre of the polity, but what we notice is the tenseness of this figure. The curator-author-editor fails to make explicit something that seems to us highly significant. This is the tense ambiguity of the figure of Justice, in the one hand with scales held carefully in balance, and in the other, with sword ready to smite.

The baldachin features an arranged combination of generic icons – copied perhaps from baldachins previously designed and woven by Flemish weavers, and known to those master craftsmen employed in the Helsingør tapestry workshop, or from books like Regentenbuch (Sovereign's Book) – and icons specific to the two ruling houses of Denmark. The depictions on the tapestry build up in a highly symmetrical fashion from the tension-ridden figure of Justice. Justice both connects and separates the armorials. The cardinal virtues are equally tense with contradiction. Temperance, depicted in the act of pouring wine from a vessel into a bowl, is leaning backwards to balance herself as she does so. Fortitude is clutching the column of Samson while gazing sagaciously on the world, her virtue girded with helmet and shield. These virtues stand on the same level as Justice, attending the armorials. The tensions created by these contradictory figures travel to the four corners of the cloth seemingly held in check there by a crowned FS monograph, which most commentators agree signals Frederick and Sophie, as intertwined monarchs.

For anyone with even a passing familiarity with the history of the Danish monarchy, it is significant that ambiguity and ambivalence lies at the centre of this baldachin. Absolutism was not a feature of the Danish monarchy at the time this baldachin did its work in the Kronborg Castle banquet hall. An unambiguous absolute monarch was foisted on the kingdom in 1660 in a vainglorious move by the grandson of the pair, who would sit under the baldachin 'living, breathing and framed against a tapestry surround'. In 1660, in what was (and perhaps still is) seen by many Danes as Denmark's shame, it led Europe in instituting absolute monarchy, abandoning elective monarchy, thus disempowering nobles and those to whom they were in some degree accountable, and putting an end to the complex, emergent baroque polity that had come into being some thirty years previously.

In 1648 the aristocratic nobles had extracted high concessions in terms of ceding powers, in electing King Frederik III. Subsequently, riding on a wave of popular support arising from an interim victory in the war against Sweden (in the course of which the baldachin was lost to Sweden), the monarch intervened decisively in the force field between the Danish monarchy and the Danish aristocracy, abolishing by fiat the elected monarchy and the vision expressed so eloquently in the baldachin. A baroque sensibility was no longer salient in the Danish monarchical context and the baldachin became war booty, no doubt bundled up in a storeroom in some northern European fortress.

However, at the time the baldachin was woven to adorn the palace walls at Helsingør, Denmark had emerged from the Middle Ages with a thoroughly transformed aristocracy:

> An era of upheaval [...] characterized by religious-political crisis, existed until 1533. With Christian III's complete rule, the framing of the Lutheran-monarchical state began [...] Frederik II culturally reaped the fruits of the new age. Humanistic scholarship was consolidated; national self-assertion promoted the study of the kingdom's ancient history [...] Simultaneously Tycho Brahe engaged in both the conquest of the sky and the deciphering of the course of an individual's life as expressed in the planets (Jansen 1993: 91).

The baldachin was designed to perform within the tense shifting landscape of partnerships associated with an aristocracy vigorously reorganising itself as it emerged out of the crisis of the late medieval. There was a shift from 'vertical to horizontal social integration' (Christianson 1981: 292), with a better-off peasantry and a surge in the urban middle classes, and secular magnate families.

Denmark became one of the most advanced countries in Europe in terms of aristocratic development [...] Sixteenth century Denmark offers a prime example of a reconstructed early modern aristocracy in Scandinavia. Denmark thus offers [an example of] the rare phenomena [*sic*] of a Protestant country where the aristocracy was at its height during the sixteenth century, when a tremendous redistribution of power and landed wealth occurred in conjunction with the Reformation. In Denmark, the fruits of this redistribution came to be enjoyed by a wary but indomitable alliance of crown and noble magnates (Ibid: 293).

The baldachin was a device that performed in a force field – 'a wary but indomitable alliance of crown and noble magnates' (Christianson 1981: 293). Understanding its working as a diagram in association with texts, the speech, and bodily gesture of court events, we take the baldachin as displaying a baroque sensibility.

So what is a baroque sensibility, and how is it revealed in the baldachin? Imagining the baldachin in place in Kronborg at Helsingør in the second half of the sixteenth century during the various proceedings of the court of King Frederick and Queen Sophie, we see it as a diagram ambiguously and ambivalently spoken from and spoken to. In speaking to a vivid vision of a just polity, the diagram that is the baldachin equivocates over how that vision might be achieved. In speaking from the diagram that figures the baldachin's surface in proposing how a just society might be achieved, the figuration equivocates over what a just society is. Just as a pudding is proved in eating, a baroque diagram's felicity is proved in its ability to assist collective passage through complexity.

CONCLUSION

In juxtaposing the baldachin and the diagram of technological innovation, we name something that we feel characterises the different performances of the baldachin and the model as material semiotic devices that intervene in the 'happening of the real' (Lury and Wakeford 2012; Winthereik and Verran 2012).

With its single and contained set of specified relations the five-step innovation model performs by eschewing contradiction and equivocation. In contrast, the baldachin elaborately figures both equivocation and contradiction and non-equivocation and non-contraction (it equivocates about contradiction).

Picking up Netz' argument and making it our own, we identify diagrams as capable of effecting dual rhetorical shifts. Diagrams – graphics and their associated texts – effect possibilities of moving between speaking from, and speaking to, and equally open up (dramatic, shocking) possibilities for equivocating over contradiction. We propose the baldachin as offering a model of meaning-making with a baroque sensibility, seeing such sensibility as concerned with collective way-finding through complexity while also representing truthfully (and equivocating over what exactly is represented). Attending to innovation model and baldachin as diagrams shows how representations are never stale; they press upon others their presence as participating entities and offer pilotage to innovation collectives in the sense that they open up a space for equivocation over contradictions (see Schick and Winthereik 2013). Attending to the iconography of innovation as diagram opens up a space for asking the question: 'what are we doing here together? What kind of pilotage does this diagram offer and to whom?'

In baroque form we juxtapose an engineering object with an art object, attending to them both as diagrams. This is a way of abandoning the idea that these objects are essentially different. Ending the comedy that is our paper with ritual, we give the final word to the historian of art Henri Focillon, who in 1934 published 'Vie des forms', sixty years later translated as the English text 'The Life of Forms in Art':

> In the life of forms baroque is certainly the freest, the most emancipated [...] either abandon[ing] or denatur[ing] that principle of intimate propriety, an essential aspect of which is a careful respect for the limits of the frame. [Baroque forms] live with passionate intensity, a life that is entirely their own (Focillon 1992: 58).

NOTES

1 We use 'comedy' here in the technical sense of literary criticism (see Frye 1957: 163). The action begins in difference and obstruction, and as the text proceeds, some device precipitates a novel set of connections and associations. Often this is made obvious with ritual – for example, a wedding.

2 <http://www.danwec.com/en/about_danwec/about_danwec.htm> [accessed 30 October 2015]

3 For more information on the research project visit <http://www.alienenergy.dk> [accessed 30 October 2015]

4 The fieldwork spoken about in the text has been carried out in context of the Alien Energy collective research project. Laura Watts and Brit Ross Winthereik are co-investigators of the project. Whenever an 'I' figures in the text as part of excerpts from field visits, it refers to the second author. The field notes in the text function as portals aiming to transport readers back to times and places where the innovation diagram was presented. The photos displaying geographical locations and the baldachin have similar functions. In juxtaposing the devices as diagrams, two ethnographer-analysts in the flesh have been translated into ethnographer-analysts in the text.

5 Translation of the Danish text – Step 1: Applied science, and model testing in test pool. Step 2: Design optimisation and feasibility studies as well as supplementary model testing at a larger scale. Step 3: Development and testing of components and materials as well as small prototype tests. Step 4: Close to full-scale testing, e.g. at DanWEC in Hanstholm connected to the grid. Step 5: Full-scale commercialisation of wave-energy devices placed in offshore parks consisting of several units.

6 This diagram features in discussions as a follow-up to Fig. 7.1, adding to the sense of certainty and optimism evoked in imagining innovation as a single progression, but also precipitating disagreements over where exactly on the wave of progress any particular entrepreneurial effort is located, since when the two diagrams are taken together they seem to adjudicate funding possibilities and sources for a particular business.

7 This workshop was actually the result of importing a large team of Flemish weavers into Denmark and paying them to source and import all the materials and technology. The high quality of the tapestry is not a surprise; it was made in a Flemish weaving centre that happened to be located in Denmark.

8 The tapestry was woven during the reign of Frederik II King of Denmark and Norway, and Sophie of Mecklenburg-Schwerin, a German-speaking province of Denmark. It adorned the main banquet hall of Kronborg Castle during a period when Denmark's elected monarchy thrived, and Helsingør expanded as a commercial centre. The tapestries are part of the Swedish National Museum's collections.

9 Shows the two reigning families joined (and separated) by Justice – the core figure of the reign as affirmed by the presence of her personal baldachin in the image. She figures as

a taut balance between discourse (scales) and physical violence (sword), and each of those iconic features is itself a moment of balance, the scales ready to tip, the sword ready to sweep.

BIBLIOGRAPHY

Campbell, T. P., 'Throne Baldachin', in T. P. Campbell, ed., *Tapestry in the Baroque: Threads of Splendor* (New York: The Metropolitan Museum of Art, and New Haven, CT: Yale University Press, 2007), pp. 28–35

Cassin, B., 'Managing Evidence', in B. Latour, and P. Weibel, eds., *Making Things Public: Atmospheres of Democracy* (Karlsruhe: ZKM, and Cambridge, MA: MIT Press, 2005), pp. 858–64

Christianson, J. R., 'The Reconstruction of the Scandinavian Aristocracy, 1350–1660', *Scandinavian Studies*, 53 (1981), 289–301

European Commission, 'Contractual Public-private for Research and Innovation in the Manufacturing, Construction, Process Industry and Automotive Sectors', 2013 <http://ec.europa.eu/research/industrial_technologies/> [accessed 6 January 2015]

Hackett, E. J., 'The Vilnius Declaration', *Science, Technology, & Human Values*, 39.1 (2014), 3–5

Focillon, H., *The Life of Forms in Art* (New York: Zone Books, 1992)

Frye, N., *Anatomy of Criticism: Four Essays* (Princeton, NJ: Princeton University Press, 1957)

Green, J. F., *Rethinking Private Authority: Agents and Entrepreneurs in Global Environmental Governance* (Princeton, NJ: Princeton University Press, 2013)

Jansen, F. J. B., 'From the Reformation to the Baroque', in S. Hakon Rossel, ed., *A History of Danish Literature* (Lincoln: University of Nebraska Press, 1993), pp. 71–120

Latour, B., 'Review Essay: The Netz-Works of Greek Deduction', *Social Studies of Science*, 38 (2008), 441–459

Law, J., *After Method: Mess in Social Science Research* (London and New York: Routledge, 2004)

Lury, C., and N. Wakeford, eds, *Inventive Methods: The Happening of the Social* (London, Abingdon, and New York: Routledge, 2012)

Netz, R., *The Shaping of Deduction in Greek Mathematics: A Study in Cognitive History* (Cambridge: Cambridge University Press, 1999)

Stengers, I., *Power and Invention: Situating Science* (Minneapolis: University of Minnesota Press, 1997)

Schick, L., and B. R. Winthereik, 'Innovating Relations – Or why Smart Grid is not too Complex for the Public', *Science and Technology Studies*, 3 (2013), 82–102

Winthereik, B. R., and H. Verran, 'Ethnographic Stories as Generalizations that Intervene' *Science Studies*, 25.1 (2012), 37–51

8

LONDON STONE REDUX

Hugh Raffles

IT'S A WET NOVEMBER EVENING AND THE ONLY MOVIE THAT TEMPTS US IS Patrick Keiller's *London* at the NFT. We take a crowded tube to Embankment and with heads lowered against the sting of slanting rain, we brave the swaying footpath on the Jubilee Bridge, dark outlines hurrying over the darker river. When we reach the South Bank, the theatre, all drab concrete brutalism, is one with the movie – all unforgiving camera and mournful voiceover.[1]

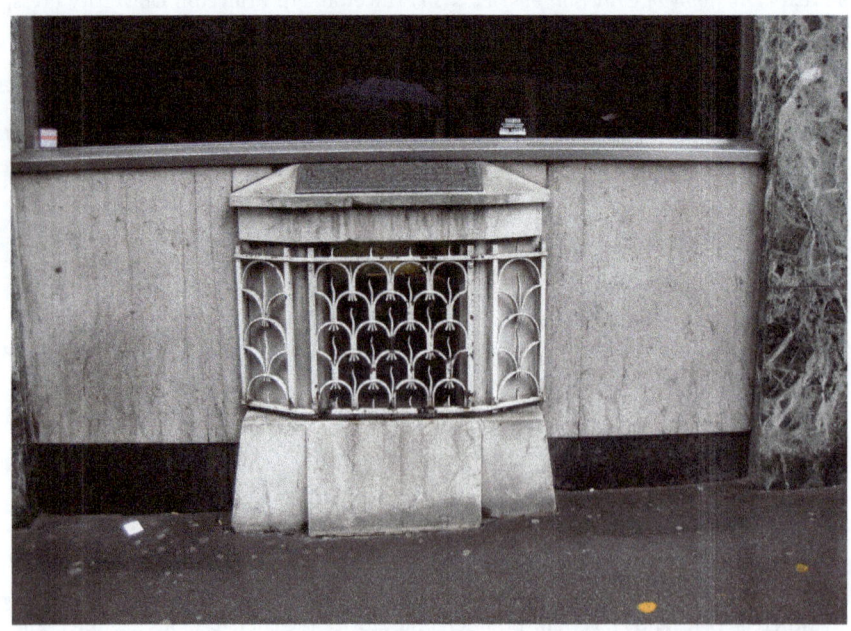

FIG. 8.1

A distanced view of a distant world – London 1992 – the interminable Thatcherite decline. Long, static takes of deserted streets and distracted pedestrians, neglected monuments and vacant office buildings, roadworks, traffic, swirling river water, and the two protagonists always off-camera: Robinson, the disenchanted academic type, and the anonymous Narrator with his doleful commentary; world-weary ex-lovers reconnecting on meandering walks through the dejected city. It takes forty-five minutes for Keiller to get them to 111 Cannon Street, an undistinguished 1960s office building. And, there, jutting out to the sidewalk in its glassed-in ironwork cage, is London Stone.

They stop and stare down. 'This', says Robinson,

> is the airborne vessel on which the magician Bladud flew to London, where he crashed on Ludgate Hill, the last stone of a circle that stood on the site of St. Paul's [...] This is the stone that Jack Cade, the Kentish rebel, struck with his staff when he took possession of the city.

The Narrator interjects that *he* thought the stone was a Roman milestone. But Robinson, absorbed, inspired, declares the route of the Number 15 bus – which runs along Cannon Street – to be a sacred route (Keiller 1994).

It's a wet November night, and when we wake up the next morning, rain still falls from a dark grey sky. We exit the Circle Line at Mansion House, unfurl our umbrellas, and locate the stone on a helpful map outside the station.

We take St. Swithin's Lane to Cannon Street – the heart of the City, London's most ancient quarter – and stare down at the yellow-grey stone in its glassed-in ironwork cage. Attached to the top is an embossed metal plaque that reads:

> This is a fragment of the original piece of limestone once securely fixed in the ground now fronting Cannon Street Station.

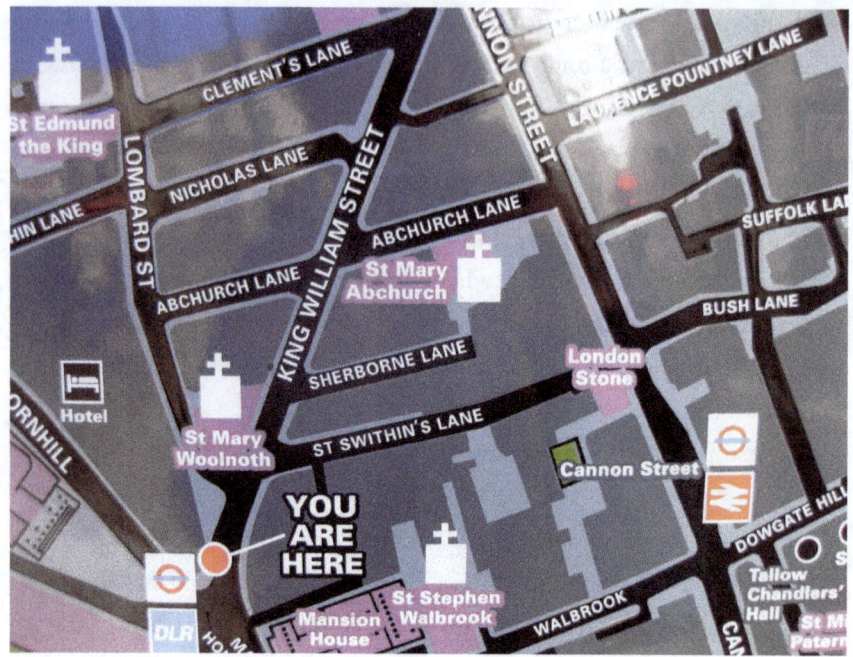

FIG. **8.2**

And:

> Removed in 1742 to the north side of the street, in 1798 it was built into the
> south wall of the Church of St. Swithun London Stone which stood here
> until demolished in 1962.

And:

> Its origin and purpose are unknown but in 1188 there was a reference to
> Henry, son of Eylwin of Londonstone, subsequently Lord Mayor of London.

Some dates, some history, a hint of mystery. A stone, a plaque, some insecure
facts. A few lines in a movie that don't make much sense. It's a familiar feeling:
we're being reeled in, wet fish on a line.

Reeled in, winched back to 1188 and just beyond, to the tenth century, when
London Stone stood in front of a large building more or less where Cannon
Street rail station is located today – a building archaeologists think was the palace

of the Roman governor. It was a prominent site and John Clark, a curator at the Museum of London, who has written with more care and erudition about this stone than anyone else, points out that placed here it was at the centre of the grid laid down by Alfred the Great when he rebuilt the city in the late 800s after it was sacked by Vikings (Clark 2010).[2]

St. Swithin's Church was constructed in the thirteenth century and London Stone stuck with it through good times and bad. The stone survived the Great Fire of 1666 that destroyed the church and most of the City, and when St. Swithin's was rebuilt, the stone, albeit 'much reduced', was protected inside a specially designed domed casing. When the church was bombed in the Blitz and finally taken down in 1962, the stone was mounted in the wall of the building that replaced it: 111 Cannon Street, then the headquarters of the Oversea-Chinese Banking Corporation (Clark 2010: 40–41). After that, in the early 2000s, the building's ground floor was occupied by a sporting goods store and, after that, by a WHSmith's.

London Stone is a block of oolitic limestone and if you're not sure what that is, the best place to look is in John McPhee's magisterial *Annals of the Former World*, where he describes oolites forming in warm lakes like underwater raindrops around tiny pieces of rock or seashell 'so tiny that in wave-tossed water they will stir up and move. They move, and settle, move, and settle', he writes, and they accumulate layer upon layer of calcium carbonate, 'building something like a pearl'. Sawn in half and viewed under a lens, you can see how they got their name: 'a stone egg, white and yolk – an oolite' (McPhee 2002: 55).

Oolites show up early in McPhee's sweeping account of North American geology. 'When a geologist finds oolites embedded in rock', he writes, his skin all puckered from bobbing on the surface of the Great Salt Lake in Utah, 'the Bahamas come to mind, and the Great Salt Lake, and, by inference, a shallow, lime-rich Cambrian sea' (Ibid.).

And, sure enough, one hundred and fifty million years ago, as the uncountable ooids were getting their start in the waning millennia of the late Jurassic, the patch of land that would be England was floating somewhere between where we now find Mallorca and Florida, growing its limestone in the shallows of a warm, salty sea. That was the dawn of the oolites. But it was only one of the British Isles' many transformative encounters with water. Three hundred and fifty million years earlier, England, Scotland, and Wales were split into two and separated by the width of the Iapetus Ocean – wider than the present-day North Atlantic – sheared along a line that would parallel the route of Hadrian's Wall, a line that continued through Ireland and whose sole visible marker today is a narrow white streak that runs diagonally up the cliff by the café parking lot at Niarbyl on the Isle of Man.[3]

That Iapetus Ocean – ancient ocean of the southern hemisphere – was slowly, very slowly, extremely slowly, maybe as slowly as three centimetres a year, slowly but inexorably closing and, in its closing, setting up the monumental collision of three seductively named microcontinents: Avalonia (which included most of what would become England, Wales, and Ireland), Baltica (from which Scandinavia and north-west Europe would emerge), and Laurentia (which would form Scotland, as well as north-east North America).

A truly complex collision; a series of staggered and uneven concussions of continents and terranes known as the Caledonian orogeny, one of the great mountain-building episodes that shaped the landscape of Britain as well as much of Scandinavia and Greenland; that pushed up a now-eroded Himalayan-scale range where England and Scotland met; that gave us the Appalachians and the Atlas mountains; that began around 485 million years ago and churned on in many episodes at many points of contact for close to 100 million years, a definitive feature of that open ocean of time that spans the Lower Ordovician, the Silurian, and Lower Devonian periods, and that ultimately led to the formation of the supercontinent Pangaea, from which the continents we know today would peel off to pursue their eternally entwined destinies.

The depth of deep time will 'awe the imagination to the point of paralysis', says McPhee. The numbers are meaningless and mind-numbing (McPhee 2002: 16). But the immensity of the near-infinite doesn't just awe us, it opens the past to geopoetry and invites geological imaginations to populate the inconceivable with elemental drama, with supercontinents unlike any we know today, with mountain ranges that rise from nowhere and erode into anonymous rubble, with temperatures fluctuating to their own scales, with immensely thick glaciers racing to blanket the land before sounding the retreat, and with oceans that open in their vastness and close so completely that only a thin white line in a cliff above a parking lot reminds us they were even there.[4]

We stand in the pouring rain at the entrance to 111 Cannon Street, wet fish, reeled in, cold and damp, stalking that storied stone in its glassed-in cage. And although the rain keeps falling from the lowering sky, when I press the buzzer the clouds part, the sun breaks through, time hiccups, and we're swimming with the ooids, and the Romans, and Avalonia, and the dismal Tories, and the magician Bladud, and WHSmith's, and Alfred the Great in the balmy saltwater shallows of the primeval Iapetus Ocean, and they're telling us that time doesn't really run in the tidy linear chronologies of historical and geological narration in which we've been dabbling so far but is probably more like the 'real duration' that the once-popular philosopher Henri Bergson described, a time of unreliable dimension, uncertain direction, and insecure features, the elastic ungraspable time that at times so estranges our senses, the time that Walter Benjamin was aiming to capture when he wrote (in characteristically gnomic prose) to his friend and fellow Jewish mystic Gershom Scholem in 1928 that the term 'origin' doesn't refer to 'the process of becoming of that [which has] emerged' – as in, say, 'the origin of life' – but to what 'emerges out of the process of becoming and disappearing' – more like 'the origin of species', a continuous making and unmaking, a circle of chewing-up and spitting-out that is also how the Earth's crust continually eats itself beneath the ocean, never growing old, and an insight that the famous critic illustrated with an image almost perfect for an oolitic lime-stone that's born in water and can't keep still, an image of the origin as standing 'in the flow of becoming as a whirlpool', an image I remembered as we walked back in the rain from seeing Keiller's gloomy *London* at the NFT, back over the flimsy Jubilee Bridge, back across the Strand and through the throngs of tipsy tourists in Leicester Square, back past the Italian cafés and the crowded gay bars on Old Compton Street and the shuttered market stalls on Brewer Street, back though Oxford Circus and along Regent Street, walking north as the sidewalks thinned and the streets emptied and we got chilled to the bone, the way you do at night in London in November, but still letting the buses pass unremarked, perhaps both feeling the connection with other nights many years before, these streets in this weather, still walking until we got home to the flat we'd rented for just a week (a strange feeling of homelessness in a city we'd once lived in so fully and for so long) on a quiet, somewhat desolate street, and, not wanting to sleep, too unsettled by too many histories and too much feeling, we opened a laptop and found ourselves watching the 1959 version of Jules Verne's *Journey to the Centre of the Earth* with James Mason as the curmudgeonly Edinburgh geologist who follows a mysterious stone to its origin on Snæfellsjökul, the mystical glaciated volcano in western Iceland, and from there through the strangeness of the Carlsbad Caverns to the lost city of Atlantis and the eruption of Stromboli in the Tyrrhenian Sea, a frantically inventive madcap movie that upended our melancholy – which, anyway, rarely lasted long – and reached a climax when the scientific adventurers finally located the centre of the Earth in the middle of an ancient ocean and discovered that the beginning and end of everything is a ravenous whirlpool (a whirlpool in the flow of becoming) into which their home-made craft is relentlessly, remorselessly, terrifyingly – though also exhilaratingly – drawn (Bergson 1911, 1913; Benjamin in Buck-Morss 1991: 9).

So we're still standing on Cannon Street – although now it's 1450 and everyone knows it as Candlewick Street – and we're outside St. Swithin's and here comes Jack Cade at the head of his peasant revolt against Henry VI, the last of the Lancastrian kings.

Henry's stock is low. He's on the point of losing France in the Hundred Years' War and he'll misplace his mind three years later. Finally, he'll lose his life in one of those murky backstairs corners of the Tower. Cade is a loyal but frustrated subject. Like so many before and since, he resorts to arms because he can't think how else to achieve a more just and better-managed country (Clark 2007, n.d.; Harvey 1991; Kaufman 2009). The rebels advance, the king retreats. But soon the battle swings in Henry's favour. His people negotiate a surrender that includes immunity for the insurgents and a hearing for their grievances. But it's a trick and Cade flees. The king's troops corner him near Lewes in Sussex and mortally wound him. They bring his corpse back to London, draw and quarter it, and send parts out for display in what, for now, remains Henry's kingdom.

Cade was an effective tactician. Early in the rising he defeated a royal army and assembled a huge force at Blackheath, then outside London. In July, he entered the capital. At Candlewick Street, he circled London Stone on horseback and struck it emphatically with his sword (some people still see the gash), declaring on pain of death that none of his men should rob or pillage the city. Then, off he cantered – frantic metallic clippety-clops on the cobblestones – to behead Henry's despised Lord Treasurer, James Fiennes, Lord Saye, whose taxes had done much to spur the revolt.

Cade was an effective tactician but an ineffective disciplinarian. And, soon, the occupied city was robbed and pillaged. Roused to action, the city's militia saw off the rebels in a bloody battle on London Bridge. Then surrender, deception, and death in Sussex.

It was a brief but traumatic rebellion, and Jack Cade and London Stone would form a lasting pair. The persisting image comes in Shakespeare's *Henry VI, Part 2*, a hundred and fifty years later. Cade is centre stage in act IV, seated astride the stone like Al Pacino in *Scarface*, 'lord of this city'. An erratic buffoon, a plundered city, a looted stone throne. On strides Dick the Butcher with his famous request: 'The first thing we do, let's kill all the lawyers'. And the rebel commander with his reply: 'Nay, that I mean to do'. No matter your view of lawyers, it's an unsympathetic portrait.[5]

Shakespeare's play premiered in 1594. Eight years earlier, William Camden published *Britannia*, the first detailed geographical survey of Britain and Ireland, and a catalogue of the antiquities he encountered on his travels. Camden was the most prominent of the early antiquarians, forerunners of today's archaeologists and empirical historians (Parry 2007; Sweet 2004; Vine 2010). They scoured the landscape of the British Isles, looking for ancient objects and monuments, seeking a newly historical sense of what it meant to be British; eager, as Camden wrote in the opening lines of *Britannia*, to 'restore antiquity to Britaine, and Britaine to his antiquity' (Camden 1806, I: 'To the Reader').

The antiquarians looked first to the much-admired classical civilisations of Greece and Rome. But, as they stumbled over barrows and cairns and dug up more and more pre-Roman artefacts, they were soon chasing a more stirring story, an earlier and more heroic Britain peopled by noble Celtic warrior tribes led by cultured Druid priests standing resolutely against Roman invaders. *Britannia*, a detailed gazetteer and a guidebook to national identity, quickly became an 'inspiration for all British antiquaries' (Sweet 2004: 57).

Every ancient object had something to say. London Stone was impressive. It was a 'great stone [...] fixed in the ground verie deepe, and bound with bars of iron' but it was also of unclear significance and unknown provenance; debtors had paid their creditors there and it was considered to mark the centre of the city (Stow 1908, I: 224). However, when Camden rode down Cannon Street his mind was on the old city walls and the role of the Emperor Constantine in their construction. The stone barely drew his attention. In passing, he suggested it was a Roman mile marker (Camden 1806, II: 80).

A hundred years later, William Stukeley – whose tales of Druid rituals started a craze for Stonehenge, Avebury, and the rest of Britain's ancient monuments – entered London from the east, passed the stone in his carriage and, as if stating an established fact, noted it was 'the *lapis milliaris* from which distances are reckon'd' (Stukeley 1724: 112). A hundred years after that, Charles Dickens described the stone as not only the centre of the capital but 'the theoretical centre of Roman England' (Dickens 1886: 210).

There were, though, other opinions. In 1720, John Strype, clergyman, historian, and follower of Stukeley, suggested that the stone could be of 'greater Antiquity than the Times of the Romans' – that it was, in fact, 'an Object or Monument of Heathen Worship', a view dramatised not long after by William Blake in his hallucinatory poems of the New Jerusalem rising from London's ruins that figured London Stone as Druid Albion's centre of Justice, a sacrificial altar for the execution of the Satanic Moral Law ('They groan'd aloud on London Stone') (Stow 1720, II: 194; Clark 2010: 43–44; Blake 1965: 171).[6] Soon after, Thomas Pennant, a Welsh zoologist and friend of Linnaeus who published popular, illustrated antiquarian *Tours* of the British Isles and amassed a notable collection of rocks, minerals, and fossils, wrote that the stone was 'preserved like the *Palladium* of the city', a comment mysterious today but not at all obscure then to men and women of classical education who knew the Palladium as the wooden

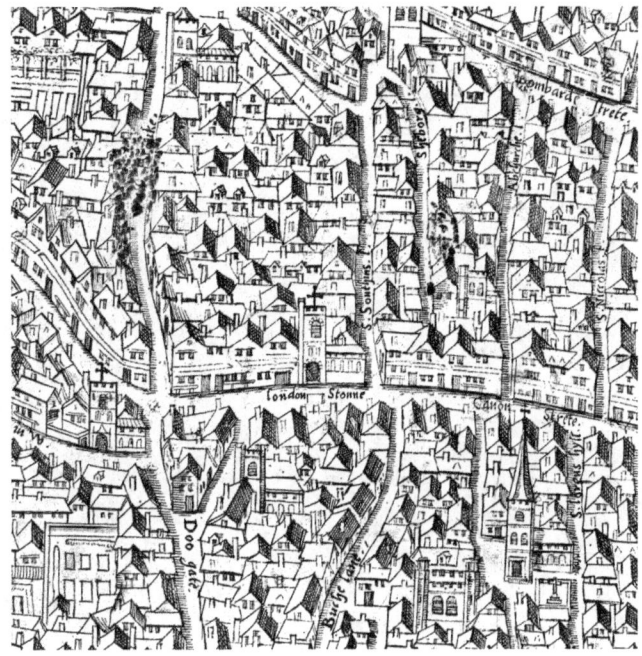

FIG. **8.3**

statue of Athena, goddess of wisdom, that kept Troy safe until Odysseus and Diomedes broke into the citadel and stole it, opening the city to the Greeks (Pennant 1813: 5).

And then, in 1862, Richard Williams, an Anglican minister and activist in the Celtic revival movement, elaborated Pennant's remark of seventy years earlier into an 'ancient saying' that he translated from the Welsh for the curious gentlemen readers of *Notes and Queries*: 'So long as the Stone of Brutus is safe, so long will London flourish' (Clark 2010: 45–53; Merrion 1862).[7] Williams, like all antiquarians, was not only familiar with the Palladium but also had read and debated Geoffrey of Monmouth's twelfth-century *History of the Kings of Britain*, so knew the story of London's founding as New Troy around 1100 BC by Brutus, the great-grandson of Aeneas, who sailed north from fallen Troy to slay the giants of Albion and establish Britain as his kingdom (Geoffrey of Monmouth 1977: 73–74).

John Clark thinks talk of Druids and Brutus is nonsense. He's in no doubt that the stone arrived in London with the Romans, hauled into the newly

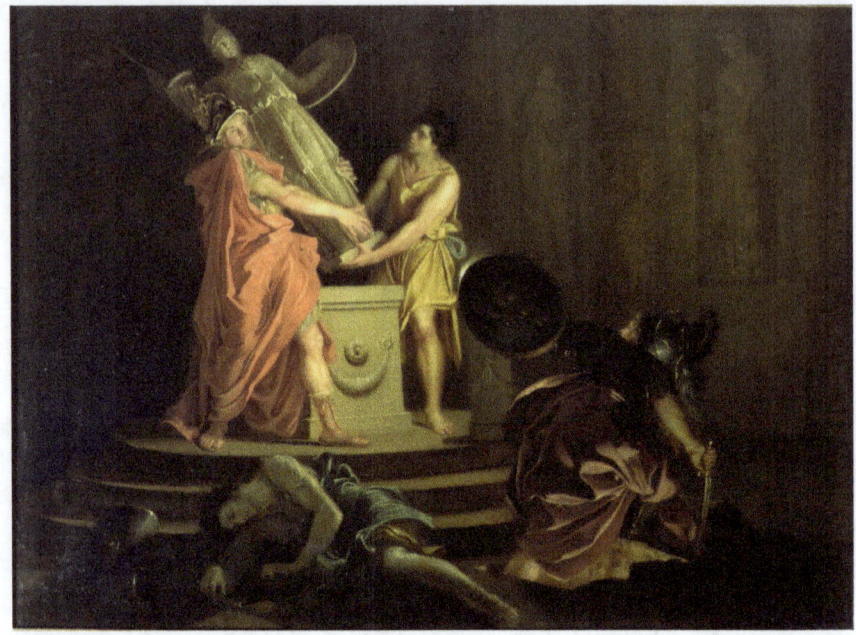

FIG. 8.4

founded settlement along with blocks of Portland Stone, Bath Stone, and the rest of the 150-million-year-old oolitic limestone from which the buildings and monuments of Londinium were raised, creamy-coloured limestone cut from quarries in Dorset, the Cotswolds, and other sites along the broad middle-Jurassic band that sweeps up in a north-easterly arc from England's south coast all the way to Yorkshire, a bed of limestone once topped with an ancient track beside which, in the first half of the first century AD, as the Romans consolidated their invasion, they built Fosse Way, the military border and supply route that ran 230 miles from Exeter to Lincoln, separating the conquered east from the recalcitrant Iron Age west.

But the Reverend Williams' London Stone arrived by a different and deeper route. His stone was the plinth of Athena's Palladium, a gift to Brutus from Aeneas after the fall of Troy, ferried proudly across the shiny Aegean Sea through the uncertainties of the Mediterranean and out over the dark depths of the Atlantic, blustering north to the uncivilised wildness of the British Isles and installed as the altar in the Temple of Diana that Brutus raised on the site of what is now St. Paul's Cathedral. It was on this stone that the ancient British monarchs swore their coronation oaths, and it was this same stone – the plinth taking on the powers of the statue it once bore – that cast its protective aura over the modern city from its berth in the wall of St. Swithin's. Antiquity to Britain and Britain to his antiquity. If Pennant and Williams hadn't come to this so late it would explain why Jack Cade stopped at Candlewick Street to proclaim his rule.

Because this is London Stone restored to the nation. More than a milestone, more than a sacrifice-stone in a Druid temple, more than a pillar in a stone circle, more than a Roman vanity, and more than just a forebear of the Stone of Scone, Scotland's Destiny Stone press-ganged into serving England's rulers. This is London Stone as the ur-stone that binds the nation to its long-discarded origins deep in the foundational moments of Western civilisation; binds the present to the time of heroes, gods, and giants; binds it fast to the prehistory of the nation, the originary nation that only yesterday rose up in the salty eddies of the Iapetus Ocean, that warm and shallow sea which disappeared so inexorably into the monumental mountain-building collision known as the Caledonian orogeny.

It's a cold and wet November morning and we're still sheltering in the entrance to 111 Cannon Street. It's raining heavily, but when I press the buzzer the clouds part and the sun breaks through. Waiting at the door, I remember a story from 2006 on the BBC website: 111 Cannon Street is scheduled for demolition and Chris Cheek, the manager of the first-floor sporting goods store, has braced himself between London Stone and a team of construction workers preparing to attack it with sledgehammers.

'Do you share the ancient belief that the stone really is London's Palladium and that the well-being of the city and its people depend on it?' the reporter asks. 'Yes, I do, really', Mr. Cheek replies. 'I'm not into hocus-pocus but there is something about this stone. For some reason it's been kept, there's something special about it' (Coughlan 2015).

We stand and shiver. It takes forever for someone to answer the door. The building is again undergoing redevelopment, and when we get inside we discover that the sports store is now the construction project-management room and

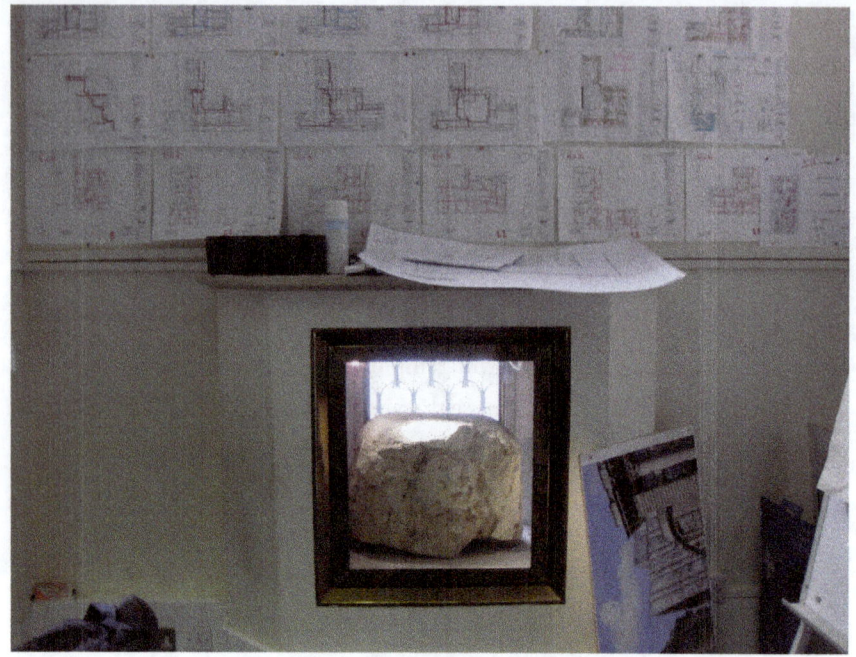

FIG. 8.5

that the stone is hidden behind a presentation easel and upstaged by architects' drawings, schedules, and floor plans. Outside, everyone hurries past without glancing at it, just as they do in Keiller's movie. But it's still there, surviving great fires, great wars, forgotten rebellions, public apathy, and official neglect, surviving even when it was in the way, persisting where so many other stones have failed.

But there's always room for doubt. John Aubrey, best remembered now for his tart sketches of contemporaries in *Brief Lives*, was also a pioneering antiquarian. In 1666, he toured a charred, still-smouldering London with his friend, the polymath experimenter Robert Hooke, recently and lucratively appointed as one of three surveyors organising the reconstruction of the ruined metropolis following the Great Fire. Among Aubrey's notes are some brief entries on London Stone. 'London Stone was not a *lapis milliaris* as supposed', he wrote. 'It was rooted a matter of ten foot deep [and it] was a kind of Obelisque [that] stands about the middle of London (i.e., between Ludgate and Aldgate). It was so fast set with Roman mortar that Mr. Hooke was [obliged] to get a Derbyshire miner to break it up, and he was 2 or 3 dayes before he could fetch up a little core. This was for the foundation of a Cellar. The stone remaynes still, but now *scarce* peeps his head above ground'. Moreover, 'the stone that stands there now', Aubrey continues, 'is only a mock-stone; [and] I have known one or two worn out in my time with carts' (Aubrey 1980: 508–09).

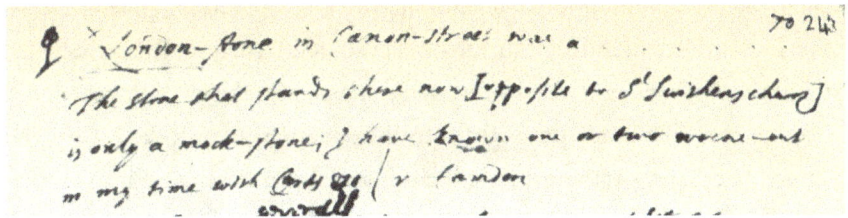

FIG. 8.6

I download Keiller's *London* and compulsively watch and rewatch the few seconds starring London Stone. I'm looking for something but not sure what.

The more time I spend with Robinson, the more I feel for the Narrator. Then I decide that, sour and misanthropic though they often are, these two enjoy each other. Under leaden skies and drizzling rain, they fit with London's mood, shuffling though the city, sifting the suburbs for their secrets, contemporary antiquarians tangling time at every turn. At first, I thought theirs was the kind of history that turns the present into a rubbish tip. Then I realise there are other ways of feeling this: for some people, these histories might one day send the rubbish tip up in flames.

Because they're not alone. London Stone sets off other anxious wanderers, scouring the metropolis, upturning paving-stones in search of buried power. 'The point about London Stone', writes the novelist Iain Sinclair, 'is that while everyone agrees it is significant, nobody knows why'. Blake in his glorious madness took the stone, he says, as a 'point from which to move the world'. Here's the revolutionary gesture: 'Break the glass, strike the stone. If it is to be treated as a trophy from a colonial war, encased like a fire extinguisher, it will demand justice' (Atkins and Sinclair 1999: 168).

You wonder what he knows. One man's hocus pocus is another's religion. One person's religion is another's occult paranoia.[8] Sinclair has a map in mind, a speculative pre-Christian geography of the London encountered by Brutus.

This is how E. O. Gordon, writing in 1914, saw the geometry of New Troy on the Thames, a symbological force field 'little less imposing than the London of today' (Gordon 2003: 8).

London was a ritual amphitheatre bounded by mounds and crowned by 'the mighty unhewn monoliths of the Druidic circle' that Gordon – like Camden, Williams, Robinson, and Sinclair, too – believed stood where St. Paul's Cathedral stands today. That circle was the fortified enclosure for the High Priest of New Troy, an area that maps perfectly onto the square mile of today's City, too perfectly perhaps, neatly mapping the transmutation of religion into money. Gordon's England looks like a grey version of Mexico, Christian conquerors raising flags on the ruins of indigenous temples, the faint pulse of pantheism beneath the steely wheels of capital. All these topological traces – a mound, a river, a stone – a national grid whose power is accessed now only by initiates through arcane books and obscure websites. Silenced, hidden, skewed, wounded, barely visible in its remains.

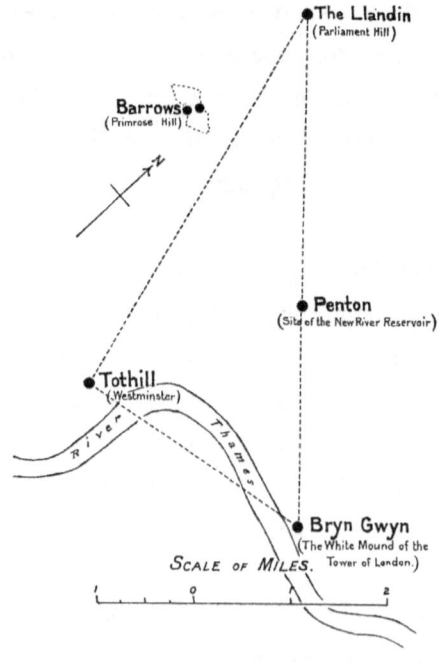

FIG. 8.7

The mighty circle is long gone, its absence marked only by London Stone, that 'single obeliscal pillar', as Gordon puts it, that 'index stone, preserved behind iron bars', constant as the eternal flame at Delphi (2003: 13).

'The new alignment hurts', writes Sinclair. 'It's part of a process whereby all the ritual markers of the original city have been shifted, not by much, by just enough to do damage; to call up petty whirlwinds, small vortices of bad faith' (Atkins and Sinclair 1999: 168).

NOTES

1 My thanks to John Law, Evelyn Ruppert, Annemarie Mol, and the other participants in the 'When Authorities Meet' workshop. An earlier, abbreviated version of this essay was published in *Cabinet* 53 (Spring 2014).

2 Clark also discusses the view of prominent late nineteenth-century British folklorists such as Laurence Gomme that London Stone was a 'fetish stone', the symbolic founding stone of the original settlement and the site at which the most important village rituals were performed. See also Clark (n.d.) for his most extended discussion.

3 There's much debate on the precise location of the suture. See, for example, Todd, Murphy, and Kennan (1991). A brief description of the complex features of the timing and nature of the closure of the Iapetus Ocean can be found in Barclay et al. (2005: 13–16).

4 'Geopoetry' is from Hess (1962).

5 The outline of Shakespeare's portrayal can be found in some of the contemporary chronicles discussed in Kaufman (2009). For a sharply contrasting view of Cade's organisational capacity and politics, see Bohna (2003).

6 For Blake, the Druids were the codifiers of custom into Law and punishment who tolled the death knell of the original Jerusalem and, therefore, as Beer (1969: 182) points out, London Stone was 'a true rock of anti-vision since it marked the point from which all distances were measured and was thus a point of reference for the world of abstract calculation'.

7 On the invented traditions of Welsh patriots in the period just prior to Williams' generation, see Morgan (1983).

8 The phrase is from Coverley (2006: 123).

BIBLIOGRAPHY

Atkins, M., and I. Sinclair, *Liquid City* (London: Reaktion Books, 1999)

Aubrey, J., *Monumenta Britannica, or, a Miscellany of British Antiquities: Parts One and Two*, J. Fowles, and R. Leggett, eds. (Sherborne: Dorset Publishing, 1980)

Barclay, W. J., et al., *The Old Red Sandstone of Great Britain*, Geological Conservation Review Series, No. 31 (Joint Nature Conservation Committee: Peterborough, 2005)

Beer, J. B., *Blake's Visionary Universe* (Manchester: University of Manchester Press, 1969)

Bergson, H., *Creative Evolution*, A. Mitchell, trans. (London: MacMillan, 1911)

—— *Time and Free Will: An Essay on the Immediate Data of Consciousness*, F. L. Pogson, trans. (London: George Allen, 1913)

Blake, W., 'Jerusalem: To the Jews', in D.V. Erdman, ed., *The Complete Poetry and Prose of William Blake* (Berkeley: University of California Press, 1965)

Bohna, M., 'Armed Force and Civic Legitimacy in Jack Cade's Revolt, 1450', *The English Historical Review*, 118 (2003), 563–582

Buck-Morss, S., *The Dialectics of Seeing: Walter Benjamin and the Arcades Project* (Cambridge, MA: MIT Press, 1991)

Camden, W., *Britannia; or, A Chorographical Description of the Flourishing Kingdoms of England, Scotland, and Ireland, and the Islands Adjacent; From the Earliest Antiquity, Translated from the Edition Published by the Author in 1607 by Edward Gough*. 4 vols. (London: J. Stockdale, 1806)

Clark, J., 'Jack Cade at London Stone', *Transactions of the London and Middlesex Archaeological Society*, 58 (2007), 169–89

—— 'London Stone – History and Myth', unpublished paper, n.d.

—— 'London Stone: Stone of Brutus or Fetish Stone – Making the Myth', *Folklore*, 121.1 (2010): 38–60

Coughlan, S., 'London's Heart of Stone', <http://news.bbc.co.uk/2/hi/uk_news/magazine/4997470.stm> [accessed 7 August 2015]

Coverley, M., *Psychogeography* (London: Pocket Essentials, 2006)

Dickens, C., *All the Year Round: A Weekly Journal* N.S., vol. 39 (London: Chapman & Hall, 1886)

Geoffrey of Monmouth, *The History of the Kings of Britain*, L. Thorpe, trans. (London: Penguin, 1977)

Gordon, E. O., *Prehistoric London: Its Mounds and Circles* (Muskogee, OK: Artisan Publishers, 2003)

Harvey, I. M. W., *Jack Cade's Rebellion of 1450* (Oxford: Clarendon Press, 1991)

Hess, H. H., 'The History of Ocean Basins', in A. E. J. Engels, H. L. James, and B. F. Leonards, eds., *Petrologic Studies: A Volume in Honor of A. F. Buddington* (Boulder, CO: Geological Society of America, 1962), 599–620

Kaufman, A. L., *The Historical Literature of the Jack Cade Rebellion* (London: Ashgate, 2009)

Keiller, P., *London* (London: BFI Films, 1994)

McPhee, J., *Annals of the Former World* (New York: FSG, 2002)

Merrion, M., [Richard Williams Morgan], 'Stonehenge', *Notes and Queries* 3rd series, 1 (1862), 3

Morgan, P., 'From a Death to a View: The Hunt for the Welsh Past in the Romantic Period', in E. Hobsbawn and T. Ranger, eds., *The Invention of Tradition* (Cambridge: Cambridge University Press, 1983), 43–100

Parry, G., *The Trophies of Time: English Antiquarians of the Seventeenth Century* (Oxford: Oxford University Press, 2007)

Pennant, T., *Some Account of London* (London: Printed for J. Faulder, 1813)

Stow, J., *A Survey of London*, C. Lethbridge, ed., 2 vols. (Oxford: Clarendon Press, 1908)

——— *A Survey of the Cities of London And Westminster: Containing the Original, Antiquity, Increase, Modern Estate and Government of Those Cities*, J. Strype, ed. (London: A. Churchill, J. Knapton, R. Knaplock, J. Walthoe, E. Horne, B. Tooke, D. Midwinter, B. Cowse, R. Robinson, and T. Ward, 1720)

Stukeley, W., *Itinerarium Curiosum. Or, An Account of the Antiquitys and Remarkable Curiositys in Nature or Art, Observ'd in Travels Thro' Great Brittan.* (London: printed for the author, 1724)

Sweet, R., *Antiquaries: The Discovery of the Past in Eighteenth-Century Britain* (London: Bloomsbury, 2004)

Todd, S. P., F. C. Murphy, and P. S. Kennan, 'On the Trace of the Iapetus Suture in Ireland and Britain', *Journal of the Geological Society*, 148.5 (1991), 869–880

Vine, A., *In Defiance of Time: Antiquarian Writing in Early Modern England* (Oxford: Oxford University Press, 2010)

9

CLAFOUTIS AS A COMPOSITE: ON HANGING TOGETHER FELICITOUSLY

Annemarie Mol

IN THE YEAR 2011, ON A RAINY DAY IN MAY, I HAPPENED TO MAKE A CLA-foutis. It turned out very well. As I was happily eating it, it dawned on me how I might tackle the question of *baroque coherence* that I was hoping to explore for the workshop that would lead to the present book.[1] This specific clafoutis, in all its modest glory, would allow me to address a few urgent so-called theoretical questions (questions that are not directly about the world, but about how to frame, articulate, and imagine the world) while avoiding abstraction. More particularly, by using clafoutis as a case I would be able to ground an exploration of *what it is to hang together* in empirical materials. Hence, these materials are granted a peculiar role in this text. While social scientists often announce that they will use this or that theory in order to talk about their materials, here I do the converse. I use clafoutis-materials to talk theory.[2] My hope is that these materials will give a new twist to theoretical questions about *what it is to hang together*. For issues to do with coherence have mostly been addressed with the icon of logical coherence in the background. In propositional logic coherence is marked by the absence of contradiction: if A happens to be true, then not-A cannot be true at the same time. One of them must be discarded in order to avoid incoherence. If a combination of propositions adds up to A, it cannot at the same time suggest not-A. Logical coherence is friction-free. As it is grounded in supposedly timeless abstractions, such as A and not-A, it is also enduring. It has a timeless soul. All of which makes it ill-suited for thinking about complex cases where tensions abound and transformations are ongoing, but where there is still a difference between 'hanging together' and 'falling apart'. Clafoutis is a case in point.

But what *is* clafoutis? The question 'what makes a clafoutis indeed "a clafoutis"' is crucially at stake in this text. Hence I will not provide you with a conclusive definition. However, to give you at least an indication, here is a recipe, one of many possible variants. Preheat an oven to 150°C. Mix flour, milk, eggs, and a pinch of salt into a smooth batter. Coat an oven dish with butter. Pour half of the batter into the dish and put it in the oven for five minutes. Take it out again and carefully add fruit with a pronounced taste. Cherries are ideal. Plums are good as well, but as these are slightly sour, you may want to add some sugar. Cover the fruit with the rest of the batter, and then you may sprinkle some sugar on top. Put the dish back in the oven. After around forty-five minutes your clafoutis is ready. It may be eaten hot, lukewarm, or cold.

A COMPOSITE

How does a clafoutis hang together? If you were to follow the recipe that I just provided, you would end up taking a dish out of the oven with an appearance of congealed solidity. There it is: a single, steaming tart and a single word – clafoutis – is enough to refer to it. But a little analysis quickly reveals that within this singularity a lot of realms, registers, regimes (what should we call them?) are being drawn together. A clafoutis is *composed* out of (let's call them) different worlds. Here, I will roughly unpack the composite.

A clafoutis, to start with, is made from ingredients. These have different provenances. Take the flour, a result of grinding wheat. If you were to make your clafoutis in the Netherlands (the geographical focal point of this text) your wheat would most likely come from France or Germany.[3] While this is not so far away, the wheat market reaches out a lot further. The price of wheat in Western Europe moves up and down as harvests in the US or China grow or fall in size.

Relevant as well is the extent to which wheat in Russia is plagued by stem rust in any given year. Recently this problem has grown due to the late sowing in response to the excessively warm weather due to climate change.[4] All of which is just a fraction of what may be said about the wheat. What about the milk? If you bought it in a local shop, it comes from a large number of cows. This may sound surprising, as any single clafoutis contains a lot less milk than the 25-litre daily yield of an average Dutch dairy cow. However, farmers pour the 'output' of their animals together, and then factories combine the milk from different farms. The eggs, in turn, bear a little stamp that states their provenance. Since 2012, EU law has stipulated that the chickens that lay these eggs should have a living space of at least 750 square centimetres, including a perch to sit on.[5] Allow me to leave out the salt.[6] More on the fruit below. You get the picture. A clafoutis includes a variety of ingredients that each have their own intricate history and specificity. Putting all these disparate ingredients together is a remarkable compositional achievement in and of itself. At the same time they all stem from what we may call an *agricultural* world. The first composite on my list.

Now for the second. A clafoutis may be composed out of ingredients, but ingredients alone are not enough to make a clafoutis. Its preparation also depends on techniques. Where do these techniques come from and how do they circulate? Cookbooks and recipe sites on the internet written in Dutch or in English tell us that the original recipes for clafoutis are French. If they give a regional specification, it is the Limousin. However, the recipe that my mother taught me comes from the Alsace. How French is that, or how long has it been French? In German this region is called Elzaß. Boundary contestations hide in many dishes.[7] And so, too, do diverse modes of boundary-making. During the very period that France was becoming a gastronomic nation, a country with a *cuisine*, Paris installed itself as the measure of everything French. This makes it doubtful whether in France a dish from the Limousin, let alone from the Alsace, might readily qualify as a part of *French* cuisine.[8] Other histories are at work as well. I was taught how to prepare a clafoutis by my mother, but she, in turn, learnt it from a cookbook. This might be glossed as a personal coincidence, but as with most personal coincidences, it is historically situated. In her generation (my mother was born in 1924) educated Dutch women (my mother studied geography in university) who were kept out of the labour market (with formal rules as well as the ethos of motherhood) invested their energy in such things as travelling to France (guided by the *Guide Michelin*) and using interesting cook books (her clafoutis came out of a widely applauded specimen written by the Dutch travel journalist and poet, Werumeus Buning).[9] Cooking techniques also tie up with histories of eating: as recipes lay out clafoutis as a dessert for four people or more, it indexes the family meal. Relevant as well are the availability of an oven and heat-resistant oven dishes. A fascinating curiosity at this point is the metal instrument that makes it possible to take the pits out of cherries (though Limousin recipes recommend that you leave them in for their entic-ing, bitter taste). Again there is no end to the details, but the point has been made. The techniques of making clafoutis brim with historical, geographical, and culinary specificities. How to put this well? Allow me to stretch the French term: a clafoutis is not just a part of, but also contains, a *cuisine.*

And then a clafoutis feeds. All along, clafoutis has most likely been pre-pared and eaten, among other things, for the nourishment it provides. These days such nourishment is more and more widely talked about in the language of nutritional science. As a response to the rising incidence of 'overweight' in the population, people in the Netherlands (and elsewhere) are encouraged to make 'rational and responsible choices' and to take full calculative control over what they eat.[10] As a part of this, all food packaging in Europe (and in many other places) is legally obliged to specify and quantify its contents in the terms of nutritional science. Thus, if you wished to do so, you could calculate how much energy and nutrients your clafoutis contains. Just add the numbers printed on the packages of flour, milk, sugar, and butter that you use, first the kilocalories (for the energy), and then the protein, carbohydrate, and fat content (for the nutrients). These are all specified per hundred grams, so take account of that. The eggs may pose a problem as their provenance stamp is not a full-blown label and they come in different sizes, but there are tables on the internet that allow you to make an informed guess. You may even put the fruit into the equation. But while public health advisors of various kinds may encourage you to engage in such calculative efforts, they cannot force you to do so. What is more, there are contrasting voices out there that warn you that maybe you shouldn't. For investing so much in accounting might well stop you from appreciating clafoutis' nourishing qualities with your senses. Maybe it is wiser to concentrate on feeling its capacity to feed in your grateful mouth and your satisfied stomach.[11]

Is your clafoutis finished? Sit down quietly with a bowl or a plate with a serving of this enticing dish in front of you. Do you prefer to eat it with a spoon or a fork? Take a bite. Allow yourself to be surprised by the crunchiness of the top layer, the crust. Beneath it you will find a softer layer of cooked batter, for which the English language has no separate word; it uses 'crust' again. Then, beneath that, the juicy layer of warm, enticing fruit. Textures and tastes vary. The crust is modest, the fruit, by contrast, comes out as strong (this is why, according to Werumeus Buning, clafoutis should not be made with, say, apples: their taste is not pronounced enough). Visually, too, the soft brown of the surface and the pale yellow of the layer beneath it nicely contrast with the vaguely red and purple (plums) or the stark, dark red (cherries) of the fruit. The smells waft around seductively. Though some recipes suggest eating it cold and others lukewarm, I recommend it hot. Once chewed and swallowed, clafoutis, neither too sweet nor too fat, tends to please the stomach. It is filling but light. All in all, clafoutis is gratifying – which is not say that it *contains* its gratifications within it, for these only *happen* if they are brought out. If indeed you sit down quietly. And attend to your food.[12]

Pleasure is a shared achievement that stretches out in time. Over the years clafoutis has been adapted to the tastes of those who eat it, while clafoutis-lovers (from the Limousin to way further north) have learnt to appreciate its specific textures, flavours, warmth, and stomach sensations. This is co-constitution.[13] The sensitivities of clafoutis aficionados are already there, absent/present within the dish that seeks to sensually appeal to them. A clafoutis, then, is not just multiple. It does not simply juxtapose elements drawn from the agricultural world (where it *is* a dish made of locally sourced ingredients); the world of cuisine (where it *is* a French dessert); the world of nutrition (where it *is* rich in carbohydrates and proteins); and the world of sensuousness (where it *is* tasty and gratifying).[14] A clafoutis is also *composed*. The diverse worlds in which it figures, are, in their turn, absent/present within it.[15] It is the character of this composition that forms the topic of the present text. How do the worlds of agriculture, cuisine, nutrition, and sensuousness hang together in a clafoutis? Not romantically. For romantic coherence inherits from logical coherence the dream of a friction-free whole. Since the way in which a clafoutis hangs together is full of tensions, it is baroque.[16] This is not to say that if one of its elements were called A, any of the others would be non-A. They would more likely fit other symbols (think of @ or आ). That is to say, the diverse worlds that a clafoutis contains do not jointly fit into a shared Euclidian space. The X- and Y-axes against which they might be projected, do not map onto each other. Accordingly, the qualifications relevant to them are not commensurable either. In an agricultural world clafoutis may be valued in terms of how and where its ingredients grow, how much they cost, and how perishable they are. In a world of cuisine what counts for more are such things as its layered flavours, the social ties it fosters, the memories it evokes, and its ease of preparation. In a world of nutrition, clafoutis may be valued by measuring the kilocalories, proteins, carbohydrates, and fats that it contains; or by appreciating its contribution to a person's overall sustenance. And in a sensual world, finally, a clafoutis is *good* if it looks good, smells good, tastes good, and gives the eater a wonderful stomach sensation.[17] All in all, it is quite an achievement that the fascinatingly heterogeneous worlds that meet in a clafoutis hang together in it in such a felicitous way.

COAGULATION

Baroque coherence emerges from the encounter of diverse worlds in a composite figure, such as a clafoutis. However, this does not mean that any encounter qualifies. If worlds come together the result may as well be incoherent. Which raises the question of what 'coherence' and 'incoherence' mean in a composite that brings together such diverse figures as an A, an @, and an आ. Here we may draw inspiration from baroque composites that so far have attracted more attention than clafoutis. Take a baroque church: putting saintly statues together erratically is not enough to evoke the almightiness of God. The gathering of images and imaginations in a church requires a certain strength to be evocative – it needs to be *just so*. Likewise with music: combining three or four random voices doesn't produce a polyphonic devotional song that calls up the Spirit and moves the listeners to tears. Rather this depends on a compelling harmonic interdependence as well as striking counterpoints between the different voices. Even camp only works its wonders if what it draws together titillates and transgresses in a tantalising combination.[18] What, in the light of these analogies, makes a clafoutis cohere in a felicitous manner, *just so*?

Interestingly, a clafoutis is not just a composite object in which worlds come together. It also offers a model for what it may be to coagulate.[19] For as you prepare a clafoutis, you mix flour, milk, eggs, and a pinch of salt and, once you have done this, it is impossible to retrieve the separate ingredients. A new entity, a batter, has come into being. Half of this batter goes into a dish made non-sticky with butter. When this dish is put into the oven for five minutes, the batter will solidify just a bit. If you carefully add the fruit, the second half of the batter will stay separate from the first. Thus, after the suggested forty-five minutes in the oven, the clafoutis that emerges has contrasting layers. A crusty upper layer, 'nicely browned with slightly puffed edges' as one of the recipes puts it, a soft doughy layer, a juicy fruit layer, and finally another soft doughy layer below.[20] At the sides, where the batter has mixed with the butter coating the dish, there is more crust. The fruit has gone mellow and its sweetness has become more pronounced (if you are using prunes, the additional sugar has melted and mixed with the fruit). Thus, the clafoutis that comes out of the oven has irreversibly coagulated while it is also full of contrasts within.

Its composite character seduces me into calling clafoutis' coherence 'baroque', even though whenever it may have been cooked up for the first time, clafoutis only spread through France in the course of the nineteenth century and the term first made its way into a dictionary in 1864.[21] But the contrasts within a clafoutis are striking enough: between the hard crust and the mellow fruit; between the modest dough and the stark fruity flavours. And then there are contrasts in time. In its classic versions, logical coherence was timeless: if A contradicts not-A, it does so forever. In a clafoutis, however, there is change. It goes into the oven in a viscous mode and by the time it comes out it has coagulated into a soft solidity. I would like to mobilise that as a model for how, historically, the worlds of agriculture, cuisine, nutrition, and sensuousness came to cohere in a clafoutis. This opens up various questions about the possible endings as well as the tenacity of this dish.

Without going into too much detail, it is relatively easy to see how (to start with these two) the worlds of *agriculture* and *cuisine* came together in clafoutis. For a long time, wheat was deemed to be the most attractive grain in France, but as it was difficult to grow it was expensive. More modest grains such as rye, buckwheat, and oats, were more widely eaten. In the nineteenth century, as growing techniques altered, wheat became affordable for all but the very poor. Hence the flour. Milk was widely available all over France (there were cows), while many people had their own chickens to provide them with eggs.[22] North of a line dividing Europe, the ideal fat was butter, derived from churning milk; south of that line, it was olive oil. The Alsace and even the Limousin are above the divide, which fits with butter being used to coat the pot. When fruit was ripe it was abundant, which made it worthwhile concocting a variety of ways of serving it. What is more, as clafoutis goes into the oven you may use preserves. Fresh fruit is not required. Ovens, in turn, were in widespread use in the nineteenth century in rural areas as well as in towns (although, again, not in the houses of the poor). All in all, then, the world of agriculture and that of cuisine were not randomly juxtaposed in a clafoutis, but formed a marvellous fit. In the twentieth century this coagulation endured while spreading out geographically. This is indexed by the situation of my mother, who, in the 1960s, living a few hundred kilometres north of France, had enough money and skills to run a comfortable household. The necessary ingredients were easy to procure. Fresh cherries were rare, but preserved cherries were for sale in the grocery store in town. In August we had plums from a tree in our garden. My mother would preserve these for the winter, first in large glass jars and later in a newly bought freezer. Our kitchen was equipped with an oven and our family would eat family meals every evening, usually with a dessert. In this way, time and again, clafoutis got made and remade.[23]

There are also stories to tell about the ways in which the *nutrition* world and that of a clafoutis' *sensuousness* readily join up, even if such stories are more speculative. It is likely that its specific combination of nutrients helps to ensure that after you have eaten clafoutis you feel satisfied and filled but not heavy. The dish is sweet thanks to the fruit and (if need be) the added sugar, but not oversweet – which is enticing for many French (and Dutch!) adults.[24] As a clafoutis contains more protein and less fat and sugar than most other tasty hot desserts that she served (apple crumble, rhubarb pie, hot semolina pudding, and so on), my mother used to stress that this dessert was *healthy*. And – let me add some cuisine to nutrition and sensuousness here – a clafoutis holds a certain appeal for those invested in vegetarian (though not vegan) cooking. With its flour, milk, and eggs it nicely complements, say, a lentil soup. Being a grain, the wheat of the tart works together with the pulses of the soup to assure an optimal uptake of their joint proteins, while the eggs add yet more proteins. And it is not just the nutrients that are complementary: so, too, are the tastes. I dished up quite a few lentil soup and clafoutis meals when I was a student and my friends and I would take turns cooking for each other. It fitted with our vegetarian habits and we also liked it. What more to desire than a protein-rich, soul-warming dish that pleases the stomach, is interesting to chew, smells delicious, and tastes good?

Thus, while the different worlds that come together in a clafoutis are made up of disparate entities, fit within different scales, and are open to diverse evaluations, they successfully came together here. Nothing highbrow is going on; we are not talking perfection and evoking the presence of God, or the Spirit may well be asking too much of a clafoutis. Nevertheless, it has a certain blessed propitiousness. As different worlds got together in this dish, they came to cohere there. They held each other in place since the way the elements emerged from one world happened to accord with the way they made up another. The story may be told starting out from the cuisine. Then it becomes a heroic tale about the recipe for clafoutis that helped to transform locally available agricultural products into a nourishing dish capable of satisfying the senses of those who learnt to like it. It is also possible to start with the agricultural world and its cultivars; with the task of cooking for and feeding a family or another gathering; or with the senses that readily learnt to appreciate this particular grain, milk, egg, and fruit combination (don't forget the pinch of salt). But whichever way the story is told, somehow the worlds of agriculture, cuisine, nourishment, and sensuousness came to coagulate strikingly well in clafoutis. Hence, clafoutis is not just an arbitrary juxtaposition, but a composite that hangs together in a felicitous way.[25]

DISINTEGRATION

But however impressive the coagulation of different worlds into a clafoutis may be, they do not necessarily continue to hold. After all, shifts and changes of just a single element may lead to the gradual or sudden disintegration of its composite. Since I am shamelessly engaging in self-ethnography all along, let me give you an example that involves my bowels. At some point, and without me immediately realising what was going on, wheat started to disagree with them. Meals including pasta, bread, or indeed clafoutis, would invariably be followed by bowel pain. But since the average Dutch person would include wheat in her meals almost every single day – I certainly did – it was not a disagreement I found out about right away. It took me a few years of bowel pain (and an undermining list of other symptoms) to realise what was going on. Or rather (after those years of dwindling health) it took me a few experimental days. During those days I avoided eating wheat altogether. All of a sudden my bowel pain stopped and it was a revelation. Since that time I have abstained from wheat.[26] *Exit clafoutis.*

Thus, the failure of just a single element may be enough for a composite to disintegrate. This tells us that there are many ways in which 'clafoutis' may fall apart.[27] Who still has a garden with cherry trees? If you don't, cooking with cherries may feel wasteful. They tend to be so expensive that it is enough of a treat to eat them fresh. You may eat a handful of cherries a few days in a row, or lots of cherries in a big splash, but either way none are left for baking tarts. The instrument to take out cherry pits is still sporadically available, but the patience to use it has suffered somewhere along the way. At the same time, having to deal with pits in your mouth does not quite fit with most present-day (French? Dutch?) standards of what it is to be delicious (in fact a similar sensitivity may have given rise to the invention of the de-pitting tool a long time ago. As Paris became the standard for French cuisine, the clafoutis might have disintegrated had it not been for this instrument, for, as a culinary historian put it, 'locals from the Limousin might accept the cherry pits in a *clafoutis*, but not Parisian travellers accustomed to a higher degree of culinary refinement').[28] And then there is the preparation. Who musters the energy necessary for preparing a clafoutis after a full day of paid work? My mother's investment in cooking was linked to the fact that she, like other women of her generation, in the Netherlands even more than in nearby countries, was forcibly kept out of the labour market. Married women had to care for their families. My mother went into local politics as well, but it was only in the seventies (when there was a severe shortage of geography teachers) that a local secondary school sought her out to do a paid job. From the *Guide Michelin* and her collection of cookbooks, she turned to geography teaching materials. That may seem an altogether different story – or another that is merely personal – but it was part of a wider trend, one that feeds fairly directly into the *conditions of possibility* of a clafoutis. That since the early seventies (tediously slowly at first, slightly faster in my generation, and almost completely only recently) women began to participate in the labour market while men, by and large, did not pick up equal amounts of care work at home, makes these conditions of possibility falter.[29]

Then there are other dissonances that may spoil clafoutis' tune, such as assaults from the nutrition sciences. Traditionally clafoutis was a dessert. But who needs nourishing desserts in an era when overweight has become an enemy of the state? My mother may have praised clafoutis' healthiness, but if you were to meticulously keep account of your 'food intake', you would be likely to find that you no longer need its calories at the end of your mostly sedentary day. Not after your so-called main course. The potential endurance of clafoutis, then, may depend on a shift in what is considered a proper meal, notably the willingness to let go of the main course.[30] Those who are prepared to skip this may combine soup and clafoutis, as I used to do as a lentil-soup-eating student. In my subsequent role as a mother in my turn, I tried something similar, using other soups. Though for a long time resistant to lentil soup, my children used to love clafoutis. This had to do with one of its particularly strong points: its sensuous qualities. Are these impressive enough to consolidate this dish? That remains to be seen. Maybe clafoutis' sensuous gratifications are not enough to withstand considerations to do with nutrition, that may, in their turn, shift from limiting calories to limiting carbohydrates (of which, thanks to the flour and the fruit, a clafoutis has ample quantities). Or maybe sensuousness will stay relevant, but food preferences will move in another direction (to spicy stuff? to rougher textures?). There are endless contingencies relevant to what will become of clafoutis in the future.

This is the lesson: baroque coherence may be temporary. It does not necessarily endure. Worlds that get together in felicitous ways in some site, for some while, may stop doing so elsewhere, or a little later. In this way clafoutis might easily disintegrate. How to think about this: what to mobilise as a model for disintegration? It is tempting to call upon the process of eating here. For once it has been chewed, a clafoutis is no longer the same. It has lost its enticing looks. In this state it may be swallowed and provide a satisfying sensation to the stomach. But digestive systems go on to break clafoutis down. Once it is absorbed, your clafoutis' nutrients still leave a trace: they may give you a sugar rush or a sense of vitality. But after a short while it is all over. Your clafoutis has thoroughly fallen apart. It has helped to build and fuel you. Mixed with other indigestible stuff, some of its remnants are propelled by your bowels to your colon, from where they are excreted as faeces.[31] Its molecules don't miraculously vanish, but even so your clafoutis is no more. Eating, then, provides a fascinating model of disintegration. But there is a problem with drawing upon this model here, in the context of the question of how worlds may first cohere, and then, after a while, stop cohering in a dish. Which is that eating is an irreversible process. The disintegration of what has been eaten cannot be undone. This is not necessarily the case for the disintegration of the composite figure of clafoutis.

TRANSFORMATION

Eating may not provide a suitable model for clafoutis' disintegration, but for an exploration of clafoutis' endurance, it is highly relevant that it is eaten. For the destruction implied in eating tells us that the *figure* of a clafoutis only endures if new clafoutises are prepared again and again at one site or another. Once they are cast in stone, churches (baroque or otherwise) tend to last for quite a while. They obviously need maintenance, lightning may strike, or a fire may consume them. But just a little travelling through France with a *Guide Michelin* reveals that many still stand strong long after God left them. Music is more ephemeral. If it is to last, a concerto or a sonata has to be performed over and over again. The event in which listeners attune to sounds is never quite the same. And what music is and does may alter over time. A polyphonic fugue that started out as a vehicle of Bach's humble devotion to God may change to become an expression of Bach's genius.[32]

What might all of this mean for clafoutis? No single clafoutis lasts. Like music, food has to be 'performed' afresh over and over again, but unlike music, food cannot be recorded. Listening to it variously in different ways is simply not possible. Instead, for clafoutis to endure its ingredients have to be grown, harvested, and traded from one year to another and someone has to put effort into preparing the dish in some well-equipped kitchen. So clafoutis is ephemeral. It substantiates for just a few hours (or, if there are leftovers, for at most a day or two) along with its material instantiation. And then it vanishes again. This implies that there are endless possibilities for the worlds that coagulate in a clafoutis to fail to come together ever again. But at the same time clafoutis is resilient, quite like churches and music. It just has different tactics.

This is where we hit upon issues to do with transformation. For while the resilience of a church is in the stubborn strength of its stones, that of clafoutis is in its remarkable adaptability. Early in this text I presented you with a clafoutis recipe. It is a simplified version of the recipe from my mother's cookbook. It lacks precise quantifiers. It doesn't even include the personally tailored kitchen measurements that tend to serve kitchens better than standard metrics. 'One manages to make one's clafoutis, this personal dish that one still calls clafoutis, by using so many spoonfuls of flour (that personal spoon, highly laden) and of sugar (the same spoon, but flattened off). And if the utensils disappear, the conversion of the personal unities to abstract unities is not always easy'.[33]

Clafoutis, like many other dishes, gets adapted as it gets made. It comes to fit local idiosyncrasies, household tools, and eating habits. Its ingredients are not necessarily quantified in abstract units that easily transport between sites. But all this intractable variability does not prevent anyone from 'still calling their dish clafoutis'. This surprised me as a child. I remember the day that I stayed over at a friend's house. In the afternoon, while drinking our lemonade, we were presented with what *his* mother called clafoutis. But it was far flatter than my mother's, its texture was smoother, and its taste sweeter. How could such a different dish still bear the same name?

Clafoutis comes in varieties. Cooks freely tinker with it, and written recipes are diverse, too. Leaf through a few cookbooks, or look up 'clafoutis' on the internet, and you will be faced with endless variations.[34] Some recipes suggest adding ground almonds, others crushed vanilla, yet others cherry liqueur. Some want you to use sugar in the batter (I found an *English* website saying that this is what the *French* do). Some turn up the oven and reduce the cooking time. And there are even recipes for savoury dishes to be served as a main course that are still called 'clafoutis' (i.e. 'Clafoutis with red bell pepper and goat cheese').[35] What all these recipes have in common is that they mix together flour, eggs, milk, and a pinch of salt. Are these ingredients, then, the defining characteristic of the dish? Do they index what has to be included for a clafoutis to cohere as 'a clafoutis' and not some other dish? The answer is: no.

It is at this point that I would like to explain how in May 2011, having abstained from wheat for almost a decade, I still ate a clafoutis. It was the result of an experiment. Home alone and seeking to eat something that would suit me, I improvised. I made a batter that contained milk and eggs, but instead of wheat flour I used fonio flour. Fonio is not a grain that is readily grown in France or Germany. Instead, fonio – 'the most tasty of all grains'[36] – originates in West Africa. Mine was imported from Burkina Faso. Since fonio requires a lot of labour it fell out of fashion in the course of the twentieth century. However, early in the twenty-first century, French aid projects began supporting farmers to grow fonio again because it contains more protein and fibre than wheat and withstands drought a lot better. They thought that besides being good local food, it might also be a good cash crop for export, as it is gluten free. Hopes were high that the likes of me would be pleased with it. So I used fonio, along with the milk, eggs, and pinch of salt. What prompted my experiment was that I had rhubarb that urgently needed to be eaten before it would rot. I heated the rhubarb, and to spice it up and counter its sour taste I added some ginger and syrup from a jar of ginger in syrup. To make my dish non-sticky I used olive oil. So all in all, it was only the eggs, the milk, and the salt that came down from the clafoutis my mother had taught me to make forty years before. And still somehow my dish cohered in a felicitous way.[37] *This was it.* As I ate the gratifying dish I joyfully realised that I was eating clafoutis.

While there are many ways for clafoutis to disintegrate, then, there are also many ways for it to endure – and here endurance does not necessarily mean staying the same. A certain coherence may re-emerge in a quite different composite. Along with the Alsace, suddenly Burkina Faso finds itself absent/present in my dish. In this way, while eating, I do not just relate to French nation-building within Europe, but also to French colonial history. At the same time, using fonio engenders the ambivalences that come with eating food that has been grown in an African country for the European market. On the package and their website, the aid organisation suggests that the fonio-growing farmers are pleased that my money allows them to earn a living. But then again, the nutrients from Burkina Faso's soil that I ingest will *not* feed someone living there.[38] The rhubarb comes from a Dutch organic farm that, while not able to save the world, still offers some hope. It combines so well with the Chinese ginger in its sugary syrup that they jointly outdid prunes (though not cherries: that is a leap). My experimental clafoutis was small, made just for me. This might well index the crisis of the family meal or even the collective meal. Together all these variations result, or so it might seem, in a quite different composite. Not even its taste safeguarded the category: this particular clafoutis tasted quite unlike any other I had eaten before. But still, somehow, it was a clafoutis. Was this the case just for me, given my particular layered history with this dish? I don't know. Had I been able to share it, my table companions, or at least some of them, might have agreed. But I could never have convinced them with words. And while writing, I likewise fail to find the words that might express what made clafoutis' soul so obviously present in my food. Even so, I am sure that out of the somewhat erratic ingredients that I used, I had made a clafoutis. *This was it.* What endured in my dish – or rather what re-emerged in it – was a striking *just so.* A remarkable composite with an inarticulable but unmistakably baroque coherence.[39]

CONCLUSION

Like other cases, that of clafoutis is a tale in its own right. But at the same time it is possible to draw out some of the lessons about *coherence* that it provides and articulate these in the form of theory. That is to say, it is possible to partially disentangle lessons from the specificities of this case and articulate these in a way that might inspire analysis in other cases – pertinent to other sites and situations. These will come with their own specificities. The lessons they generate are likely to fit partially with what we learnt from clafoutis but will also, in turn, add to, shift, or even radically transform our collective understanding of what it is to cohere. As we work in this way, by unravelling specific cases, disentangling lessons, and moving on to further cases, *theory* provides neither an overview, nor a fixed set of solid handholds. Instead, it is a repository of sensibilities, a lexicon of verbal tools, a repertoire that allows the articulation of varied concerns and gets enriched in unfolding conversations. As it happens (but this is no coincidence), the implication is that the coherence of the *theory* emerging in this way is actually quite like that of *clafoutis.*

What kind of coherence is this? Classic propositional logic worked with entities that had the potential to contradict each other, as they met on a level plane. They were homogeneous: A versus not-A. The entities that hang together in a baroque ensemble are different. They do not necessarily fit in the same lexicon or sign system at all. I suggested as an analogue the way A relates to @ and आ. And then I translated this analogue into clafoutis-terms: this dish contains elements pertaining to worlds as diverse as agriculture, cuisine, nutrition, and sensuousness. In a coherent composite such worlds are not juxtaposed in a random way, but hang together. For instance, as clafoutis got concocted, an emerging cuisine drew on available ingredients to cook up a dish that established itself as being both nourishing and tasty. An achievement indeed. At the same time, tensions loom. Cherry pits may give clafoutis an enticingly bitter taste, but outside the Limousin people may dislike having to deal with pits in their mouth. Clafoutis may be nutritious, but in contexts where overeating becomes a problem this strength may turn into a weakness. And so on. A composite that hangs together in a baroque way does not have an eternal soul; its soul dies along with the mortal body that it inspires. There are ever so many elements implied in it and a change in just about any of these may be enough for the assemblage to collapse. Calorie-counting, wheat allergies, cherries becoming expensive, women working in paid jobs while men dread the kitchen: all these contingencies and many more may lead on to clafoutis' demise.

However, while the baroque heterogeneity of a clafoutis makes its coherence precarious, it also makes it robust. For if there is no obligatory passage point, if no single element is essential, there are many possibilities for modulation. Cherries may be pitted, prunes may be appreciated, fonio may replace wheat. Overfeeding may be avoided by leaving out the so-called 'main dish' from a meal, or by transforming clafoutis itself from a dessert into a main dish. And so on. But that all but endless adaptations are possible does not mean that anything goes. And here we come to the core of baroque coherence. This core is a speechless moment. A mysterious revelation. *This is it*. Churches may evoke the presence of God, but may also fail to do so. Music may move listeners to tears, or rather leave them cold. Analogously, clafoutis, too, may either be a gratifying dish or fall apart. Whatever it is that makes the difference between a random juxtaposition and a felicitous composite, I cannot put into words. This may be *my* failure, but articulating the mystery of baroque coherence may as well be too much to ask of *words*.[40] For words may do a lot: they may describe a situation, express a concern, call up a memory, convey an order, encourage a sensation, seduce an acquaintance, substitute for a sigh, and so on – but at some point they hit their limits. Here is one such point. My clafoutis was soothingly warm, surprisingly tasty, pleasantly textured, and caringly filling. But that it was a *true clafoutis* depends on more than these qualities alone. It eludes articulation. It was *just so*.

NOTES

1 For their role in the substantiation of this text, I would like to thank the organisers and participants of a 2011 CRESC workshop in Manchester on the empirical baroque. More particularly I would like to thank John Law, whose intellectual inspiration is easy to trace in this text, and Mattijs van de Port for his lessons about *the baroque*. In addition, I thank Marilyn Strathern for her interest and comments and Mieke Aerts for her enduring support. Thanks as well to the European Research Council for its Advanced Grant AdG09 Nr. 249397 that allows me to study 'The Eating Body in Western Practice and Theory' with a spirited research team. Thanks to the team (including, if not all at the same time): Emily Yates-Doerr, Sebastian Abrahamsson, Anna Mann, Filippo Bertoni, Rebeca Ibáñez, Michalis Kontopodis, Cristobal Bonelli, Else Vogel, Tjitske Holtrop, Hasan Ashraf, and Carolina Dominguez. Thanks as well to Jan Mol, my father. After I told him that I was writing about clafoutis (a dish he too has fond memories of) he sent me helpful internet links to the provenance of the recipe and the word. My mother I can no longer thank: she died a few years ago. But if this text were an ode, it would be an ode to her.

2 The *empirical philosophy* that I engage in here finds among its ancestors Foucault (who, for example, theorised power by comparing kings with therapists), Deleuze and Guattari (who drew entangled rhizomes into theory to counter unidirectional roots), and Serres (who, for example, modelled relations on cloth, clouds, rivers, and other 'things' that are *not* solid boxes). See respectively Foucault (1975), Deleuze and Guattari (1980), and Serres (1979).

3 This geographical localisation of the ingredients fits with the investment in *what* is being eaten. For the argument that this is a Euro-American preoccupation see Strathern (2012), who argues that in Melanesia the question is rather *who* feeds whom.

4 These details come from a website written for investors concerned with the price of wheat: <http://www.debeurs.nl/debeurs/discussies/onderwerp.aspx?Id=1249924#lastpost> [accessed May 2011].

5 Obviously there is a lot more to say, e.g. about the quest for better living conditions for chickens; about salmonella harboured in eggs; or about infections of chicken with 'bird flu'; see for instance Hinchliffe et al. (2013). The geographic tropes articulated there resonate with those that I try to work with in the present text.

6 Even though salt is utterly fascinating; see Kurlansky (2002).

7 Annelies Moors brought to my attention the case of falafel, that is famously claimed as a national dish by both Palestinians and Israelis; see Raviv (2003).

8 See for the emergence of French *cuisine* Parkhurst Ferguson (2000).

9 See Werumeus Buning (1939), which was reprinted for decades. Its title translates into English as *100 Adventures with a Ladle*. This beautifully indexes what kinds of adventures its users best aim for in life. The author mobilised his impressive writing skills to make

these adventures sound thrilling and full of wonders.

10 The persistent use of the term 'choice' in (Dutch) health advice that at the same time tells you what you *should* do, is striking. It fits with the general overinvestment in 'choice' that I tried to counter in Mol (2008).

11 For an analysis of Dutch dieting advice see Mol (2013); for alternatives that encourage food pleasures, Vogel and Mol 2014; and for the idea that tasting may stretch out from fingers to the sensations in one's stomach, Mann et al. (2011). Counting nutrients, meanwhile, is not only done in the context of watching one's weight. All kinds of specific health problems come with their own calculative repertoires (e.g. people with diabetes may learn to monitor their carbohydrate balance; people with kidney problems may variously keep track of their protein and mineral intake). But that is another story.

12 As Teil and Hennion (2004) tell us, taste is neither in the food nor in the person who eats it. Instead, it is a performance: tasting has to be achieved again and again. This achievement depends on the tasters' investment, but also on the contexts in which they taste. For the latter, see Mann (2015).

13 A lot of writing effort has been spent on moving beyond the liberal fantasy that entities are first given and then relate, so as to bring out instead how entities make each other be. This was one of the points of early actor-network theory that took De Saussure's model of the ways in which words inform each other and transpose it to things (see Akrich (1993), and Mol (2010)). There are various other models of co-constitution around: for example, Darwinian ones of how species make each other be (see Pollan 2001 for the great example of how apples seduced humans into giving them their current shape). The present article participates in outlining the relational constituting of a heterogeneous 'composite' out of varied *kinds* of elements.

14 Multiplicity is not plurality since it tends to come with intricate interdependencies between the varied versions of entities; see for this Mol (2002), Moreira (2006), and Akrich and Pasveer (2000).

15 Those familiar with *Aircraft Stories* will have noticed the striking similarity between the way in which I analyse my clafoutis here and the way John Law, in the chapter 'Hidden Heterogeneities' of that book, unpacks a formula for the form and the size of the wings of a war plane, the TSR2 (Law 2002). This is how theory, while never abstracted, may yet travel between different cases.

16 Here I draw inspiration from the contrast between romantic and baroque combinatory logics as presented in Kwa (2002).

17 For a more extensive analysis of the way foods may be qualified with the case of 'good tomatoes', see Heuts and Mol (2013).

18 For baroque churches, see the introduction to this book; for music, see Hennion (2015); and for an analysis of camp as baroque, see Van de Port (2011). Once the present text was all but finished, I learnt that the notion of 'baroque food' has been used in a quite different way by Michel Onfray for chocolate, an alleged stimulant and aphrodisiac. See Onfray (1995).

19 What I need here is a term for getting to hang together irreversibly. There is a Dutch word, *stollen*, that I would prefer to use. It translates as *solidify*, or *coagulate*. In English *coagulation* tends to be used for the way proteins come to hang together as they are cooled (blood) or heated (eggs). Even if a clafoutis contains no blood and is composed out of more than eggs alone, I venture to use this term as it better indexes transformation than the alternative 'solidify'. Verran (2009) uses the term 'clotting' for the way entities assemble together out of heterogeneous elements. But this evokes blood even more directly and hence does not quite fit with the case of clafoutis.

20 <http://www.joyofbaking.com/breakfast/CherryClafoutis.html> [accessed November 2013]

21 <http://fr.wikipedia.org/wiki/Clafoutis#mw-head> [accessed November 2013]

22 The story of milk differs even between adjacent countries. For example, in France in the twentieth century, people got used to sterilised milk, while in the Netherlands and the UK the investment is in fresh milk. It would be worthwhile to try to write milk's comparative history, but see for France: Vatin (1990), for Britain: Atkins (2012), and for the fascinating travels of milk to India and China (where most adults cannot digest it): Wiley (2011).

23 There is a lot of food literature that relates how local ingredients and local cuisines make (or used to make) each other be. For a good argument against 'naturalising' the first while 'culturalising' the latter, see Yates-Doerr (2015), which asks whether meat comes from animals, and Yates-Doerr and Mol (2012), which makes a contrast between versions of meat.

24 What is enticing to whom obviously differs. The question of how to specify such differences is one of the contentious issues in the interdisciplinary field of food studies. Is it bodily needs, bodily sensitivities, cultural priming, cultural pride, another 'variable', or any combination of these that goes into *taste preferences*? Overall, the ideal is one of addition (see Wilk (2012)). The holism implied in that ideal is, in terms of the present text, romantic in kind. This raises the question of what baroque explorations of eating practices would bring to bear, a question that the present text does not answer but helps to open up.

25 As my investment is in the *form* of clafoutis' baroque coherence, I have not even begun to write a proper history of exactly how and why clafoutis coagulated and travelled. This would be a daunting task. It is no accident that many compelling histories have been written of individual foodstuffs (to give just a few good examples: sugar (Minz 1986); the potato (Zuckerman 1998); corn/maize (McCann 2005), but hardly any of composed dishes). As De Certeau, Giard, and Mayol put it, '[e]very alimentary custom makes up a minuscule crossroad of histories' (1998: 171). Hence, to unravel an 'alimentary custom' requires an exploration of all the histories that meet within it. For a widely cast and still fascinating history, not of a single dish but of 'food', see Jones (2007).

26 This happened in the early 2000s. Interestingly, wheat aversions have grown impressively since that time (even if, for instance, in the Netherlands a lot more slowly than in a hotspot like Seattle). It is quite puzzling what is going on with this grain that a few decades ago did not seem to pose any problems, except for people with a deviant gene and the concomitant diagnosis of coeliac disease. Quite a few commentators suspect a fad. See Raffaetà (2011) for an analysis that proposes that people 'claiming' to be sensitive to gluten engage in 'medicalisation from below'. The generalised critical term 'medicalisation' was problematic when applied to professionals to begin with, but when shifted to 'ordinary people' it becomes strangely moralising. My own and other people's (literal) *gut feelings* deserve a more subtle and complex analysis.

27 This resonates with the stories that Madeleine Akrich (1993) told a long time ago about technologies that stop working because a single element goes missing or falls apart. See also the wonderful exploration of the array of explanations for why the transport system *Aramis* failed in Latour (1996).

28 This quote stems from an article that wonders whether Paris is (a part of?) France. Or not. See Parkhurst Ferguson (2000: 1061).

29 This is obviously a simplified abbreviation of the many complexities involved. For an analysis of one of these, notably the gendering of using ovens, see Silva (2000). And I won't even start on the way clafoutis is affected by postmodern family life, restaurant eating (clafoutis may be on their menu), and so on.

30 Mary Douglas' family, or so she noted, was not prepared to settle for soup and pudding. It became the starting point for her famous deciphering of a *meal*; see Douglas (1972).

31 Social science work on defecation and faeces is relatively sparse. But for further examples see van der Geest (2007); Abrahamsson (2014).

32 These insights I borrow from Antoine Hennion's long-term investigations into the ways bodies/people learn to be affected. See Hennion (2007), and Hennion (this volume).

33 This is a quote from one of the rare articles that I found when putting Google Scholar to work on 'clafoutis'. See Weber (1996: 13), my translation.

34 This fluid adaptability ties up with that other of other figures, from anaemia (Mol and Law 1994) and the water pump (De Laet and Mol 2000) through to a German ambulance that became a collective taxi in Ghana (Beisel and Scheider 2012). However, the links between clafoutis versions are not all fluid in kind; sometimes they resemble more what Strathern (2004) called *partial connections.*

35 Not everyone so forgivingly allows for transformations! On the French Wikipedia page on *clafoutis* I learn that even substituting cherries with plums is, for those who are serious about this, enough to drop the name. With plums the dish is to be called *flaugnarde*. See <http://fr.wikipedia.org/wiki/Clafoutis#mw-head> [accessed November 2013]

36 This is a translated quote from the site: <http://www.fonio.nl/index.php> [accessed May 2011; no longer accessible in November 2013]. For an English language site see: <http://www.agriculturalproductsindia.com/cereals-pulses/cereals-fonio.html> [accessed November 2013]. Fonio is also sold in the kernel, to use in a way one might use rice or quinoa for a 'main dish'.

37 The ingredients inform the cuisine. It is among the assets of gluten that it helps foods to physically hang together: bread, pie, or quiche made without gluten easily fall apart. Clafoutis made with other grains than wheat may still cohere, though, thanks to the eggs. See, for the chemistry involved, McGee (2004).

38 In this respect, fonio is like other kinds of food transported around the globe. See for questions around their transportation, the contributions by Goodman and Watts (1997), and Inglis and Gimlin (2009). And for the general state of food inequalities and externalities, see Carolan (2011).

39 Since that May day of 2011, I have continued to experiment. As I am tinkering with the last version of the present text, I lunch on a clafoutis made with equal, small amounts of quinoa flour and rice flour, an egg, milk, a pinch of salt, and de-pitted fresh apricots. There were fresh apricots in my favourite version of the open fruit pies (made with bread dough) that were the specialty of Limburg, the region where I grew up. Fond memories of those pies happily resonate in the gratification provided by this particular version of clafoutis. See for the memories resonating in the dishes of his Greek informants, Sutton (2001).

40 For further explorations of words affecting bodily engagements with foods, see Mol (2014), Van de Port and Mol (2015). The first traces the Dutch word *lekker* while the second differentiates between *chupar* and *comer* fruits in Bahia, Brazil.

BIBLIOGRAPHY

Abrahamsson, S., 'An Actor Network Analysis of Constipation and Agency: Shit Happens', *Subjectivity*, 7.2 (2014), 111–130

Akrich, M., 'Essay of Technosociology: A Gasogene in Costa Rica', in P. Lemonnier, ed., *Technological Choices. Transformation in Material Cultures since the Neolithic* (London: Routledge, 1993), pp. 289–337

Akrich, M., and B. Pasveer, 'Multiplying Obstetrics: Techniques of Surveillance and Forms of Coordination', *Theoretical Medicine and Bioethics*, 21 (2000), 63–83

Atkins, P., *Liquid Materialities: A History of Milk, Science and the Law* (Farnham: Ashgate, 2012)

Beisel, U., and T. Scheider, 'Provincialising Waste: The Transformation of Ambulance Car 7/83-2 to Tro-Tro Dr. Jesus', *Environment and Planning D*, 30.4 (2012), 639

Carolan, M., *The Real Cost of Cheap Food* (Oxon: Earthscan, 2011)

de Certeau, M., L. Giard, and P. Mayol, *The Practice of Everyday Life* (Minneapolis: University of Minnesota Press, 1998)

De Laet M., and A. Mol, 'The Zimbabwe Bush Pump: Mechanics of a Fluid Technology', *Social Studies of Science*, 30 (2000), 225–263

Deleuze, G., and F. Guattari, *Mille Plateaux* (Paris: Éditions de Minuit, 1980)

Douglas, M., 'Deciphering a Meal', *Daedalus*, 101 (1972), 61–81

Foucault, M., *Surveiller et Punir* (Paris: Éditions Gallimard 1975)

Geest, S. van der, 'The Social Life of Faeces: System in the Dirt', in R. van Ginkel, and A. Strating, *Wildness and Sensation: Anthropology of Sinister and Sensuous Realms* (Amsterdam: Het Spinhuis, 2007), pp. 381–397

Goodman, D., and M. Watts, *Globalising Food: Agrarian Questions and Global Restructuring* (London: Routledge, 1997)

Hennion, A., *The Passion for Music: A Sociology of Mediation* (Farnham: Ashgate, 2015).

Heuts, F., and A. Mol, 'What is a good tomato? A case of valuing in practice', *Valuation Studies*, 1(2), (2013) 125–146.

Hinchliffe, S., et al., 'Biosecurity and the Topologies of Infected Life: From Borderlines to Borderlands', in *Transactions of the Institute of British Geographers*, 38.4 (2013), 531–543

Inglis, D., and D. Gimlin, *The Globalization of Food* (Oxford: Berg, 2009)

Jones, M., *Feast: Why Humans Share Food* (Oxford: Oxford University Press, 2007)

Kurlansky, M., *Salt: A World History* (New York: Walker Publishing Company, 2002)

Kwa, C., 'Romantic and Baroque Conceptions of Complex Wholes in the Sciences', in J. Law, and A. Mol, eds., *Complexities: Social Studies of Knowledge Practices* (Durham, NC, and London: Duke University Press, 2002): pp. 23–53

Latour, B., *Aramis or the Love of Technology* (Cambridge, MA: Harvard University Press, 1996)

Law, J., *Aircraft Stories. Decentring the Object in Technoscience* (Durham & London: Duke University Press, 2002)

Mann, A., *Tasting in Mundane Practices. Ethnographic Interventions in Social Science Theory*, PhD Thesis, University of Amsterdam, 2015

Mann, A., et al., 'Mixing Methods, Tasting Fingers: Notes on an Ethnographic Experiment', *HAU, Journal of Ethnographic Theory*, 1.1 (2011), 221–43

McCann, J., *Maize and Grace: Africa's Encounter with a New World Crop 1500–2000* (Cambridge, MA: Harvard University Press, 2005)

McGee, H., *On Food and Cooking: The Science and Lore of the Kitchen* (New York: Scribner, 2004)

Mol, A., *The Body Multiple: Ontology in Medical Practice* (Durham: Duke University Press, 2002)

—— *The Logic of Care: Health and the Problem of Patient Choice* (London, New York: Routledge, 2008)

—— 'I Eat an Apple: On Theorising Subjectivities', *Subjectivity*, 22 (2008), 28–37

—— 'Actor-Network Theory: Sensitive Terms and Enduring Tensions', *Kölner Zeitschrift für Soziologie und Sozialpsychologie. Sonderheft*, 50 (2010) 253–269

—— 'Language Trails: "Lekker" and its Pleasures', *Theory, Culture & Society*, 31.2.3 (2014), 93–119

Mol A., and J. Law, 'Regions, Networks and Fluids: Anaemia and Social Topology', *Social Studies of Science*, 24 (1994), 641–671

Moreira, T., 'Heterogeneity and Coordination of Blood Pressure in Neurosurgery', *Social Studies of Science*, 36.1 (2006), 69–97

Onfray, M., *La raison gourmande* (Paris: Grasset, 1995)

Pollan, M., *The Botany of Desire: A Plant's-Eye View of the World* (New York: Random House Trade Paperbacks, 2001)

Parkurst Ferguson, P., 'Is Paris France?', *The French Review*, 73.6 (2000), 1052–1064

Raffaetà, R., 'The Allergy Epidemic, or when Medicalisation is Bottom-up', in S. Fainzang, and C. Haxaire, eds., *Of Bodies and Symptoms: Anthropological Perspectives on their Social and Medical Treatment* (Tarragona: Universitat Rovira i Virgili, 2011), pp. 59–78

Raviv, Y., 'Falafel: A National Icon', *Gastronomica: The Journal of Food and Culture*, 3.3 (2003), 20–25

Serres, M., *Le Passage du Nord-Ouest* (Paris: Éditions de Minuit, 1979)

Silva, E., 'The Cook, the Cooker and the Gendering of the Kitchen', *The Sociological Review*, 48.4 (2000), 612–628

Strathern, M., *Partial Connections* (Oxford: Rowman & Littlefield, 2004)

—— 'Eating (and Feeding)', *Cambridge Anthropology*, 30.2 (2012), 1–14

Sutton, D., *Remembrance of Repasts: An Anthropology of Food and Memory* (New York: Berg, 2001)

Teil, G., and A. Hennion, 'Discovering Quality or Performing Taste?', in M. Harvey, ed., *Qualities of Food* (Manchester: Manchester University Press 2004), pp. 19–37

Van de Port, M., '(Not) Made by the Human Hand: Media Consciousness and Immediacy in the Cultural Production of the Real', in *Social Anthropology*, 19.1 (2011), 74–89

Van de Port, M., and A. Mol, 'Chupar frutas in Salvador da Bahia: A Case of Practice-specific Alterities', *Journal of the Royal Anthropological Institute*, 21.1 (2015), 165–80

Vatin, F., *L'industrie de lait. Essai d'histoire économique* (Paris: L'Harmattan, 1990)

Verran, H., 'On Assemblage', *Journal of Cultural Economy*, 2.2 (2009), 169–182

Vogel, E., & Mol, A. 'Enjoy your food: On losing weight and taking pleasure', *Sociology of Health and Illness*, 36(2) (2014) 305–317

Weber, F., 'Réduire ses dépense, ne pas compter son temps. Comment mesurer l'économie domestique?', *Genèses*, 25.1 (1996), 5–28

Werumeus Buning, J. W. F., *100 avonturen met een pollepel* (Amsterdam: H.J.W. Becht, 1939)

Wiley, A., 'Milk for "Growth": Global and Local Meanings of Milk Consumption in China, India, and the United States', *Food and Foodways*, 19 (2011), 11–33

Wilk, R., 'The Limits of Discipline: Towards Interdisciplinary Food Studies', *Physiology & Behavior*, 107.4 (2012), 471–475

Yates-Doerr, E., 'Does Meat Come from Animals? A Multispecies Approach to Classification and Belonging in Highland Guatemala', *American Ethnologist*, 42.2 (2015), 309–323

Yates-Doerr, E., and A. Mol, 'Cuts of Meat: Disentangling Western Natures-cultures', *Cambridge Anthropology*, 30.2 (2012), 48–64

Zuckerman, L., *Potato: How the Humble Spud Rescued the Western World* (New York: North Point Press, 1998)

MATTERING PRESS TITLES

On Curiosity
The Art of Market Seduction

FRANCK COCHOY

Practising Comparison
Logics, Relations, Collaborations

EDITED BY

JOE DEVILLE, MICHAEL GUGGENHEIM, AND ZUZANA HRDLIČKOVÁ

Modes of Knowing
Resources from the Baroque

EDITED BY

JOHN LAW AND EVELYN RUPPERT

Imagining Classrooms
Stories of Children, Teaching, and Ethnography

VICKI MACKNIGHT

www.ingramcontent.com/pod-product-compliance
Lightning Source LLC
Chambersburg PA
CBHW072132170526
45158CB00004BA/1342